Valuation of Interest-Sensitive Financial Instruments

SOA Monograph M-FI96-1

David F. Babbel
Wharton School
University of Pennsylvania

Craig B. Merrill
Marriott School of Management
Brigham Young University

Produced for the Society of Actuaries by Frank J. Fabozzi Associates, New Hope, Pennsylvania

Printed in the United States of America
1 2 3 4 5 6 7 8 9 0

Preface

Undoubtedly the most important contribution of the financial economics literature over the past twenty five years is the development of contingent claims valuation methodologies, commonly referred to as option pricing models. We prefer the broader "contingent claims valuation" term to the narrower "option pricing" term because it encompasses the full gamut of valuation approaches directed toward the pricing of contingent claims. Upon reflection, virtually all financial institution liabilities and assets may be characterized as contingent claims. The payment of a liability is typically contingent upon a loss event or a consumer choice (e.g., surrender, account withdrawal). Those that are not contingent upon a loss event or a consumer choice, such as GICs or CDs, are conditional upon the firm being solvent. Other payments, such as dividends paid to mutual financial institutions' customers/owners, may depend upon profitability. On the asset side of the balance sheet, most assets have payments that are contingent upon various factors, such as solvency, interest rate levels, call features, prepayment features, and the like. Thus, it would seem natural for a financial institution to be interested in methodologies that were developed especially for the valuation of contingent claims.

During the past decade, financial economists have turned their attention specifically toward those types of contingent claims that are of most concern to financial institutions. Included under the umbrella of techniques generally referred to as "fixed income pricing," they include the full range of models designed to price government, corporate, and mortgage-backed securities with and without call features, prepayment provisions, accelerated and regular sinking funds, convertibility, and so forth. They also include options and futures on fixed income securities, floating rate securities, indexed bonds, fixed income derivative securities, putable bonds, strips, perpetual floaters, inverse floaters, interest-only and principal-only mortgage strips, and a bevy of "second generation" options such as caps, collars, floors, swaps, swaptions, caputs, Asian options, binaries, and many others. These models have been applied in recent years to the valuation of most bank, pension, and life insurance liabilities as well, and even some property-casualty insurance liabilities. Thus, a proper understanding of the development and underpinnings of these models would seem essential to the financial analyst or valuation actuary. It is the purpose of this monograph to foster this basic understanding, and to serve as a convenient and helpful springboard into the technical economic and finance literature on these subjects.

There are some subjects which are natural adjuncts to the topic of this monograph that we do not treat here. For example, asset/liability management depends first on having consistent valuation models that address both sides of the balance sheet. Measurement of effective duration and convexity also hinges crucially on having such valuation models. We, along with numerous others, have treated these adjunct topics elsewhere. Nonetheless, we have found that when forays into asset/liability management and measurement of interest rate sensitivities are taken without a clear understanding of the requisite economic valuation principles, and without grounding the endeavor in a manner consistent with rigorous valuation methodologies, more harm than good is often done. Therefore, we commend to your perusal our efforts at elucidating these principles and methodologies.

David F. Babbel
Craig R. Merrill

Acknowledgments

We would like to express our gratitude to several individuals who have painstakingly reviewed various chapters of this monograph, including Elias Shiu of the University of Iowa, Lester Seigel at the World Bank, David Becker of Lincoln National, Frank Fabozzi of Yale University, and Algis Remeza of the Wharton School. We would also like to express our appreciation to others who provided comments and suggestions regarding its content, including Darrell Duffie of Stanford University, Hal Heaton of Brigham Young University, Phelim Boyle of Waterloo University, Michael Gibbons of the Wharton School, Irwin Vanderhoof of New York University, and John Zacharias. The authors, of course, assume all responsibility for any remaining errors.

A special thanks is given to the Society of Actuaries, and its Financial Reporting, Product Development, and Investment Special Interest Sections, without whose support and encouragement this monograph would never have been completed. Two groups had oversight of this project. The Option Pricing Project Oversight Group, chaired by David N. Becker, with members Christian J. DesRochers, Arnold A. Dicke, Mark W. Griffin, Thomas Ho, Roger W. Smith, and James A. Tilley, provided direction and valuable assistance throughout the project. The Committee on Life Insurance Research, chaired by Irwin T. Vanderhoof, with Edward A. Lew, Chairperson Emeritus, Robert J. Johansen, Vice-Chairperson, and members Faye Albert, Daniel F. Case, Douglas C. Doll, Jeffrey C. Harper, Timothy F. Harris, Owen A. Reed, Klaus O. Shigley, Courtland C. Smith, and staff members Karen Haywood, Jack Luff, Pam Leonard and Zain Mohey-Deen, helped us refine our monograph and get it ready for publication.

Table of Contents

Table of Contents—*Continued*

Table of Contents—*Continued*

Table of Contents—*Continued*

Spot Interest Rates, Forward Interest Rates, Short Rates, and Yield-to-Maturity

1. Introduction

In this chapter we distinguish between four types of interest rates that are sometimes confused with each other. These distinctions will be crucial to understanding different valuation techniques discussed in the ensuing chapters. It will be shown there that in the valuation of interest-sensitive financial instruments, the short rates of interest are of primary importance. However, the process governing the movement over time of the short rates used in valuing such instruments must be consistent with the observable spot interest rates and implied forward interest rates, which in turn determine the yields-to-maturity associated with various financial market instruments. Before we embark on this quest, let us state the ground rules. We will ignore default risk, taxes, transactions costs, and market imperfections and focus only on the core of the valuation process. Elsewhere can be found treatments of how to incorporate these other factors into the valuation process.[1]

We first turn our attention to time lines and a precise definition of time points and time periods. We then relate the various types of interest rates to these time points and time periods. Next, we discuss the functional relationships between the types of interest rates. Finally, we end with a discussion of the term structure of interest rates that is fundamental to the valuation of fixed cash flow instruments, and crucial to the valuation of interest-sensitive cash flows as well.

2. Time Points, Time Periods, and Time Lines

In Figure 1.1 we represent the passage of time on a simple horizontal line with today designated as Time 0. One period from now, Time 1 will occur. Two periods from now, Time 2 will occur. Time 0, Time 1, and Time 2 are examples of what are called *time points*. A time point lasts for an instant, and no longer. A *time period* is the time interval between two time points. For example, Period 1 is the time interval between Time 0 and Time 1, and Period 2 is the time interval between Time 1 and Time 2.

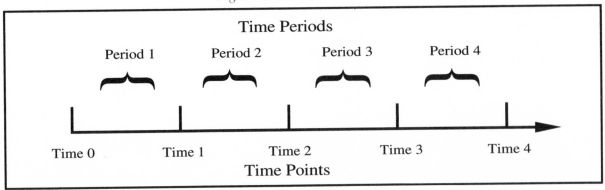
Figure 1.1. A Time Line

Time periods may be of any length. They may last a month, a year, or any other arbitrarily chosen amount of time. (Most often in securities valuation, they are set equal to a month long.) Time points are important, because it is at time points that information is revealed and observed. It is also at time points that cash flows may occur, and are valued. Information may be revealed during time periods, but it is not observed or, if observed, is not used in valuation until one of the time points is reached.

3. Spot and Forward Rates of Interest

In this section, we introduce the concepts of spot and forward rates of interest, which are used in valuing fixed income securities. One way to distinguish between spot and forward rates of interest is by analogy to certificates of deposit (CD) that may be acquired at commercial banks. A CD may be purchased with a lump sum payment today (Time 0), maturing in one, two, three, or more years, at which time the lump sum payment, together with accrued interest, is paid to the purchaser. It offers a prespecified rate of interest over the time period stipulated on the certificate. A bank will offer different rates of interest on its CDs, depending on the length of time for which the money is to be left on deposit. For example, the bank may offer an interest rate of 8% per annum (p.a.) on a one-year CD, 8.75% p.a. on a two-year CD, 9.33% p.a. on a three-year CD, 9.79% p.a. on a four-year CD and 10.13% p.a. on a five-year CD.

In this illustration, we can show the differences between what are referred to as spot rates of interest, and their closely related adjuncts, forward rates of interest. A *t-period spot rate of interest* is the per period rate of interest that can be earned on an investment made today (Time 0), which would be repaid in a lump sum with interest on a specified date in the future (Time *t*). The spot rates in our example are 8.0%, 8.75%, 9.33%, 9.79% and 10.13% per annum.[2]

A *forward rate of interest* is the rate of interest, implicit in currently quoted spot rates, that would be applicable from one time point in the future to another time point in the future. Forward interest rates are typically cast as single-period rates.[3] Because forward interest rates are rarely observed in the market, we have to infer what they are from other available data. Nonetheless, they are important in pricing securities and can even be "locked in" today for future borrowing or savings rates.

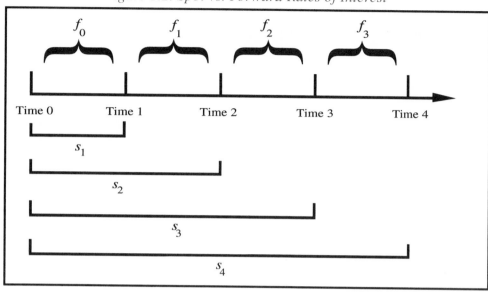

Figure 1.2. Spot vs. Forward Rates of Interest

The difference between spot and forward rates of interest is more easily explained with a time line illustration, based on our previous illustration. In Figure 1.2, the line segments appearing below the time line represent lengths of time (measured in time periods) over which various spot rates of interest, s_t, are applicable. If money were deposited for one year, from now (Time 0) until a year from now (Time 1), it would earn 8% p.a. (denoted s_1) in our hypothetical example. Therefore, the line labeled s_1 runs from Time 0 to Time 1. The subscript attached to s refers to the length of time over which the spot rate of interest applies. If money were deposited for two years (Time 0 to Time 2), s_2 would be 8.75% p.a.

At this juncture it is useful to point out a notational convention used here and elsewhere. Because spot rates of interest always refer to an interest rate applicable to a time interval beginning at Time 0, we distinguish them from one another with a subscript that denotes the time point at the end of their applicable time intervals. Forward rates of interest,

on the other hand, carry a subscript denoting the time point at the beginning of the single periods to which they are applicable. Because they are single-period rates, if we know the beginning time point, we also know the ending time point. Hence, it is sufficient to distinguish them one from another with a single subscript. This can lead to some confusion if this convention is not kept in mind. For instance, s_1, which covers the time interval from Time 0 to Time 1, is identical to f_0, which applies to the same time period.

Notice in Figure 1.2 that s_2, i.e., the 8.75% two-year spot rate in our example, covers a period of time that partially overlaps with that of the 1-year spot rate, s_1. The amount paid on this two-year instrument beyond the amount received on the one-year instrument can be stated in terms of an interest rate and computed by knowing s_1 and s_2. This second year single-period rate is a forward rate of interest. Notice that it must be computed because it is not observed. Accordingly, it is sometimes referred to as the implied forward rate. How high must it be? Obviously, it must be much higher than 8% for the two-year spot rate, which is in some sense an "average" of the forward rates, to be 8.75% p.a.

To compute the implied forward rate of interest applicable to the second year, we can do the following. First we calculate the return from the two investments.

$10,000 @ 8.00% one year later

$$= \$10,000(1 + 0.0800)^1 = \$10,800.00$$

$10,000 @ 8.75% two years later

$$= \$10,000(1 + 0.0875)^2 = \$11,826.56$$

We now have enough information to figure out the implied forward rate of interest that the bank would be paying during the second year. If we had $10,800 at the end of the first year, and $11,826.56 at the end of the second, our rate of return during that second year must have been (11,826.56÷10,800.00−1=) 9.5%. We would call this the forward rate of interest at Time 1, denoted f_1.[4]

Similarly, we could compute the forward rate of interest applicable to the third year as follows:

$10,000 @ 8.75% two years later

$$= \$10,000(1 + 0.0875)^2 = \$11,826.56$$

$10,000 @ 9.33% three years later

$$= \$10,000(1 + 0.0933)^3 = \$13,068.27$$

Therefore, f_2 would be ($13,068.27÷ $11,826.56−1=) 10.5%. The same procedure would result in an implied forward rate of interest of applicable to the fourth year, f_3, of 11.2%, and f_4 of 11.5%.

The implied forward rates of interest can be extracted from a schedule of spot rates of interest very simply, by using the following formula:

$$f_{t-1} = (1 + s_t)^t \div (1 + s_{t-1})^{t-1} - 1$$

This is equivalent to the procedure that we just went through to arrive at our implied forward rates. We compounded the investment (assumed to be $1 in the above formula) at 1 plus a rate of interest for the longer period, divided that product by the investment compounded at 1 plus a rate of interest for the shorter period, and then subtracted 1 from the quotient.

Applying this formula to a schedule of spot rates of interest to extract all of our implied forward rates, we would have:[5]

$$s_1 = 0.0800, \therefore f_0 = (1 + 0.0800)^1$$
$$\div (1 + 0.0000)^0 - 1 = 8.0\%$$

$$s_2 = 0.0875, \therefore f_1 = (1 + 0.0875)^2$$
$$\div (1 + 0.0800)^1 - 1 = 9.5\%$$

$$s_3 = 0.0933, \therefore f_2 = (1 + 0.0933)^3$$
$$\div (1 + 0.0875)^2 - 1 = 10.5\%$$

$$s_4 = 0.0979, \therefore f_3 = (1 + 0.0979)^4$$
$$\div (1 + 0.0933)^3 - 1 = 11.2\%$$

$$s_5 = 0.1013, \therefore f_4 = (1 + 0.1013)^5$$
$$\div (1 + 0.0979)^4 - 1 = 11.5\%$$

Note that the spot rates of interest are very close to simple arithmetic averages of the forward rates of interest. For instance, the two-year spot rate of 8.75% is close to the mean of the 8.0% first-year forward rate and the 9.5% second-year forward rate. Similarly, the three-year spot rate of 9.33% is close to the mean of the first three forward rates of interest (8.0%, 9.5%, and 10.5%)—close, but not quite. If we had included enough digits in our computations, the discrepancy would have been apparent.[6] This is because the multi-year investments pay a constant interest rate throughout their term. Therefore, in the case of the two-year CD, for example, the lender receives 8.75% in the first year, which is higher than the one-year rate of 8.00%. When computing the implied forward rate, one must take account of the difference in the compound one-year return from both investments. That is why the spot rates of interest are actually geometric averages. The precise formula for converting forward rates of interest into spot rates is given below.

$$ s_t = \sqrt[t]{(1+f_0)(1+f_1)...(1+f_{t-1})} - 1 $$

To illustrate this formula, let us compute s_3, the three-year spot rate of interest. We compute this by substituting in the above formula the three single-year forward rates of interest applicable to years one, two, and three. Then solving by taking the third root of the product, we get:

$$ s_3 = \sqrt[3]{(1+0.08)(1+0.095)(1+0.105)} - 1 = 9.33\% $$

4. Short Rates and Yield-to-Maturity

Short rates of interest are *future* short-term rates of interest that *might* arise over time. By convention, they are single-period rates of interest. Hence, we identify them with a single subscript denoting the time point at the beginning of their applicable period.

It is useful to distinguish short rates from forward rates. At Time 0 there is, implicit in the spot rates applying to different lengths of time, a vector of single-period forward rates. For each future time period, there exists at Time 0 one and only one applicable forward rate. This does not mean that at Time 0 we actually know what the future single-period rate of interest will eventually be at Time 1, for example. But regardless of what future rates of interest unfold, it does mean that today, at Time 0, we can "lock in" a single-period rate of interest that will apply to the period beginning at Time 1.[7]

The future short rate that transpires one year hence may or may not be equal to the forward rate applicable to that time period. It could be any one of several hundred possibilities. Indeed, we cannot even say that the *expected* future short rate is equal to the forward rate currently implied for that period. (We will demonstrate the validity of this assertion in Chapter 2.) What we can say is that there is an array of possible short rates for each future time point, and that each possible short rate has varying probabilities of actually occurring. We can also say that the probabilities of these different short rates occurring at future time points are consistent with the term structure of spot and forward rates manifest at Time 0. (We will demonstrate the validity of this assertion over the next six chapters.)

Another kind of interest rate, called yield-to-maturity (YTM), is often reported in the financial pages of our newspapers. For instruments like a CD or a zero-coupon bond, where there is a single cash inflow to the purchaser, the YTM is the same as the spot rate.[8] However, this is not generally the case. For coupon bonds and other financial instruments which feature payments throughout their lives, the YTM will depend on the spot rates of interest associated with each cash flow provided. This is because a coupon bond, as well as other financial instruments with multiple cash flows, can be thought of as a collection of zero-coupon bonds. Each cash flow can be valued as an individual zero-coupon bond. Therefore, each payment is valued by a different spot rate of interest. The instrument's YTM depends on the entire collection of spot rates used in valuing its cash flows.

Exactly what would the average yield be on such a financial instrument? This is the question that led to the development of the concept of YTM. The YTM is a complex weighted average of spot rates of interest, where the weights depend on the pattern of cash flows receivable on a particular instrument over all points in time.[9] Accordingly, it is quite specific to a particular instrument and cannot be used to estimate the fair value of other instruments.[10] Indeed, the YTM can be determined only after the market value of an instrument is already known and its payment stream indicated. It is unique to that instrument at that time. Therefore, little more will be said about it in subsequent chapters.

Yields and short rates can be contrasted with forward and spot rates on a time line similar to that used in Figure 1.2. We have done this in Figure 1.3, where short rates at Time t are denoted r_t and YTMs are denoted y. With the exception of Time 0, there are several short rates shown for each time point. Note, however, that YTMs carry no time subscript. That is because there is no unique yield associated with any given time period, but only with a given financial instrument. Another fact is apparent from glancing at the figure. At Time 0, the one-period short rate, spot rate, forward rate, and the yield-to-maturity on a zero-coupon bond maturing at Time 1 will all be identical, i.e., $r_0 = f_0 = s_1 = y$. Beyond the first period, these various interest rate measures will generally not be equal to one another, except that spot rates equal the YTMs on zero-coupon bonds.

Figure 1.3. Spots, Forwards, Short Rates and Yield-to-Maturity

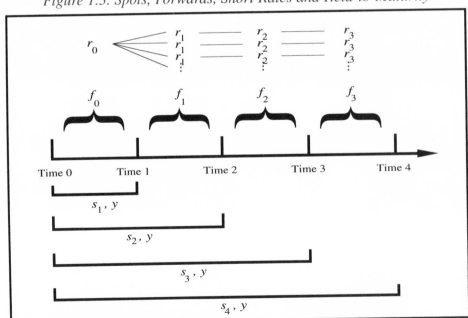

5. The Term Structure of Interest

As we have seen, there are different rates of interest quoted for different lengths of time. The *term structure of interest rates* is the name given to the pattern of interest rates available on instruments of a similar credit risk, but of different terms to maturity. Most often among economists and market analysts, the interest rates referred to when discussing the term structure of interest are spot rates of interest applicable to the valuation of U.S. government-issued securities. This is the case because they want to be exact and not confuse the discussion with issues of different borrowers or different types of financial instruments. Most often in the popular press, however, the term structure referred to is based on government coupon bonds and their YTMs. In this monograph, when we speak of term structures of interest, we will be referring to the spot rate term structure unless otherwise stated. We will also occasionally make use of the forward term structure, but here too it will be derived from the spot rates applicable to government bonds.

Figure 1.4 plots the spot and forward rate curves of our numerical example given above, while Figure 1.5 provides a sample of actual term structures of spot interest rates for various dates in the past. These curves, which represent the term structure, are known as yield curves. Several items are striking about the yield curves shown. First, the general levels of interest rates over time have undergone substantial changes. Second, the term structures exhibit varying slopes, some positive, some negative, and some virtually flat across maturities. Third, there are differing levels of curvature, or bend, to the shapes of the term structures of interest. Some exhibit smooth, gradual curvature and others sharper, rougher bends.

Figure 1.4. Hypothetical Term Structure of Interest

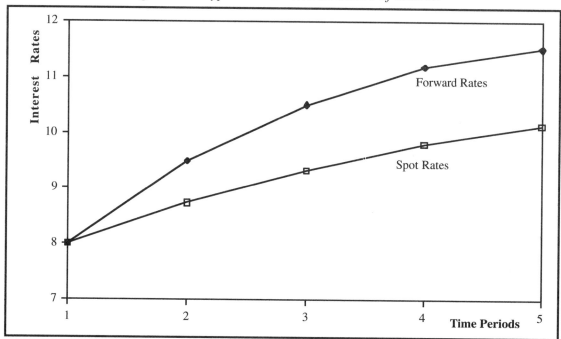

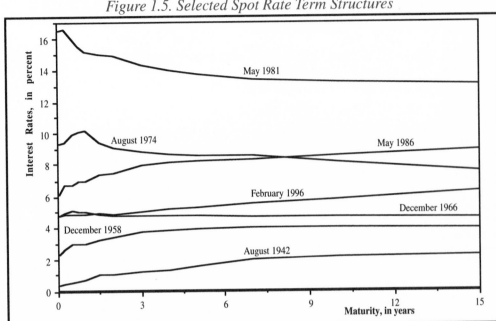

Figure 1.5. Selected Spot Rate Term Structures

Figure 1.6 extracts two of the spot rate term structures from Figure 1.5—the May 1981 and May 1986 curves—and displays them along with their corresponding forward rate curves. Two items are of particular note. First, the forward rate term structure exhibits sharper, more sudden bends than the spot rate term structure. This is because the spot rate, which is a geometric average, of sorts, of the forward rates, cannot bend as sharply because the averaging process dampens any sharp shifts in the forward rates. Second, if the forward rate curve resides above the spot rate curve, the latter will tend to rise as term is increased. Conversely, if the forward rate curve is below the spot rate curve, the latter will tend to fall as term is extended. This, again, is a simple reflection of the averaging process implicit in the conversion of forward rates of interest to spot rates. As higher forward rates are included in the geometric average, they will tend to pull the average higher, but as lower forward rates are included, they will tend to pull the average downward.

6. Concluding Remarks

As will be seen in ensuing chapters, the term structure of interest rates is fundamental to the valuation of fixed cash flow streams, and serves as an anchor to generating random short rate processes that are consistent with observed market prices. At this point we conclude this chapter without an elaboration of traditional theories of the term structure. The interested reader can pursue such information in a large number of textbooks on capital markets and institutions.[11] However, some of the traditional and modern theories of the term structure of interest will be discussed in subsequent chapters.

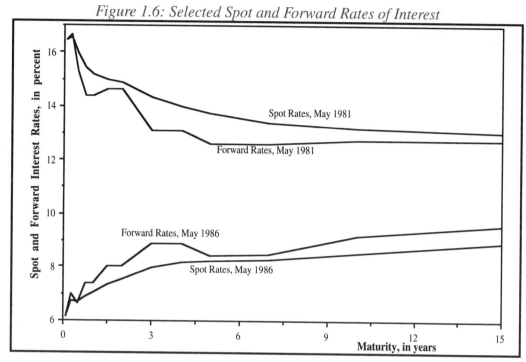

Figure 1.6: Selected Spot and Forward Rates of Interest

Spot Rates, May 1981

Forward Rates, May 1981

Forward Rates, May 1986

Spot Rates, May 1986

Spot and Forward Interest Rates, in percent

Maturity, in years

End Notes

1. See, for example, Babbel and Santomero, *Financial Markets, Instruments, and Institutions*, Irwin Press, 1996, or Bodie, Kane, and Marcus, *Investments*, 3rd edition, Irwin Press, 1996.

2. The bank may report to the Internal Revenue Service interest earnings on your multi-year CD even though you have not yet received it. Typically it is merely a book entry in your account. The actual cash payment will come at the maturity of the CD. However, to make payment of your tax more convenient, it is often possible to collect the interest on an annual basis, even though your CD has not matured. Nonetheless, the receipt of interest does not preclude the bank from reducing your principal if you attempt to withdraw your funds prior to maturity.

3. There are also implicit forward rates that apply to several time periods. For example, there could be a two-period forward rate applicable to the time interval between Time 3 and Time 5. In this monograph, all forward rates are single-period rates unless otherwise stated.

4. As stated in endnote 2, the fact that a bank may credit an account during the first year of a two-year CD with interest earnings based on the two-year spot rate does not mean that the depositor actually earns that much interest during the first year. This won't come as a surprise to any who have tried to withdraw their money early. The "severe interest penalty for early withdrawal" will leave the depositor who closes out a two-year CD account after only one year with interest earnings more in line with what is implied by the one-year rate, or less.

5. Note in the equation for f_0 that the spot rate of interest earned from Time 0 to Time 0 is zero—no time has elapsed, so no interest is earned.

6. A more precise calculation of the implied forward rates gives $f_0=8\%$, $f_1=9.5052\%$, $f_2=10.4993\%$, $f_3=11.1816\%$, and $f_4=11.5006\%$.

7. Forward rates of interest for *saving* can be locked in by taking a long position in one instrument, and a short position in another, with a maturity one period shorter than the instrument held in the long position. On the other hand, forward rates of interest for *borrowing* can be locked in by taking a short position in

one instrument, and a long position in another, with a maturity one period shorter than the instrument held in the long position. To be concrete, the forward rate applicable to period 2, $f_1 = 9.5052\%$, can be secured for future saving by purchasing a two-year zero-coupon bond with a face value of $1 million for $845,554.23 (=$1 million$\div[1+0.0875]^2$) and financing the purchase by selling short an equal dollar amount of one-year zero-coupon bonds carrying an 8% yield. At the end of one year the short position must be closed for $913,198.57 (=$845,554.23$\times[1+0.08]$). This process leaves no net cash inflow or outflow at Time 0, but a cash outflow of $913,198.57 at Time 1 and a cash inflow of $1 million at Time 2. Thus, the interest rate locked in at Time 0 but applicable to the time interval between Time 1 and Time 2 is 9.5052% (=[$1,000,000$\div$$913,198.57]-1), which is exactly equal to the sought forward rate, f_1.

8. This yield to maturity is not to be confused with the "bond equivalent yield" reported by many newspapers. The latter computes a semiannual YTM and then doubles (rather than compounds) it to annualize it. This results in a slight distortion. There is another distortion that stems from the tax code. Zero-coupon bonds are treated for tax purposes and traded as original issue discount bonds. They are taxed on imputed interest using the constant or scientific yield method. Spot rates implied from zero-coupon bond prices will therefore differ from those implied by coupon-bearing bonds. See Frank Fabozzi, *Handbook of Fixed Income Securities*, 4th ed., p. 820.

9. The yield-to-maturity may be approximated by taking the spot rates applicable to each cash flow and applying dollar duration weights to them. This is shown in Appendix B to Chapter 2.

10. An exception is the YTM on a zero-coupon bond, which is identical to the spot rate of interest. These YTMs can be used as spot rates to value other streams of fixed cash flows.

11. A recent example is Babbel and Santomero, *op cit.*

Practice Exercises

1. Suppose the spot rates of interest are as follows:

    one year: 7.0%
    two years: 7.8%
    three years: 8.4%
    four years: 8.8%
    five years: 9.0%

    What are the implicit single-year forward rates of interest for each of the years?

2. Using the spot rates given above, what would be the total cumulative value of a 4-year certificate of deposit at maturity?

3. Using the spot rates given above, what would be the total cumulative value of a 3-year $1,000 certificate of deposit at maturity?

4. Using the cumulative values computed in questions 2 and 3 above, compute the implied forward rate of interest extending from Time 3 to Time 4.

5. Suppose the single-year forward rates of interest are as follows:

    first year: 8.0%
    second year: 8.9%
    third year: 9.6%
    fourth year: 9.8%
    fifth year: 9.9%

    What are the associated spot rates of interest for periods of 1, 2, 3, 4, and 5 years?

6. Using the data in question 5, what is the implicit three-year forward rate extending from Time 2 to Time 5?

7. Distinguish the notion of "short rates" from that of forward rates of interest? Why do we care about short rates?

8. Returning to the spot rates given in question 1, how could we, at Time 0, "lock in" the forward rate of interest extending from Time 3 to Time 4?

9. What is the difference between internal rate of return and YTM?

10. Why don't we use YTM when plotting the term structure of interest? Why don't we use YTM when valuing securities?

An Introduction to Valuation of Fixed and Interest-Sensitive Cash Flows

1. Introduction

In the previous chapter we focused our attention on various notions of interest rates and their relation to each other. In this chapter we turn our attention to prices. In ordering the topics in this monograph, we could have taken the approach seen in most treatises by beginning with prices and then moving to interest rates. After all, prices of various securities are inextricably linked to interest rates. Indeed, it can be said that interest rates are merely an adjunct to prices—a way of stating the price at one time in terms of the price at another time—and that prices are the fundamental element that drives interest rates. On the other hand, interest rates are, in some sense, themselves prices—the prices of money over periods of time. We prefer to focus on interest rates first because they foster helpful intuition, are amenable to interpolation between discrete time points, and are useful in valuing a wide variety of securities.

An analogy will suffice to make the point. A meteorologist may say that a particular wet air mass currently over Peoria will arrive in Bloomington, Illinois in approximately an hour; alternatively, she may report that wind is blowing from the west at 50 miles per hour. The reference to location is analogous to a reference to prices, whereas the reference to wind velocity is analogous to interest rates. Either way of communication conveys somewhat different information to the residents in Bloomington. They must prepare for rain soon, but because of the strong wind, an umbrella will be of no use. In our view, knowing the speed of the traveling storm is more helpful. Sure, the meteorologist could state that the storm will hit Morton in 12 minutes, Mackinaw in 32 minutes, and Danvers in 41 minutes, and perhaps report on the estimated time of storm arrival for a dozen or more other towns, but it would be a tedious way to report the weather.[1] Similarly, an analyst could report the prices of hundreds of government securities, or report a few dozen interest rates that can be used to price all government securities, as well as a host of related securities.

Table 2.1. A Schedule of STRIP Prices

Maturity	STRIP Prices	Spot Interest Rates	Implied Forward Interest Rates
1	$925.93	8.00%	8.00%
2	$845.55	8.75%	9.50%
3	$765.21	9.33%	10.50%
4	$688.25	9.79%	11.18%
5	$617.27	10.13%	11.50%

2. Valuing Fixed Cash Flows

In valuation, two approaches are generally taken. The first approach is to take the prices of traded securities of different characteristics as given. Zero-coupon bonds (commonly called STRIPS) are often used for this purpose. Then the particular instrument that is being valued is replicated by a portfolio of these simple traded securities. Summoning the value additivity principle, which says that the value of the whole is the sum of the values of the parts, we can arrive at the ultimate value.

2.1 Value Additivity

In Table 2.1 we show an example of this approach. The prices of STRIPS with maturities varying from one to five years are displayed. Adjacent to the prices are the related spot rates of interest, as well as the implied forward rates.

Now consider a security that provides two fixed and certain cash flows: $100 at the end of Year 3 and $500 at the end of Year 5. What is its value? We know from the above chart that the price of a STRIP with a face value of $1,000 which matures in 3 years is $765.21. Similarly, we know the price of a $1,000 STRIP maturing in 5 years is $617.27. Accordingly, we can take those prices and multiply them by the proportion of $1,000 due on each date. Our calculation would proceed as follows:

(1)	(2)	(3)	(4)
Year of Cash Flow	Value of Cash Flow per $1,000	# of $1,000 Cash Flows during Year	(2)×(3)
3 years	$765.21 per $1000 face	1/10	$76.52
5 years	$617.27 per $1000 face	1/2	308.63
		Sum:	$385.15

Therefore, the present value of this instrument with multiple cash flows is $385.15, which is the present value of each cash flow combined.

2.2 Valuation Using Interest Rates

The second approach is to focus on interest rates of some sort that are related to value. Several come to mind. For instance, we could use a series of spot or forward rates to translate future cash flows into their present value counterparts. Consider the instrument introduced above that has cash flows of $100 at the end of Year 3 and $500 at the end of Year 5.

2.2.1 Valuation Using Spot Rates

In Figure 2.1, we show our hypothetical term structure of spot rates of interest. The actual numerical values of the spot rates shown were taken from Table 2.1. These spot rates can be used in valuing fixed and certain cash flows by incorporating them into the discount factors, as follows:

$$\frac{\$100}{(1 + 0.0933)^3} + \frac{\$500}{(1 + 0.1013)^5} = \$385.15$$

Figure 2.1. Hypothetical Term Structure

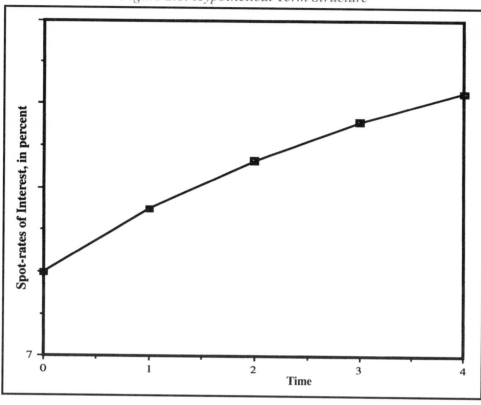

The general formula for using spot rates to value a stream of arbitrary cash flows, which are paid at various time points in the future, is as follows:

$$V_0 = \sum_{t=1}^{T} \frac{CF_t}{(1 + s_t)^t}$$

where V_0 is the present value at Time 0 of the stream of cash flows, s_t designates the t-year spot rate of interest, CF_t denotes the cash flow occurring at Time t, and T is the time point of the final cash flow.

2.2.2 Valuation Using Forward Rates
We can also use forward interest rates to value the same cash flows, as follows:

$$\$100 \div [(1 + 0.08)(1 + 0.095)(1 + 0.105)]$$
$$+ \$500 \div [(1 + 0.08)(1 + 0.095)(1 + 0.105)$$
$$(1 + 0.1118)(1 + 0.115)] = \$385.15$$

The general formula for using forward rates to value a stream of arbitrary cash flows, which are fixed, certain, and paid at various time points in the future, is as follows:

$$V_0 = \sum_{t=1}^{T} \frac{CF_t}{\prod_{n=1}^{t}(1 + f_{n-1})}$$

where f_n denotes the single-period forward rate of interest implicit in the term structure of spot rates at Time 0 for the period beginning at Time n.

2.2.3 Valuation Using Short Rates

Another approach to valuation is to discount the projected cash flows by the multiplicity of interest rate paths that could arise in the future. Under this approach, the discount rates used are based on the sequences of short rates (single-period spot rates) that might unfold. Typically, hundreds, and even thousands of paths of possible future short rates are used in practice.

In this subsection we illustrate the valuation approach using only five distinct paths. Figure 2.2 shows the five paths that interest rates might follow. The plot is based on the short rates shown in Table 2.2. Each path is defined by a series of short rates, and is assumed to have equal probability of occurring as any of the other paths; moreover, their probabilities sum to one. Thus, the "average" shown below each

Figure 2.2. Display of Interest Rate Paths

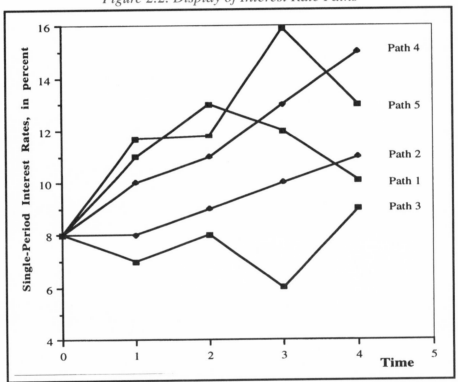

Table 2.2. Simulating Interest Rate Paths

	Time 0	Time 1	Time 2	Time 3	Time 4
Path 1:	8.0%	11.0%	13.0%	12.0%	10.1%
Path 2:	8.0%	8.0%	9.0%	10.0%	11.0%
Path 3:	8.0%	7.0%	8.0%	6.0%	9.0%
Path 4:	8.0%	10.0%	11.0%	13.0%	15.0%
Path 5:	8.0%	11.67%	11.79%	15.87%	13.0%
Average:	8.0%	9.53%	10.56%	11.37%	11.62%

time point represents the short rate currently expected to prevail at that moment. (This average short rate is not used in valuation, but is computed only for pedagogical purposes.) Note that these expected future one-period rates, or short rates, are not equal to the forward interest rates shown earlier, although they are fairly close. With the exception of the first short rate, all averages are higher than their respective forward rates.[2] In subsequent chapters, we will show how appropriate interest rate paths can be constructed for this purpose. In particular, we will demonstrate how particular types of paths preserve the "no arbitrage" (i.e., no "free lunch") principle, and are consistent with partial and general equilibrium economic models.

We will now apply the "discounting by paths" approach to valuing our hypothetical security that provides a $100 cash flow at Time 3 and a $500 cash flow at Time 5. The value of the $100 cash flow may be determined by discounting $100 by the sequence of short rates shown in each path, then summing the present values across all paths and multiplying each derived value by the probability of its associated interest rate path, which in this case is ⅕ for each path.

Path 1: $100÷[(1.08)(1.11)(1.13)]   = $73.82

Path 2: $100÷[(1.08)(1.08)(1.09)]   = $78.65

Path 3: $100÷[(1.08)(1.07)(1.08)]   = $80.13

Path 4: $100÷[(1.08)(1.10)(1.11)]   = $75.83

Path 5: $100÷[(1.08)(1.1167)(1.1179)] = $74.17

$V_0 = (73.82 + 78.65 + 80.13 + 75.83 + 74.17) ÷ 5 = \$76.52$

Similarly, we may obtain the value of the $500 cash flow. Since this amount is paid further into the future, we must discount it by a longer series of short rates than was used in valuing the $100 cash flow. After summing the present values across all paths and applying

the appropriate weights, we arrive at the value of the $500 payment.

Path 1: $500÷[(1.08)(1.11)(1.13)(1.12)(1.101)]=$299.32

Path 2: $500÷[(1.08)(1.08)(1.09)(1.10)(1.11)] =$322.09

Path 3: $500÷[(1.08)(1.07)(1.08)(1.06)(1.09)] =$346.74

Path 4: $500÷[(1.08)(1.10)(1.11)(1.13)(1.15)] =$291.78

Path 5: $500÷[(1.08)(1.1167)(1.1179)(1.1587)(1.13)]=$283.24

$V_0 = (299.52 + 322.09 + 346.74 + 291.78 + 283.24) ÷ 5 = \$308.63$

Now, to get the value of the hypothetical security, we simply sum the computed values of the two cash flows, as shown below:

$$\$76.52 + \$308.63 = \$385.15$$

Note that this is the same price we obtained earlier when discounting by spot or forward rates. Therefore, our set of future short rates is consistent with the spot and forward rates of interest given above. Indeed, by using these same five short-rate paths to value zero-coupon bonds maturing at the end of one, two, three, four, or five years, we could have replicated exactly the prices given in Section 2.1.[3]

2.2.4 Valuation Using Yield-to-Maturity

As noted in Chapter 1, there is considerable attention given to yield-to-maturity in the financial markets. In addition, this figure is frequently reported in the financial press for individual bonds. We can use our current discussion on valuing cash flows to explain how this figure is calculated, as well as what it does and does not explain.

Suppose we knew the market value of our hypothetical financial instrument, V_0, was $385.15, and that the instrument featured the same pair of cash flows as described earlier. We could derive the yield-to-maturity by solving for y in the following general formula:

$$V_0 = \sum_{t=1}^{T} \frac{CF_t}{(1+y)^t} = \frac{\$100}{(1+y)^3} + \frac{\$500}{(1+y)^5}$$

$$= \$385.15$$

The yield-to-maturity that solves this equation can be found by an iterative search procedure. Recall from Chapter 1 that the yield-to-maturity carries no subscript. In other words, it is the single "interest rate" that is used to discount all of the cash flows irrespective of their timing. However, note that the yield-to-maturity can be derived only if we *already know* the market price. This is because we use the price to derive the yield, not vice versa.

Whereas spot and forward rates can be used to determine the value of any stream of fixed cash flows, the yield-to-maturity is unique to a particular pattern of cash flows and hence is valid only for discounting the cash flows of an instrument exhibiting exactly the same pattern, as is shown in Appendix A to this chapter. On the other hand, it offers a simple, single number in place of the numerous yields associated with all of the cash flows. It is, in essence, a complex average of the spot rates that results from the valuation of the cash flows of the financial asset under consideration.[4]

In our example here, the yield-to-maturity is 10.0274%. We can use this figure along with the equation above to derive the present value of the two cash flows under consideration.

$$V_0 = \frac{\$100}{(1+0.100274)^3} + \frac{\$500}{(1+0.100274)^5}$$

$$= \$75.08 + \$310.07 = \$385.15$$

Note that by construction the appropriate YTM produces the correct present value of the entire cash flow stream. However, using YTM will not allow us to obtain the correct present value of each cash flow separately. To show this, we have repeated the final result from each of our calculation methods in Table 2.3.

All of the individual cash flow values are consistent with each other except for the YTM result, which provides different present value information for each of the two cash flows. When taken together, they produce offsetting errors by construction so that the cumulative present value is correct. It is only in the case of the valuation of a single cash flow, or zero-coupon bond, that these differences do not arise, i.e., the YTM equals the spot rate for an instrument with a single payment.

3. Valuing Interest-Sensitive Cash Flows

In this section we will discuss the valuation of interest-sensitive cash flows. We will not consider default risk, illiquidity, or uncertainty of cash flows apart from any uncertainty devolving

Table 2.3. Valuing Cash Flows: Comparisons of Different Approaches

Approach	PV(CF$_3$)	PV(CF$_5$)	Price
Value additivity:	\$76.52	+ \$308.63	= \$385.15
Spot rates:	\$76.52	+ \$308.63	= \$385.15
Forward rates:	\$76.52	+ \$308.63	= \$385.15
Short rates:	\$76.52	+ \$308.63	= \$385.15
Yield-to-maturity:	\$75.08	+ \$310.05	= \$385.15

Chapter 2

from which interest rates will arise in the future. The traditional approaches to valuing interest-sensitive cash flows involved taking the expected cash flows and discounting them by yields, spot rates, or forward rates. The only problem with these approaches is that they are wrong. Substantial adjustments must be applied to the discount factors in order to have the derived prices approximate those observed in the marketplace. But the extent of adjustments necessary could not be determined without already knowing the prices of the instruments, or instruments of like character. Applying the "discounting by paths" methodology, however, can produce appropriate values not only for fixed cash flows, but also for interest-sensitive cash flows.

We will illustrate this concept by recalling our five interest rate paths from Table 2.2, and valuing an instrument whose expected cash flows are both equal to the certain cash flows of our prior instrument. However, the realized cash flows will be determined entirely by the level that interest rates reach at the time point that precedes the cash flow. The cash flows are shown below, to the right of the short rates that precede them in time.[5]

	Time 0	Time 1	Time 2	Time 3
Path 1:	8.0%	11.0%	13.0%	$123.11
Path 2:	8.0%	8.0%	9.0%	$85.23
Path 3:	8.0%	7.0%	8.0%	$75.76
Path 4:	8.0%	10.0%	11.0%	$104.17
Path 5:	8.0%	11.67%	11.79%	$111.65
Average:	8.0%	9.53%	10.56%	$100.00

	Time 3	Time 4	Time 5
Path 1:	12.0%	10.1%	$434.60
Path 2:	10.0%	11.0%	$473.32
Path 3:	6.0%	9.0%	$387.26
Path 4:	13.0%	15.0%	$645.44
Path 5:	15.87%	13.0%	$559.38
Average:	11.37%	11.62%	$500.00

We calculate the present value of each cash flow by discounting it using the path of short rates that could give rise to it. Below we show the values for each path.

	Time 3	+	Time 5	=	Total
Path 1:	$90.88	+	$260.17	=	$351.05
Path 2:	$67.04	+	$304.90	=	$371.94
Path 3:	$60.70	+	$268.56	=	$329.26
Path 4:	$79.00	+	$376.65	=	$455.65
Path 5:	$82.81	+	$316.88	=	$399.69
Average:	$76.09	+	$305.43	=	$381.52

In the bottom line we see the estimated present value of the financial instrument is $381.52. Note that this diverges significantly from the value computed by applying spot rates, forward rates, or yield-to-maturity to the expected cash flows of $100 and $500 for Time 3 and Time 5, respectively. These other methods would have estimated value at $385.15. Note also that the estimated present value of the first cash flow is $76.09, which is lower than that produced using spot or forward rates. Similarly, the estimated present value of the second cash flow is $305.43, which is lower than that produced using spot or forward rates. However, using the "discounting by paths" approach does not always produce lower estimated values than those produced using spot or forward rates applied to expected cash flows. Indeed, if the expected cash flows had remained the same, but the pattern of contingent cash flows were reversed, where the larger cash flows were associated with the lower interest rates, the estimated values of the cash flows would have exceeded those produced by applying spot or forward rates of interest to the expected cash flows. Technically, this divergence in prices estimated when discounting by interest rate paths versus those estimated via more traditional approaches occurs because the present value of expected values does not equal the expected value of present values.

So which estimated values are correct? We will show in subsequent chapters that interest-sensitive cash flow present values estimated by the path-related discount rates, with some slight modifications to accommodate the "market price of risk," are consistent with economic principles, whereas those estimated by spot rates, forward rates, and yields-to-maturity are not. But don't stop here. If it were that easy, people who estimate the values of such cash flows for a living wouldn't be earning exorbitant sums of money and we wouldn't have written the remaining six chapters!

4. Conclusion

In this chapter we have provided an introduction to several approaches used in valuing cash flows. For fixed and certain cash flows, all methods except for the yield-to-maturity approach provide accurate estimates of present value. For interest-sensitive cash flows, only the approach that considers interest rate paths associated with each cash flow produces estimates of present value that are consistent with basic economic principles and, equally important, consistent with much of observed market pricing.

In the next chapter, we will demonstrate how interest rate paths can be formulated in a "discrete-time" lattice framework. The short rates produced are shown to be consistent with the "no arbitrage" principle heralded in financial economics. Then in Chapter 4 we will consider "continuous-time" models of interest rates. In Chapter 5 we will compare and contrast the discrete-time and continuous-time single-factor valuation models. Subsequent chapters will accommodate greater complexity

by including additional random factors besides the evolution of the short rate.

End Notes

1. The authors are well aware that it is not *ground level* wind speed that dictates time of storm arrival, but this is, after all, only an analogy!

2. This is why forward rates are considered to be a biased estimate of the future short rates. In deterministic models of interest rates, one of the traditional theories of interest was that the forward rate was an unbiased estimate of the expected future spot rate. Arbitrage arguments were used to invoke the proof. However, in stochastic interest rate models, a bias exists. Nonetheless, there is a set of spot and forward rates of interest that is *consistent* with (but not *equal* to) the random interest rate paths used in valuation.

3. We leave this as an exercise for the ambitious reader, although by adjusting for scale, we have already performed the necessary calculations to replicate the zero-coupon bonds maturing at the end of Year 3 and Year 5. All that needs to be done is to multiply value of the $100 cash flow by 10 and the $500 cash flow by 2 to achieve the same prices shown for the $1,000 zero-coupon bonds maturing at those same times. The ambitious reader will be rewarded by discovering that the combination of these five short-rate paths produces the same present values, spot rates, and forward rates that were shown in Section 2.1 for the zero-coupon bonds.

4. The complex weighting scheme used to develop YTM is described in Appendix B to this chapter.

5. The cash flows in this example were set to equal the ratio of the preceding short rate to the average short rate for that time point, multiplied by the expected cash flow. For example, $434.60=(10.1\%\div11.62\%)\times\$500$.

Practice Exercises

1. Suppose that the prices of $1,000 zero-coupon bonds are as follows:

One year:	$950
Two years:	$890
Three years:	$830
Four years:	$770
Five years:	$720

   What would be the value of an instrument paying $1,500 at the end of Year 2 and $2,000 at the end of Year 5?

2. Compute the spot rates of interest associated with the zero-coupon bond prices given in Question 1.

3. Compute the implicit single-year forward rates of interest based on the information given in Question 1.

4. Using the spot rates of interest derived in Question 2, what would be the value of a bond that paid $100 at the end of each of the first four years, and $1,100 at the end of the fifth year?

5. Using the forward rates computed in Question 3, what would be the value of a zero-coupon bond that paid $10,000 at the end of Year 4? Does the computed value match the price shown in Question 1?

6. Suppose that interest rates can follow two paths over time, with equal probability. The first path is given by single-year short rates of 8%, 5%, 4%, 3%, and 6%, whereas the second path is given by single-year short rates of 8%, 10%, 14%, 15%, and 11%. What would be the value of a zero-coupon bond that pays $10,000 at the end of five years? What would its YTM be?

7. Using the same two paths of short rates given above, what would be the value of an instrument that pays $15,000 if the first path is followed, but $5,000 if the second path is followed? What would its YTM be?

8. Using the same two paths of short rates given in Question 6, what would be the value of an instrument that pays $5,000 if the first path is followed, but $15,000 if the second path is followed? What would its YTM be?

9. In Questions 6, 7, and 8, we used the same two interest rate paths to value the three instruments. All three instruments paid a single cash flow at Time 5, whose expected value was $10,000. However, the prices and YTMs were substantially different. Why?

10. In Appendix B to this chapter, we show that YTM is approximated by a dollar-duration weighted average of the underlying spot rates used to compute the value of a bond, or portfolio of zero-coupon bonds. Consider the two zero-coupon bonds described below:

	Par Value	Maturity	Applicable Spot Rate
First Zero-Coupon Bond:	$1 million	2 years	8.0%
Second Zero-Coupon Bond:	$1 million	10 years	10.0%

   What are the values of each zero-coupon bond, and the portfolio of these two bonds? What is the exact YTM of the portfolio of these two bonds? What is the approximate YTM of this portfolio, based on the dollar-duration weighted spot rates of interest? Suppose the spot rate applicable to the second zero-coupon bond is 12%. What is the exact YTM of the portfolio of these two bonds? What is the approximate YTM of this portfolio, based on the dollar-duration-weighted

Recall $DD = \frac{dA}{dY} = -\frac{\sum t A_t}{(1+Y)^{t+1}}$

$A = \sum \frac{A_t}{(1+Y)^t}$

DD of $2 Yr = -\frac{2 \times 10^6}{(1+Y)^3}$, $Y = 8.3875647\%$

spot rates of interest? Why is this latter YTM a worse estimate of the exact YTM than the first one was to its corresponding exact YTM?

Appendix A. The Uniqueness of Yield-to-Maturity

One of the most common uses of yield-to-maturity is in the quoting of bond prices. Let us consider two default-free three-year bonds. Bond A offers an interest payment, called a coupon, of $40 each year, while Bond B provides a coupon of $130 each year. Both bonds have a face value of $1,000 to be repaid, along with the final coupon, at the end of the third year.

Now suppose that the spot rates of interest for one, two, and three-year periods are: $s_1 = 5.0\%$, $s_2 = 7.0\%$, $s_3 = 8\%$. The values of these bonds may be computed as follows:

$$P_{\text{Bond A}} = \frac{\$40}{(1+0.05)^1} + \frac{\$40}{(1+0.07)^2} + \frac{\$1040}{(1+0.08)^3}$$
$$= \$898.62$$

$$P_{\text{Bond B}} = \frac{\$130}{(1+0.05)^1} + \frac{\$130}{(1+0.07)^2} + \frac{\$1130}{(1+0.08)^3}$$
$$= \$1,134.39$$

After determining the appropriate prices, we can solve for yield-to-maturity by keying in the prices and cash flows and using the YTM or IRR (internal rate of return) function built into most financial calculators. For Bond A, the YTM is 7.93%. For Bond B, the YTM is 7.80%.

There are three things noteworthy in this example. First, the appropriate yield-to-maturity cannot be calculated until after the correct price has already been determined. Second, as long as

the cash flows are fixed and free of default, we can just as easily use the schedule of spot rates of interest in the valuation of different cash flow streams. Third, each cash flow stream will be associated with a unique yield-to-maturity. In our example, Bond A elicited a higher yield-to-maturity than Bond B. The reason for this is that a yield-to-maturity is a complex weighted average of the spot rates of interest. (See Appendix B.) In this case, Bond A has lower early cash flows, and hence a lesser weighting on the lower, shorter-term interest rates, coupled with a relatively greater weighting on the higher, longer-term interest rates than the weightings given by Bond B.

Appendix B. The Relation between YTM and Spot Rates of Interest

To understand the relation between YTM and spot rates of interest, it is useful to be familiar with the notion of dollar duration (DD). This term is used to convey the approximate change in price of a financial instrument associated with a change in its yield. With this notion in mind, we may now explore the relationship of yield-to-maturity to spot rates of interest. As we will discover, these interest rates are linked to each other through dollar duration weighting. We will demonstrate this relationship first through a simple numerical example. Then we will do so more generally with a mathematical derivation.

Suppose you were to put $2,000 in a two-bond portfolio and divide your money equally among the two bonds. One of the bonds is a 1-year zero with a face value of $1,100, and the second bond is a 10-year zero with a face value of $3,707.22. (These face values may appear strange at first blush, but the justification for their choice will become apparent.) Suppose also that the 1-year spot rate is 10% and the 10-year spot rate is 14%. Then each zero is worth $1,000:

$$\$1,000 = \frac{\$1,100}{1.10^1} \text{ and } \$1,000 = \frac{\$3,707.22}{1.14^{10}}$$

Question: What is the yield-to-maturity on the two-bond portfolio? Since the bonds are equally weighted in your portfolio, in terms of their present values, it is tempting to venture a guess that the portfolio yield is midway between the 10% and 14% spot rates applicable to the bonds. But a 12% YTM would be a wrong guess. Its actual YTM is 13.641%, as verified below:

$$\$2,000 = \frac{\$1,100}{1.13641^1} + \frac{\$3,707.22}{1.13641^{10}}$$

This YTM is approximated by the dollar-duration-weighted average of the spot rates. To see this, let us compute the *DD* of each zero. If we designate modified duration with *MD* and the YTM-based present value with *V*, we can state dollar duration as: $DD = MD \times V$. Recall that the *MD* of a zero is its maturity divided by $(1+y)$, where *y* is used to denote YTM in the equations. Accordingly, the *DD* of the first zero is

$$\frac{1}{1.13641} \times \frac{1,100}{1.13641^1} = 851.77$$

The *DD* of the second zero is

$$\frac{10}{1.13641} \times \frac{3,707.22}{1.13641^{10}} = 9,081.61$$

Therefore, the *DD* of the portfolio of zeros is $851.77 + 9,081.61 = 9,933.38$. Now weighting the spot rates of interest by the dollar durations of their respective zeros relative to the portfolio dollar duration, we obtain:

$$\frac{851.77}{9,933.38} \times 0.10 + \frac{9,081.61}{9,933.38} \times 0.14$$
$$= 0.13657, \text{ or } 13.657\%$$

While this is only a first order approximation of the true 13.641% YTM, it surely comes a lot closer than the 12% that market value weighting would imply.

This numerical example could be extended to approximate the yield of a portfolio having many zero-coupon bonds in it. And since a bond can be considered simply as a portfolio of zeros, we have shown that YTMs on bonds or other portfolios are related to the dollar-duration-weighted spot rates.

Let us prove this result more generally. Consider a portfolio worth *P* dollars, comprised of an *n*-year zero worth P_n dollars and an *m*-year zero worth P_m dollars. Then,

$$P = P_n + P_m \tag{A.1}$$

Let CF_n denote cash flow at time *n*. Then,

$$P_n = \frac{CF_n}{(1+s_n)^n} \text{ and } P_m = \frac{CF_m}{(1+s_m)^m} \tag{A.2}$$

We know from the definition of YTM that *P* can be restated in terms of cash flows and *y*.

$$P = \frac{CF_n}{(1+y)^n} + \frac{CF_m}{(1+y)^m} \tag{A.3}$$

To simplify the derivation, we define new variables to represent the two right-hand-side expressions of (A.3). To emphasize their functional dependence on *y*, we make this dependence explicit in the parentheses.

$$C_n(y) \equiv \frac{CF_n}{(1+y)^n} \text{ and } C_m(y) \equiv \frac{CF_m}{(1+y)^m}$$

so that $P = C_n(y) + C_m(y)$. $\tag{A.4}$

Next, we restate the content of (A.1), but with the two new variables introduced above, adjusted to reflect the difference between YTM and spot rates. We obtain a first order Taylor polynomial approximation of P about y:

$$P = \{P_n\} + \{P_m\} \cong \left\{ C_n + \frac{\partial C_n}{\partial y}(s_n - y) \right\}$$
$$+ \left\{ C_m + \frac{\partial C_m}{\partial y}(s_m - y) \right\} \quad (A.5)$$

The expressions in braces on both sides of the second equality sign correspond to each other. In light of equation (A.4), equation (A.5) becomes:

$$0 \cong \frac{\partial C_n}{\partial y}(s_n - y) + \frac{\partial C_m}{\partial y}(s_m - y) \quad (A.6)$$

Earlier, we learned in Table 2.3 that the errors in valuing of individual cash flows, when applying the YTM of a portfolio, are exactly offsetting. In other words, the total portfolio is correctly valued, but the individual pieces are not. Equation (A.6) formalized this observation. Multiplying the partial derivatives by the expressions in parentheses and collecting terms, we have:

$$s_n \left(\frac{\partial C_n}{\partial y} \right) + s_m \left(\frac{\partial C_m}{\partial y} \right)$$
$$\cong y \left\{ \frac{\partial C_n}{\partial y} + \frac{\partial C_m}{\partial y} \right\} \quad (A.7)$$

Note that $\partial C_n/\partial y$ and $\partial C_m/\partial y$ are the *DDs* of the n-year and m-year zeros, respectively, taken with respect to the yield of the underlying bond, and when combined, as they are in the right-hand-side term in braces, they are the *DD* of the entire bond, which is a portfolio of zeros. Solving for y, we obtain:

$$y \cong \frac{s_n(\partial C_n/\partial y) + s_m(\partial C_m/\partial y)}{\partial P/\partial y} \quad (A.8)$$

The weights applied to the spot rates are the dollar durations of their respective zeros relative to the dollar duration of the entire portfolio. This, of course, is only a first-order approximation of YTM. The formula holds true only in the immediate neighborhood of the partial derivatives, but lacks precision for large absolute spreads between y and s, because it is a linear approximation to a curved function.

3

Discrete-Time One-Factor Models

1. Introduction

Our main concern in this monograph is understanding approaches to the valuation of *interest rate contingent securities*. These are securities whose future payoffs are completely determined by the evolution of the term structure of interest rates. Figure 3.1 lists several types of securities that fall into this category. A call option on a Treasury bond is an example of a security whose future payoff is related *indirectly* to the term structure of interest, but *directly* to the value of the underlying bond. We can use this security to illustrate the issues involved in valuing interest rate contingent securities.

Figure 3.1. Examples of Interest Rate Contingent Securities

Call and Put Options on Treasury Securities
Tresury Bill Futures Contracts
Treasury Bond Futures Contracts
Treasury Bond Futures Options
Floating Rate Securities
Callable Treasury Securities
Interest Rate Swaps
Interest Rate Caps
Interest Rate Floors
Interest Rate Collars
Captions
Swaptions

First, let us consider the Treasury bond. It is treated as a default-free, noncallable security. Thus, the cash flows are both known and presumed to be certain. The value of the Treasury bond is the sum of the present values of the cash flows. The interest rates used in calculating the present values are given by the term structure of interest rates. Therefore, any model of the term structure is also a model of Treasury bond value.

An option on a Treasury bond differs from a Treasury bond in that both the actual cash flow and the value of the security are dependent upon the evolution of the term structure of interest rates. If the option expires "in the money," the cash flow to the holder of the option is determined by the value of the bond relative to the strike price.[1] Although the bond value is dependent upon the term structure of interest rates, unlike the call option, its cash flows are fixed. At any time prior to the maturity of the option, it is the evolution of the term structure that determines the value of the bond and, therefore, the value of the option which is written on the bond. Another example of an interest rate contingent security is an interest rate cap. Its cash payoffs and market value depend *directly* on the term structure of interest rates. We will be discussing this security later.

The fundamental issue in valuing interest rate contingent securities is modeling the evolution of the term structure of interest rates. In this chapter, we will discuss single-factor discrete-time models of the term structure of interest rates. Then, we will use these models of the term structure to derive the value of bonds and interest rate contingent securities. In subsequent chapters, we will extend the analysis to multi-factor discrete-time, single-factor continuous-time, and multi-factor continuous-time models of the term structure of interest rates.

2. A Simple Illustrative Example

In single-factor term structure models we assume that all relevant information in the term structure of interest rates is captured by a model of the evolution of a single factor—the *short rate*. In these models the short rate is defined to be the spot rate of interest for the shortest period of time considered by the model. For a discrete-time model with one-month intervals, the short rate is the one-month spot rate of interest. For a continuous-time model, the short rate is the instantaneous spot rate of interest. Once we know the current level of the short rate, the model of the evolution of the short rate uniquely determines the rest of the term structure of interest rates. This will be illustrated later in this chapter.

The most basic model of the random evolution of the term structure of interest rates is the *single-factor binomial branching model*. In this model we assume that the short rate will either go up or down next period. The specification of how the short rate moves up or down is the key to differences between models in this category. We will begin with a general single-factor discrete time binomial model of short rate movement. The generic branch of this model is illustrated in Figure 3.2.

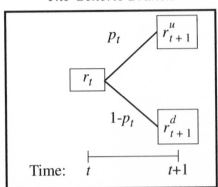

Figure 3.2. General Binomial Branching Model: The Generic Branch

The value of the short rate at Time t is denoted r_t in Figure 3.2. Over the next period r_t will either increase to r_{t+1}^u with probability p_t or decrease to r_{t+1}^d with probability $1-p_t$. If the probability and magnitude of movement are independent of previous movements in the short rate, the short rate is a *Markovian process*. The branching process then repeats. This specification allows for a branching structure that is often referred to as a recombining interest rate lattice, or tree. Figure 3.3 shows a two-period tree that illustrates the recombining nature of the process. An up movement followed by a down movement leads to the same value of the short rate as a down movement followed by an up movement. This recombining feature locally implies the path independence of a Markovian process.

In the general model the short rate moves either up or down each time period. The probability of an up or down movement and the size of the movements can vary from one period to the next. (If they do, care must be taken or the tree might lose its recombining feature.) However, we will consider an illustrative example where the probability is constant and the size of the interest rate movement is determined by a constant multiplicative ratio. We will refer to the model of the illustrative example as the *multiplicative binomial model*.

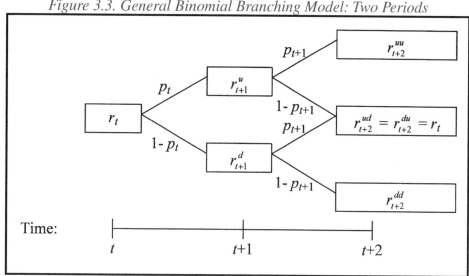

Figure 3.3. General Binomial Branching Model: Two Periods

Figure 3.4 portrays the multiplicative binomial model over a generic two-period interval. The initial short rate, which is the spot rate of interest in force from Time t to Time $t+1$, is denoted by r_t. The short rate in force at Time $t+1$ is either

$$r^u_{t+1} = r_t(1+\gamma) \text{ or } r^d_{t+1} = r_t/(1+\gamma)$$

where γ is the constant volatility parameter.

There are three possibilities for the short rate that will prevail at Time $t+2$:

$$r^{uu}_{t+2} = r_t(1+\gamma)(1+\gamma)$$

$$r^{ud}_{t+2} = r^{du}_{t+2} = r_t(1+\gamma)/(1+\gamma) = r_t$$

$$r^{dd}_{t+2} = r_t/(1+\gamma)/(1+\gamma)$$

We can construct the probability distribution for the terminal period interest rate distribution.

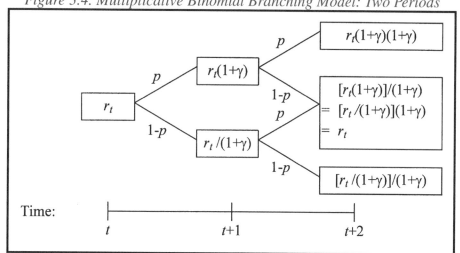

Figure 3.4. Multiplicative Binomial Branching Model: Two Periods

We will observe r_{t+2}^{uu} at Time $t+2$ only if the interest rate moves up twice. The probability of two upward movements is $p \times p$. Similarly, the probability of observing r_{t+2}^{dd} at Time $t+2$ is the probability of two downward movements in the short rate, that is, $(1-p) \times (1-p)$. The probability of observing

$$r_{t+2}^{ud} = r_{t+2}^{du}$$

in force at Time $t+2$ is $2 \times p \times (1-p)$. As the number of time periods in the lattice N becomes large, the distribution of short rates at the terminal period in the lattice approaches a lognormal distribution with lognormal parameters

$$\mu = 0$$

$$\sigma = \sqrt{N} \ln(1 + \gamma)$$

where N is the number of branching periods in the lattice up to time T.

A numerical example of the multiplicative binomial model is presented in Figure 3.5. The short rate in this example is a one-year spot rate

of interest. The current short rate is 5%. The volatility parameter, γ, is 0.25, and the probability of an upward movement in the short rate, p, is 0.5. We will use this simple numerical example to value zero-coupon Treasury bonds called Treasury STRIPS or, more simply, STRIPS.

Consider a STRIP that will pay $100 in one year. The $100 is risk-free; i.e., there is no uncertainty about the size of the cash flow and there is no risk of default. In Figure 3.6 we represent the risk-free nature of the instrument in a tree that corresponds to the first node of the tree in Figure 3.5. At Time $t+1$ there will be a $100 cash flow regardless of whether the short rate increases or decreases. Therefore, the price of the STRIP is the present value of the cash flow, or $95.24=$100/(1+0.05). The appropriate discount rate is 5% because that is the current short rate as illustrated in Figure 3.5. In general, the cash flows would be weighted by their probability of occurrence. However, this is a risk-free cash flow that is simply discounted by the appropriate short rate. This distinction will become clear in the two-period example.

Figure 3.5. A Numerical Example of a Multiplicative Binomial Branching Model

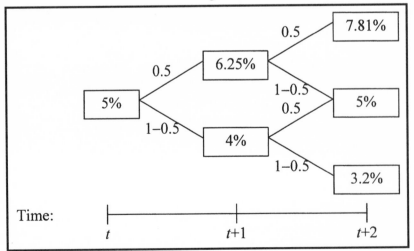

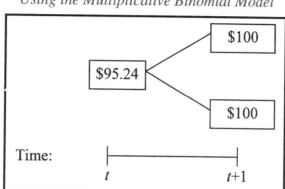

The one-year STRIP had no uncertainty about the discount rate to be used. However, the cash flow for a two-year STRIP must be discounted by a two-period spot rate, or by a series of one-period short rates. A two-year STRIP will allow us to revisit the concept of *discounting by interest rate paths*. There are two possible paths for short rates to follow: an up movement or a down movement. Each of these is assumed to have a probability of 0.5. Therefore, if we discount the $100 by each of these possible paths and then weight the results by their probability of occurring, we will know the value of the STRIP.[2] Thus the price of the two-year STRIP is

$$0.5\left[\frac{\$100}{(1 + 0.0625)(1 + 0.05)}\right]$$

$$+ 0.5\left[\frac{\$100}{(1 + 0.04)(1 + 0.05)}\right] = \$90.61$$

An equivalent, yet computationally more tractable, approach to calculating the value of the two-year STRIP is to work backwards through the tree to arrive at the price. The first step of this process is illustrated in Figure 3.7a. The branch emanating from the upper node at

Time $t+1$ has been circled and represents the value of a one-year STRIP when the spot rate is 6.25% (r_{t+1}^{u} from the tree in Figure 3.5). The price of this one-year STRIP is $94.12=\$100/(1+0.0625)$. In Figure 3.7b the price of the one-year STRIP emanating from the lower node at Time $t+1$ has been filled in. The calculation of the current price of the two-year STRIP is now reduced to the one-period problem represented by the circled branch in Figure 3.7b. Weighting each of the prices at Time $t+1$ by the probability of observing each price and then discounting at 5% yields the price of the two-year STRIP. The price then is

$$0.5\left[\frac{\$94.12}{(1 + 0.05)}\right] + 0.5\left[\frac{\$96.15}{(1 + 0.05)}\right] = \$90.61$$

As this example illustrates, the price of a multi-period security can be found by recursively pricing one-period securities beginning at maturity and working back to the present. Notice that this yields the same price as the previous approach of discounting by interest rate paths. This example also illustrates the value of placing cash flows in a lattice structure. The lattice structure will prove even more useful when valuing interest rate contingent securities.

Figure 3.7.a. Valuing a Two-Year STRIP Using the Multiplicative Binomial Model: Step One

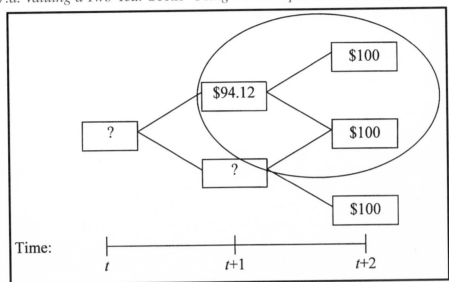

Figure 3.7.b. Valuing a Two-Year STRIP Using the Multiplicative Binomial Model: Step Two

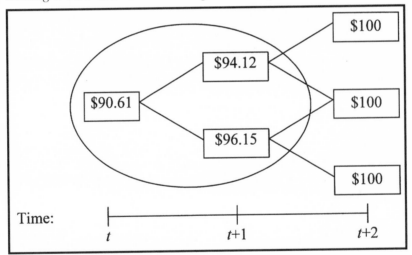

2.1 The Term Structure of Interest Rates in the Simple Illustrative Model

This simple two-period example also illustrates how the term structure of interest rates is generated by the current short rate and a binomial model of its evolution over time. The price of the two-year STRIP reveals the two-year spot rate of interest. The two-year *spot rate of interest* can be found by solving the equation

$$\$90.61 = \frac{\$100}{(1 + s_2)^2}$$

for s_2. The solution is

$$s_2 = \sqrt{\frac{\$100}{\$90.61}} - 1 = 5.054\%$$

The *forward rates of interest* are also implicit in the lattice model. Given the two-period example and recognizing that f_0 is known, there remains only one forward rate to be calculated, f_1. An assumption of no arbitrage is necessary to define the implied forward rate. An *arbitrage opportunity* is an investment strategy that meets two criteria:

- it pays a positive cash inflow to its adopter when it is first set up, and
- it cannot, under any scenario, require that its adopter suffer any net cash outflow on any date.

Arbitrage opportunities are sometimes called "free lunches," one of the few things famous for being non-existent. Arbitrage opportunities are so attractive that their availability induces virtually instantaneous and unrestricted attempts to capitalize on them by purchasing underpriced and selling overpriced securities. This buying and selling will, in a well-functioning market, cause the prices of underpriced securities to rise and the prices of overpriced securities to fall until the arbitrage opportunity has been competed out of existence.

Consider two strategies for investing now in anticipation of receiving $100 in two years. First, a one-year zero-coupon bond yielding $f_0 = s_1$ could be purchased and then in a year the proceeds could be rolled over into a new one-year zero-coupon bond. The implied forward rate, f_1, is the rate that can be locked in at Time 0 for the second one-year zero-coupon bond. Second, a two-year zero-coupon bond could be purchased. The prices of these strategies, denoted by A_1 and A_2, are

$$A_1 = \frac{\$100}{(1 + f_0)(1 + f_1)}$$

$$A_2 = \frac{\$100}{(1 + s_2)^2}$$

Consider the case where $A_1 > A_2$. Selling the first strategy and then investing in the second strategy would yield $A_1 - A_2$. The proceeds from the second strategy would fully fund the obligation incurred by selling the first strategy. This is an arbitrage profit. Similar reasoning leads to an arbitrage profit if $A_1 < A_2$. In either case the market will drive prices so that any two strategies involving Treasury securities that have the same cash flows will have the same prices. Therefore, A_1 must equal A_2 in equilibrium.

Setting $A_1 = A_2$ and rearranging terms leads to the following expression for the forward rate,

$$f_1 = \frac{\$100/(1 + s_1)}{\$100/(1 + s_2)^2} - 1$$

Notice that the numerator and denominator of the fraction on the right-hand side are the prices of one-period and two-period zero-coupon bonds, respectively. Thus, the forward rate must be

$$f_1 = \frac{P_1}{P_2} - 1$$

In general, the implied forward rates are the future one-period interest rates that can be locked in at any time, t. The general formula for the implied forward rates of interest at Time t is

$$f_t = \frac{P_t}{P_{t+1}} - 1$$

The binomial lattice models have an entire term structure of spot and forward rates of interest implicit in them. In fact, each node of the lattice could be considered as the initial time period and level of the short rate. Emanating in a rightward direction from each node is a complete binomial lattice that can be used to determine the spot rates of interest for all maturities encompassed by the lattice as well as the implied forward rates of interest for all future time periods within the lattice. Thus, a single-factor discrete-time model of the evolution of the short rate does, in fact, represent a model of the evolution of the entire term structure of interest rates.

2.2 Interest Rate Contingent Claims in the Simple Illustrative Model

Given a model of the evolution of the term structure of interest rates, interest rate contingent securities can be valued. Take an *interest rate cap* as an example. A cap is an over-the-counter security that derives its cash flows from some underlying interest rate such as LIBOR, commercial paper rates, STRIP yields, or prime rates. Cash flows occur periodically from monthly to annual intervals. The terms of the contracts are normally between three years and twelve years. The key feature of an interest rate cap is the *strike level*. The cash flows are either zero or the current level of the index rate minus the strike level of the index rate times the *notional amount*, whichever is greater.[3]

Therefore, a cap generates only non-negative cash flows to the purchaser. Stated in a formula, a cap pays

$$\text{Max}[\{(Index\ level - Strike\ level)$$
$$\times \left(\frac{Days\ in\ Period}{360}\right)(Notional\ Amount)\},0]$$

at each payment date. The index level and strike level are stated as annual percentage rates. The term (Days in Period/360) scales the interest rates to the period of the contract.

Returning to the multiplicative binomial model example from Figure 3.5, the interest rate cap can be valued by constructing a cash flow tree and then discounting based on the short rate tree. Consider a two-year cap with a strike level of 6% and a notional principal of $100. The cash flow tree for valuing this cap is illustrated in Figure 3.8. Now the lattice in Figure 3.5 is interpreted as a two-year model of the evolution of the one-year spot rate. The cash flows in Figure 3.8 are $\text{Max}[\{(r_t - \text{strike level})(\text{notional amount})\},0]=\text{Max}[\{(r_t-0.06)(\$100)\},0]$.

Figure 3.8. Cash Flows for an Interest Rate Cap with a 6% Strike Level Using the Multiplicative Binomial Model

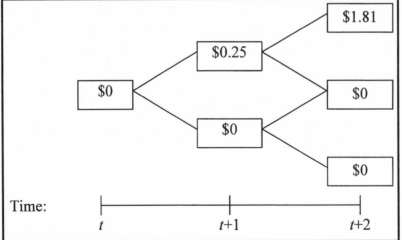

The value of the cap is found by discounting the cash flows in one-period steps, working recursively back from maturity to the present, just as with the STRIPs. The relevant discount rates are taken from the lattice in Figure 3.5. The valuation tree for a cap written on the interest rate modeled in Figure 3.5 is illustrated in Figure 3.9. The relevant calculations are for the nodes marked A and B. The value at the node denoted by A is the expected present value of the cash flows at Time $t+2$ emanating from this node plus the cash flow occurring at this node. The discount rate corresponding to this node is 6.25%. Thus, the calculation for node A is

$$\$1.10 = \frac{(0.5)(\$1.81) + (0.5)(\$0.00)}{(1 + 0.0625)} + \$0.25$$

The calculation for node B is just the expected present value of the cash flows emanating from this node. Thus, the current value of the cap is

$$\$0.52 = \frac{(0.5)(\$1.10) + (0.5)(\$0.00)}{(1 + 0.05)}$$

The interest rate cap can serve as a hedge to borrowers against rising interest rates. In effect, it is insurance against the cost of rising interest rates. Consider a three-year floating-rate loan of $100. The annual interest payments are set equal to the applicable one-year spot rates of interest. Thus, the first year's interest payment is $5.00=(0.05)($100). If the interest rate increases during the second year, then according to the model in Figure 3.5, the interest payment would be $6.25=(0.0625)($100). However, the interest rate cap would effectively cap the borrower's interest payment at $6.00 (or 6%) on the $100 loan during the second period. Notice that at a time when the interest rate payment would be $6.25, the cap pays $0.25, making the net interest payment $6.00. The same would be true for the third year. If the short rate rose to 7.81%, then the cap would pay $1.81 and the net interest payment would still be only $6.00. The hedging capability of the cap is valuable and thus a price must be paid for the cap. In this case, the price is $0.52.

Figure 3.9. Valuation of an Interest Rate Cap with a 6% Strike Level Using the Multiplicative Binomial Model

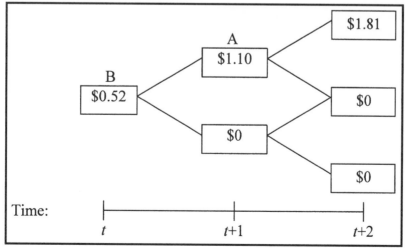

2.3 Arbitrage in the Simple Illustrative Model

The current value of an interest rate contingent claim depends upon the possible realizations of the random evolution of the term structure of interest rates. Since any models of the possible realizations are subjective constructs, we need to place restrictions on their structure to ensure that they are plausible descriptions of what may happen to interest rates in the future. The principal restriction we will impose is that a model must not allow for any arbitrage opportunities.

It is possible to construct a portfolio of Treasury securities and borrowing or lending at the riskless rate that will replicate the cash flows of an interest rate contingent security. To illustrate this, consider a one-year interest rate cap. Using the same parameters as the cap illustrated in Figure 3.8, this one-year cap has one potential cash flow. If the short rate increases, then the cap will pay $0.25 per $100 of notional value. The value of this cap would be $0.119 per $100 of notional value. All numbers in the following example will be stated in terms of $100 of notional value, but could be scaled up for larger contracts.

Consider a portfolio investment strategy to be adopted at the inception of this cap contract. The portfolio strategy will be adopted at Time t, before the random evolution of the short rate at Time $t+1$ is known. The strategy is to
- Sell short Δ two-year STRIPS at $90.6055 per $100 of face value each and
- Lend D dollars at the short rate.

This strategy has an initial cost and will generate cash flows in one year that depend upon the evolution of the short rate. The initial cost and the terminal cash flows will be functions of Δ and D of the following forms:

$$\text{Initial cost} = D - \$90.6055\Delta$$

Cash flows in one year

$$= \begin{cases} -\$94.1177\Delta + D(1+0.05) \\ \quad \text{if short rate rises to } 6.25\% \\ -\$96.1539\Delta + D(1+0.05) \\ \quad \text{if short rate falls to } 4\% \end{cases}$$

where $94.1177 and $96.1539 represent the values of the STRIP one year hence, in the case of the short rate rising or falling, respectively. (The two-year STRIP in this case is referred to as the *underlying asset*.)

Now suppose we choose D and Δ so the payoffs of this strategy match those of the one-year cap under both scenarios. That is, suppose we choose D and Δ in such a way that:

$$-\$94.1177\Delta + D(1+0.05) = \$0.25$$

$$-\$96.1539\Delta + D(1+0.05) = \$0.00$$

In this case the payoff to this strategy after one year replicates that of the interest rate cap under each of the possible scenarios. In particular, if

$$D = \$11.2434 \text{ and}$$
$$\Delta = 0.1228$$

then the proposed strategy and the interest rate cap will have the same payoff regardless of whether interest rates rise or fall. Because the position is closed out at the end of one year, there are no future cash flows associated with this strategy. Thus, the cash payoffs are truly the same as those associated with a one-year interest rate cap. We will argue that, if there are to be no arbitrage opportunities, then the cost of the cap must be the same as the initial cost of the proposed strategy which replicates its payment pattern.[4] That is,

$$C = D - \$90.6055\Delta = \$0.119$$

If the price of the cap were anything but $0.119, then there would be an arbitrage opportunity through the use of replicating portfolios. Arbitrage opportunities are exceedingly attractive, and this makes them extremely short-lived. When implementing an arbitrage strategy, there is no risk, no waiting for profits and no net commitment of funds. That is, the profits are received up front and under no circumstances is a cash contribution from the investor required; an arbitrage opportunity is infinitely profitable in a rate of return sense. A profit-motivated investor will engage in arbitrage opportunities on the greatest possible scale, buying underpriced securities, such as the interest rate cap in our example when its price is lower than $0.119, and selling overpriced securities. When arbitrage profits are to be had through the purchase of an underpriced security, only an uninformed individual would willingly take the other side of the transaction. Thus we expect the price adjustment to be virtually instantaneous when the interest rate cap is either underpriced or overpriced, and our assumption that the prices will be arrayed in such a way as to eliminate opportunities for arbitrage is highly plausible.

This example illustrates a number of important features shared by our more sophisticated, less stylized, approach to be described later. It is the ability to identify and execute a strategy involving the contingent security's underlying asset and a money market instrument which *replicates* the security's payoff pattern under all scenarios that enabled us to value the security. This in turn depends on our willingness to specify a set of scenarios for the future evolution of the term structure that we may with confidence assume is exhaustive. The example studied in this section is based on a model that is too simple to be considered exhaustive, so our confidence in the $0.119 value we derived is correspondingly low. Notice that if there are other scenarios possible which were omitted from consideration, the proposed strategy may very well lead to net cash outflows and the strategy would be disqualified as an arbitrage opportunity. This leads naturally to the question: can this approach be enhanced to accommodate richer *scenario sets* to derive values to which we can give more credence?

Consider the multiplicative binomial model of Figure 3.10. For the next example, consider the interval from Time t to Time $t+2$ to be one year. This means that at the end of one year, the short rate could be 6.25%, 5% or 4%. Notice that this is a slightly richer scenario set than the one we just used to value the one-year interest rate cap. Just as before, the short rate could move up to 6.25% or down to 4%. However, now we have introduced the possibility that the short rate could increase to 5.5902% and then increase to 6.25% or return to 5% by the end of the year. Similarly, the short rate could decrease to 4.4721% and then decrease to 4% or it could return to 5% by the end of the year. This tree was generated by setting the parameter γ equal to 0.118034. This value of γ for half-year time intervals yields the same annual volatility as setting γ equal to 0.25 for a tree with yearly intervals.[5]

Now we have four possible scenarios in our scenario set. That is, we have four possible paths that the short rate could follow over the two periods. This is more plausible than the mere two scenarios we entertained in the first example; moreover, once we learn to value this bond option under this scenario set, we will see that the technique easily generalizes to scenario sets of arbitrarily large size, provided that the set of scenarios meets certain criteria.

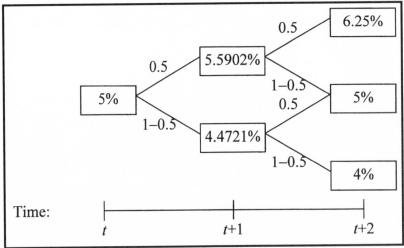

Figure 3.10. A Numerical Example of a Multiplicative Binomial Branching Model with γ=0.118034

A straightforward application of the technique we used in the first example cannot work to solve this richer problem. That is, suppose we attempt to design a strategy involving a three-period, or 18-month, STRIP and a money market transaction that replicates the payoff to the interest rate cap for each of the four scenarios envisioned. The evolution of the STRIP corresponding to the model of Figure 3.10 is shown in Figure 3.11 and the valuation tree for the interest rate cap corresponding to Figure 3.10 is shown in Figure 3.12.a. The values in Figure 3.12.a are derived using the discounting by paths method introduced at the beginning of this chapter. Now consider the following strategy to be adopted at Time *t*:

Figure 3.11. A Three Period (18-month) Zero-Coupon Bond Based on the Short Rate Lattice from Figure 3.10

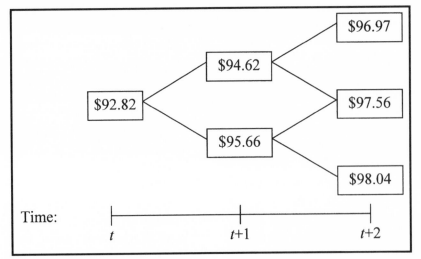

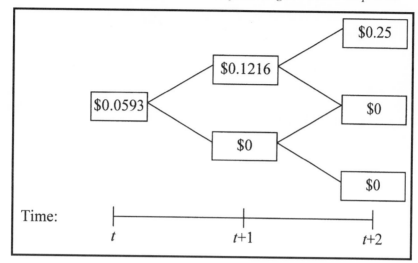

Figure 3.12.a.One-Year Interest Rate Cap Valuation Lattice Based on the Short Rate Lattice from Figure 3.10: Step One

• Sell short Δ STRIPS at $92.82 each and
• Lend *D* dollars at short rate.

To replicate the payoff on the interest rate cap at its expiration for each of the four scenarios, we must choose Δ and *D* to satisfy these conditions:

$$-\$96.97\Delta + (1 + 0.05/2)(1 + 0.055902/2)D = \$0.25$$

$$-\$97.56\Delta + (1+0.05/2)(1+0.055902/2)D = 0$$

$$-\$97.56\Delta + (1+0.05/2)(1+0.044721/2)D = 0$$

$$-\$98.04\Delta + (1+0.05/2)(1+0.044721/2)D = 0$$

If such a Δ and *D* can be found, we can argue, as we did before, that the value of the cap must be $92.82Δ−*D*, the cost of this strategy which replicates the expiration-day payoff to the cap under all four scenarios. Unfortunately, there is no pair of values for Δ and *D* satisfying these conditions. The only values that satisfy the first two equations are Δ=0.422813 and *D*=$39.234075, which fail to satisfy the third and fourth conditions. A

dynamic application of the same ideas will, however, allow us to value this interest rate cap.

We value the cap in this two-period example by solving a sequence of one-period problems, each of which resembles the previous one-period replicating portfolio example. Consider Figure 3.12b. The problem of finding the value which the cap must take at the end of the first period if the short rate rises over that period is exactly the kind of problem we just solved in the single-period interest rate cap problem. Because the remaining uncertainty affecting the payoff on the interest rate cap involves only two possible outcomes, circled in Figure 3.12b, we can find a combination of the STRIP and money market holdings that will replicate the end-of-period interest rate cap value. To be precise, let's consider the following strategy to be adopted after one year should the short rate rise during the first year to 5.5902%:

• Sell short Δ STRIPS at $94.62 each and
• Lend *D* dollars at 5.5902%.

Figure 3.12.b. One-Year Interest Rate Cap Valuation Lattice
Based on the Short Rate Lattice from Figure 3.10: Step Two

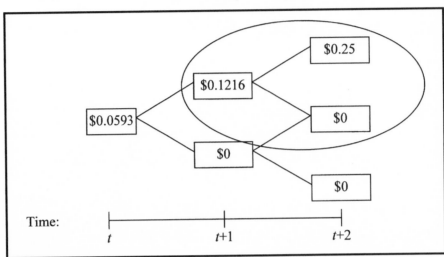

In order to replicate the payoffs on the cap for the top two nodes at expiration we pick D and Δ in such a way that:

$$-\$96.97\Delta + (1 + 0.055902/2)D = \$0.25$$

$$-\$97.56\Delta + (1 + 0.055902/2)D = 0$$

This entails

$$D = \$40.214935$$

$$\Delta = 0.423729$$

Reasoning as we did for the one-period example in Section 2.2, we conclude that, if there are no arbitrage opportunities should the STRIP's yield rise during the first year to 5.5902%, then the price of the cap would have to be $C=\$94.62\Delta-D=\$0.1216$.

Now consider Figure 3.12c. The problem of finding the value the cap must take if the short rate declines over the first year is, again, exactly the kind of problem we were able to solve in the one-period example. That is, consider the following strategy to be adopted after one year should the short rate fall during the first year to 4.4721%:

• Sell short Δ STRIPS at $95.66 each and
• Lend D dollars at 4.4721%.

We pick D and Δ in such a way that:

$$-\$97.56\Delta + (1 + 0.044721/2)D = 0$$

$$-\$98.04\Delta + (1 + 0.044721/2)D = 0$$

This is a trivial problem. Replicating a zero payoff in each state simply entails doing nothing. Thus,

$$D = \$0$$
$$\Delta = 0$$

Reasoning as we did earlier, we conclude that if there are no arbitrage opportunities should the short rate fall during the first year to 4.4721%, then the price of the interest rate cap would have to be $C=\$95.66\Delta-D=\$0$.

Finally consider Figure 3.12d. Now that we have found the value the cap must take after one year when the short rate either rises or falls, we are in a position to find the value of the interest rate cap today. Consider the following strategy:

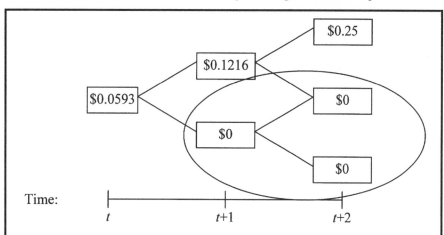

Figure 3.12.c. One-Year Interest Rate Cap Valuation Lattice Based on the Short Rate Lattice from Figure 3.10: Step Three

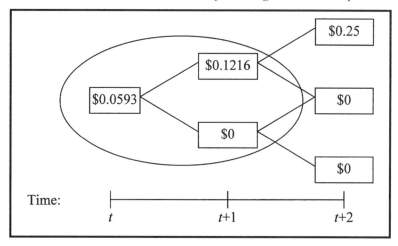

Figure 3.12.d. One-Year Interest Rate Cap Valuation Lattice Based on the Short Rate Lattice from Figure 3.10: Step Four

• Buy Δ STRIPS at $92.82 each and
• Borrow D dollars at short rate.

Now we design a strategy that replicates the values we have deduced the cap must take after one year when the yield either rises or falls. To accomplish this we choose D and Δ in such a way that:

$$-\$94.62\Delta + (1 + 0.05/2)D = \$0.1216$$
$$-\$95.66\Delta + (1 + 0.05/2)D = 0$$

This entails

$$D = \$10.91206$$
$$\Delta = 0.116923$$

Reasoning as we did for the one-period example, we conclude that, if there are no arbitrage opportunities, then the price of the cap would have to be $C = \$92.82\Delta - D = \$0.0593$.

This example is a step toward realism from the first, and it illustrates two more points not seen in the first example. First, the replicating strategy is seen to be *dynamic*. This means that to replicate the interest rate cap's payoffs at expiration we must be prepared to rebalance the portfolio of STRIPS and money market holdings over time as the uncertainty in the future term structure unfolds.

Second, it should be evident that we can extend this line of reasoning to accommodate any number of possible scenarios so long as we can trade frequently enough to keep up with the unfolding uncertainty. Thus our scenario set can have as many scenarios as needed for realism, but the uncertainty must unfold gradually enough that we can rebalance a portfolio after each change in the term structure and each such change is to one of only two possibilities.

Recall Figure 3.2 that depicts the general form of unfolding uncertainty in a one-factor model of the term structure. This branching process can be repeated as frequently as necessary within any given time interval in order to generate an adequate scenario set. With this understanding we now turn to the question of what specific restrictions are imposed on a scenario set by the twin requirements that (1) uncertainty unfold in this dichotomous or "binomial" manner, and (2) no arbitrage opportunities be admitted.

3. Restrictions on Term Structure Dynamics Implied by the Absence of Arbitrage

We will use the same sort of replicating portfolio argument we exploited in the examples of Section 2 to investigate the limitations on term structure dynamics implied by the absence of arbitrage. Consider the following strategy to be adopted at the beginning of the generic interval that is portrayed in Figure 3.13:

- Sell 1 Note at N and

- Buy $\left(\dfrac{N_d - N_u}{B_d - B_u} \right)$ Bonds at B each

where N_u and N_d are the prices of the note in the case of an upward movement in the short rate or a downward movement in the short rate, respectively. Similarly, B_u and B_d represent the bond prices that correspond to movements in the short rate. We are tacitly assuming that N_u, N_d, etc. are known at the beginning of the generic interval. The uncertainty is such that we know what is possible in the near future; i.e., one of the two branches will be followed, and we know what lies along each branch; however, we do not know which branch will be followed by the realized scenario until after we have taken this position.

We have enough information at the beginning of the interval to calculate the initial cost of adopting the proposed strategy as well as its payoff at the end of the interval for each branch.

$$\text{Cost of strategy} = B\left(\frac{N_d - N_u}{B_d - B_u} \right) - N$$

$$\text{Payoff if up move} = B_u\left(\frac{N_d - N_u}{B_d - B_u} \right) - N_u$$

$$= \frac{B_u N_d - B_d N_u}{B_d - B_u}$$

$$= B_d\left(\frac{N_d - N_u}{B_d - B_u} \right) - N_d$$

$$= \text{Payoff if move down}$$

Figure 3.13. General Binomial Branching Model: The Generic Branch with a Note and a Bond

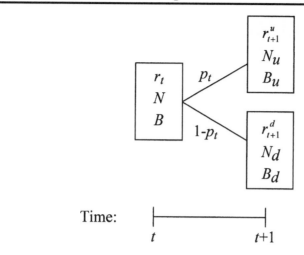

The short rate evolves according to the generic branching process. The Note and the Bond both derive their values from the evolution of the term structure of interest rates. Therefore, there will be a value for both the Note and the Bond that corresponds to each node of the short rate tree.

Because the strategy gives the same cash flow whether the unfolding uncertainty leads to the upper or lower node, the strategy is riskless across the generic interval. If there are no arbitrage opportunities, then the value of this riskless strategy must appreciate at the same rate as the riskless money market account, i.e., the short rate. Therefore,

$$\left\{ B\left(\frac{N_d - N_u}{B_d - B_u}\right) - N \right\}(1 + r) = \frac{B_u N_d - B_d N_u}{B_d - B_u}.$$

This last equation can be rewritten as

$$(1 + r)[B(N_d - N_u) - N(B_d - B_u)]$$
$$= B_u N_d - B_d N_u \qquad (3.1)$$

Let p denote the subjective probability of uncertainty unfolding in such a way that the

upper branch in Figure 3.13 is followed. Now add and subtract the quantity $p(N_d - N_u)(B_d - B_u)$ on the right side of Equation (3.1) to give

$$(1 + r)[B(N_d - N_u) - N(B_d - B_u)] = B_u N_d - B_d N_u$$
$$+ p(N_d - N_u)(B_d - B_u) - p(N_d - N_u)(B_d - B_u)$$

which can be rearranged to read

$$\frac{\{[pB_u + (1 - p)B_d]/B\} - (1 + r)}{(B_d - B_u)/B}$$

$$= \frac{\{[pN_u + (1 - p)N_d]/N\} - (1 + r)}{(N_d - N_u)/N} \qquad (3.2)$$

Note that the expected return of bond is

$$\mu_B = \frac{pB_u + (1 - p)B_d - B}{B}$$

and the variance of bond return is

$$\sigma_B^2 = p\left(\frac{B_u - B}{B} - \mu_B\right)^2 + (1-p)\left(\frac{B_d - B}{B} - \mu_B\right)^2$$

$$= \frac{p(1-p)(B_d - B_u)^2}{B^2}$$

Similarly, the expected return of the note is

$$\mu_N = \frac{pN_u + (1-p)N_d - N}{N} \qquad (3.3)$$

and the variance of return of the note is

$$\sigma_N^2 = \frac{p(1-p)(N_d - N_u)^2}{N^2} \qquad (3.4)$$

Therefore, after substituting these expressions into Equation (3.2), we have

$$\frac{\mu_B - r}{\sigma_B} = \frac{\mu_N - r}{\sigma_N}$$

Notice that we used no features of the securities B and N other than the fact that they are interest rate contingent securities. Since we could repeat this argument for any two such securities, the ratio on the left for any interest rate contingent security must be a constant which we denote λ. Thus our first important conclusion is

$$\frac{\mu_s - r}{\sigma_s} = \lambda$$

for any interest rate contingent security S.

It should be noted that our reasoning has led us to conclude that, for any node in the tree generated by iterating the generic branch from Figure 3.13, the quantity λ, defined by the ratio on the left in Equation (3.5), must be the same for any interest rate contingent security; i.e., λ is an invariant quantity for all interest rate contingent securities. Nothing, however,

about the syllogism we have explored so far leads us to conclude that λ must be the same for each node of the tree. In fact, in general it will be a randomly changing quantity or a stochastic process. Consequently, its value will be a function of its position in the tree, and a better notation for it is $\lambda(r,t)$. We will use this notation only when we need to emphasize λ's dependence upon r and t. Thus,

$$\frac{\mu_s(r,t) - r}{\sigma_s(r,t)} = \lambda(r,t) \qquad (3.5)$$

Equation (3.5) can be read to say that λ is the additional expected return above the risk-free return per unit of risk borne by holding a security and that this reward for risk bearing must be the same for all interest rate contingent securities if there are to be no opportunities for arbitrage trades. Consequently, $\lambda(r,t)$ is known as the "market price of risk."

There is a second important invariant quantity to be discovered. Starting from Equation (3.1), add and subtract the quantity $N_d B_d$ on the right side:

$$(1+r)[B(N_d - N_u) - N(B_d - B_u)]$$
$$= B_u N_d - B_d N_u + N_d B_d - N_d B_d$$

Algebraic manipulation allows us to segregate quantities involving the Note on the left side and quantities involving the Bond on the right:

$$\frac{N_d - N(1+r)}{N_d - N_u} = \frac{B_d - B(1+r)}{B_d - B_u} \qquad (3.6)$$

Once again, notice that we have used no special information about the two securities with current prices B and N other than the fact that they are assumed to be interest rate contingent securities. Consequently, we could repeat the steps leading to Equation (3.6) for any two such securities. Therefore, for any interest rate contingent security, we may conclude

$$\frac{S_d - S(1+r)}{S_d - S_u} = \pi$$

where π also is a quantity invariant across the universe of interest rate contingent securities.[6] Notice that this last equation can be written

$$S = \frac{[\pi S_u + (1-\pi)S_d]}{1+r} \qquad (3.7)$$

Equation (3.7) states, in words, that the value of any interest rate contingent security at the beginning of our generic interval is the discounted expected value of the security's value at the end of the interval where the expectation is calculated using the artificially constructed quantities π and $1-\pi$ as though they were the probabilities of the scenario following the upper and lower branches, respectively. Moreover, the discounting is done using the *risk-free* interest rate. This is peculiar: theories of risky asset valuation, such as the Capital Asset Pricing Model and the Arbitrage Pricing Theory, imply that risky cash streams must be present-valued by discounting expected future values at a rate adjusted from the risk-free rate by an amount that compensates the security holder for the risk borne.

What has, in effect, happened is that we have devised a way to adjust the probabilities so as to make the risk-free rate the only correct discount rate to use to present-value risky cash flows whose risk derives solely from the uncertainty in the evolution of the term structure. The only circumstance in which these artificial probabilities and the subjective probabilities would be identical would be if investors required no compensation for the burden of term structure risk. Such investors could be said to be *risk-neutral*. For this reason, π is sometimes called the *risk-neutral probability*. If investors do in fact require compensation for

the burden of term structure risk, π will not be the same as the actual, subjective probability of transiting along the upper branch in Figure 3.8. We will shortly see how π and p are related.

With the same reasoning we applied to conclude that λ is a stochastic process related to all interest rate contingent securities, we conclude that π is as well. Thus, π might more precisely be written as $\pi = \pi(r, t)$. We will do this only when we need to emphasize the dependence of π on r and t.

The invariant quantity π is also called a "martingale probability." A martingale is a quantity that changes randomly over time in such a way that the expected incremental change is always zero. Under the probability π, the ratio of the price of any interest rate contingent security to the value of the money market account is a martingale. To see this, let M_t be the value of the money market account at Time t and M_{t+1} be the value of the account at Time $t+1$. Now note that

$$M_{t+1} = M_t(1+r)$$

where r is the short rate at the beginning of the interval spanning t and $t+1$. Now, writing $E^\pi[\bullet]$ to denote the expected value operator using π and $1-\pi$ as the transition probabilities, we have

$$E^\pi\left[\frac{S_{t+1}}{M_{t+1}} - \frac{S_t}{M_t}\right] = \pi\left[\frac{S_u}{M_t(1+r)}\right]$$

$$+ (1-\pi)\left[\frac{S_d}{M_t(1+r)}\right] - \frac{S_t}{M_t}$$

$$= \frac{\{[\pi S_u + (1-\pi)S_d]/(1+r)\} - S_t}{M_t}$$

$$= 0$$

with the last equality following from Equation (3.7). Thus, this artificially constructed probability π makes the ratio of the price of any interest rate contingent security and the value of the money market account a martingale.

It should come as no surprise that these two invariant quantities, λ and π, are related in a simple way. Recall, from Equation (3.5),

$$\lambda = \frac{\mu_s - r}{\sigma_s} \qquad (3.8)$$

Substituting expressions for μ_s and σ_s analogous to Equation (3.3) and Equation (3.4) we get

$$\lambda = \frac{[pS_u + (1-p)S_d - S]/S - r}{[(S_d - S_u)/S]\sqrt{p(1-p)}}$$

Now simplification using Equation (3.7) leads to

$$\lambda = \frac{\pi - p}{\sqrt{p(1-p)}}$$

Or, after solving for π, we have

$$\pi = p + \lambda\sqrt{p(1-p)}$$

This shows how the adjustment from the subjective probability, p, to the martingale probability, π, depends on λ, the market price of risk.

In order to illustrate how pricing with martingale probabilities compares to pricing with the "true" probabilities, consider the problem of valuing a simple one-period interest rate contingent claim. This claim will pay \$110 if the short rate goes up and \$90 if the short rate goes down. This security can be valued using the martingale probability, π=0.5, and discounting at the risk-free rate, r=0.05.

$$\frac{\pi\$110 + (1-\pi)\$90}{1+r} = \$95.24$$

Similarly, this claim can be valued using the "true" probability, p=0.51, and a risk-adjusted discount rate. Solving Equation (3.8) for the expected return on the security, μ_s, we get the risk-adjusted discount rate

$$\mu_S = r + \lambda\sigma_S = 0.0520995$$

where λ=0.02 and σ_s=0.104979. Thus, this security's value is

$$\frac{p\$110 + (1-p)\$90}{1+r+\lambda\sigma_S} = \$95.24$$

The conclusion is that the valuation can account for risk through converting the "true" probabilities into martingale probabilities and discounting by the risk-free rate or by using the "true" probabilities and discounting by a risk-adjusted discount rate.

4. Arbitrage-Free Models

There are two fundamental approaches to modeling the term structure of interest rates in a single-factor framework. The first approach proposes a model of the evolution of the short rate. The term structure of interest rates is deduced from the model. The parameters of the model are calibrated to reflect market interest rate data. Examples of this approach are Vasicek,[7] Dothan,[8] Courtadon,[9] and Cox, Ingersoll and Ross.[10]

Ho and Lee[11] pioneered a different approach that has led to a series of models called *arbitrage-free models* of the term structure of interest rates. These arbitrage-free models provide an exact fit to the current term structure of interest rates. While Ho and Lee[12] construct a binomial tree for discount bond prices, Black, Derman, and Toy[13] model the short rate in a binomial tree framework that allows an exact fit to both the current term structure of interest rates and the current volatilities of all discount bond yields. Hull and White[14] introduce a more general set of single-factor models that are capable of providing an exact fit to both the volatility of discount bond yields and to the term structure of interest rates. They also show how the parameters of the process followed by the short rate can be determined by market data. Heath, Jarrow and Morton[15] consider the process followed by instantaneous forward rates and provide general results that must hold for all arbitrage-free models.

A single-factor model for use in interest rate contingent securities will specify one factor as the source of the stochastic uncertainty that drives all interest rate movements and, therefore, all interest rate contingent security values. The choice of driving factor varies from model to model. Ho and Lee[16] and Hull and White[17] specify the process for discount bond values. Black, Derman and Toy,[18] Hull and White[19] and Black and Karasinski[20] all specify the process for the short rate. Heath, Jarrow and Morton[21] specify the process for forward rates at all future times. However, as illustrated above, specifying any one of these three processes uniquely determines the other two through the assumption of no arbitrage. We saw an example of this earlier where we derived the implied forward rates from the model-generated spot rates.

Finally, Hull and White[22] give a detailed description of the numerical methods for implementing these models. They describe the specification of parameter values based on market data and explore practical issues for accurate implementation of these models. They also show the relationships between the various models discussed above. The constant volatility model from Hull and White[23] is relatively straightforward to implement; we will use it to illustrate how a richer scenario set can be generated and used to price interest rate contingent securities. The comparison of models will be left for the fifth chapter.

4.1 Generating the Interest Rate Tree

The particular form of a constant volatility model to be presented here is a version of the extended-Vasicek model. This is an arbitrage-free model in that the model provides an exact fit to the current term structure of spot rates of interest. The single factor is the short rate, r_t, which is defined to be the continuously compounded yield on a zero-coupon bond maturing in Δt time periods. The simple example used earlier in the chapter was a multiplicative model; i.e., the evolution of the short rate was determined by multiplying the current short rate by some parameter. This model is an additive model with the set of achievable interest rates evenly spaced. Any short rate on the tree may be written as $r_0+j\Delta r$, where r_0 is the initial value of the short rate at Time 0 and j is an integer that can be positive, negative, or zero. Time increments on the tree are also equally spaced. The first node of the tree is assumed to be Time 0 and subsequent nodes are at Time $i\Delta t$ where i is a non-negative integer. As discussed in Hull and White, the values of Δr and Δt must be chosen so that Δr is between $\sigma\sqrt{3\Delta t}/2$ and $2\sigma\sqrt{3\Delta t}$ and due to theoretical advantages, they choose to set $\Delta r = \sigma\sqrt{3\Delta t}$ where σ is the volatility parameter.[24]

It will be helpful to define some notation to be used through the rest of the presentation of this model. Let the node on the tree where $t=i\Delta t$ and $r=r_0+j\Delta r$ be referred to as the (i, j) node of the tree. Further, define the following:

$R(i)$ = the yield at Time 0 on a discount bond maturing at Time $i\Delta t$,

r_j = $r_0 + j\Delta r$,

$\mu_{i,j}$ = $\theta(i\Delta t) - ar_j$, the drift rate, or expected change, for r at node (i, j)

$p_1(i, j)$ = the probability of following the upper branch from node (i, j),

$p_2(i, j)$ = the probability of following the middle branch from node (i, j),

$p_3(i, j)$ = the probability of following the lower branch from node (i, j), and

$Q(i, j)$ = the value of a security that pays one dollar if and only if node (i, j) is reached and zero dollars otherwise.

The three possibilities for generic node (i, j) with three branches emanating from it are shown in Figure 3.14. In this model it is possible for the interest rate movement described by the middle branch to be an increase of Δr, to be no change in r_j, or to be a decrease of Δr. These possibilities are represented by panels (A), (B), and (C), respectively. In each case the upper and lower branches simply bracket the middle branch. The choice of which branching scheme will be followed is driven by the value of $\mu_{i,j}$.

The logic we will follow in developing the tree is fairly straightforward. The tree must be consistent with the $R(i)$ in the sense that zero coupon bond prices, and therefore yields, generated by the tree must exactly match the $R(i)$ observed in the market at Time 0. The first node of the tree is set equal to r_0, the current value of the short rate. Next, the drift of the interest rate process, which is the expected change in the short rate, must be calculated. Notice that the drift, $\mu_{i,j}$, is a function of an unknown function of time, $\theta(i\Delta t)$, which is constant within any given time step but can vary across different time steps, as well as a function of the current level of the short rate and a constant parameter a. The inclusion of the function $\theta(i\Delta t)$ in the specification of the drift allows for an exact fit to the yield curve given by the $R(i)$. Therefore, the value of $\theta(i\Delta t)$ must be solved for in order to be consistent with $R(0)$ through $R(i+2)$ at each time step. The solution method will be described below. Given $\theta(i\Delta t)$, we know the value of $\mu_{i,j}$, which is the drift from the (i, j) node of the tree.

At any node (i, j), the branches emanating from the node with their accompanying probabilities must be consistent with $\mu_{i,j}$ and with

Figure 3.14. Generic Branch of the Extended-Vasicek Trinomial Lattice Model

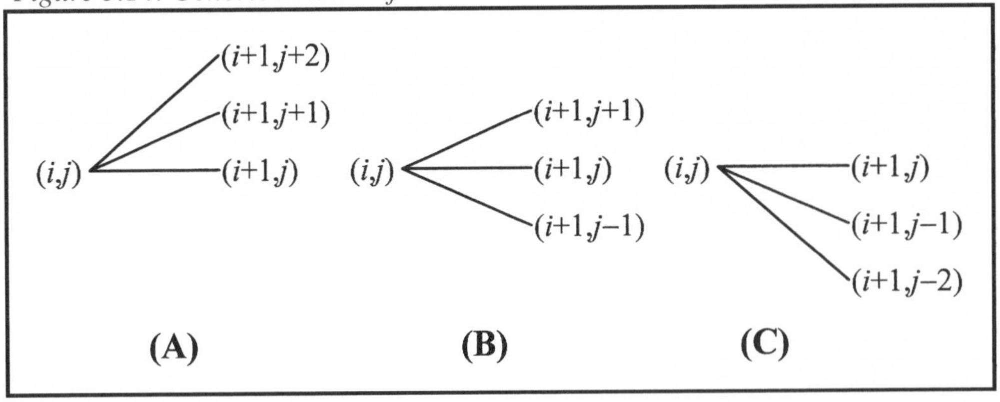

(A)   (B)   (C)

σ. This is accomplished through the specification of the probabilities and by making sure that the middle node is as close as possible to the current value of the short rate plus the drift, $\mu_{i,j}$. That is, the three branches emanating from node (i, j) will lead to three nodes centered around node k, specifically, nodes $(i+1,k+1)$, $(i+1,k)$, and $(i+1,k-1)$, where k is chosen so that the short rate reached by the middle branch, r_k, is as close as possible to the current value of the short rate plus its expected change, $r_j + \mu_{i,j}\Delta t$. The probabilities for moving along these branches are functions of $\mu_{i,j}$, σ, j and k and have the following form

$$p_1(i, j) = \frac{\sigma^2 \Delta t}{2\Delta r^2} + \frac{\eta^2}{2\Delta r^2} + \frac{\eta}{2\Delta r}$$

$$p_2(i, j) = 1 - \frac{\sigma^2 \Delta t}{\Delta r^2} - \frac{\eta^2}{\Delta r^2}$$

$$p_3(i, j) = \frac{\sigma^2 \Delta t}{2\Delta r^2} + \frac{\eta^2}{2\Delta r^2} - \frac{\eta}{2\Delta r}$$

where

$$\eta = \mu_{i,j}\Delta t + (j - k)\Delta r$$

Given our choices for Δt and Δr, these probabilities will always be between 0 and 1 and will sum to one. At this point the process repeats for the nodes at the next time step.

In order to make this process more concrete, an illustrative tree will be constructed for the first four periods. For this illustration, assume σ=0.014, a=0.1 and Δt=1 year. The yield curve to be fit is upward sloping with a one-year yield of 10%, a two-year yield of 10.5%, a three-year yield of 11%, a four-year yield of 11.25% and a five-year yield of 11.5%.

The initial node (0,0) is set equal to the current short rate of 10%. Next, the value of θ(0) must be found. This can be accomplished by using the first two discount bond yields, s_1=0.10 and s_2=0.105. Notice that there are two ways of writing the value of a bond that matures at Time t=2. Using the two-period yield, the value is

$$e^{-2(0.105)\Delta t}$$

Alternatively, the value can be expressed in terms of single-period yields as

$$e^{-0.10\Delta t}\mathrm{E}(e^{-r_1\Delta t}\,|\,r_0 = 0.10)$$

where the expectation is taken using the risk-neutral probabilities over the possible values of r_1. As shown by Hull and White,[25] the expectation can be approximated by

$$\mathrm{E}(e^{-r_1\Delta t}\,|\,r_0 = 0.10) \cong e^{-0.10\Delta t}(1 - \mu_{0,0}\Delta t^2)$$

Recall that $\mu_{0,0}$=θ(0)−ar_0; then by setting the two expressions for the value of a discount bond maturing at Time t=2 equal to each other we can solve for θ and μ. Thus, θ(0)=0.0201 and $\mu_{0,0}$=0.0101.[26]

Given the value of $\mu_{0,0}$, panel (B) of Figure 3.14 illustrates the way the short rate will branch from node (0,0). The formulas for the probabilities for each of the three branches are given above. Those probabilities are calculated to be $p_1(0,0)$=0.462, $p_2(0,0)$=0.493, and $p_3(0,0)$=0.045. At this point we have constructed a one-period tree which is illustrated in Figure 3.15. The next step will be to solve for θ(1) and then to generate the branches for the next period. In order to do this, a general formula for θ($i\Delta t$) will now be derived.

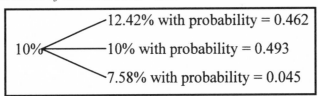

Recall that $Q(i, j)$ is the value of a security that pays one dollar if node (i, j) is reached and zero dollars otherwise. For example, $Q(1,1)=0.4177$, $Q(1,0)=0.4463$ and $Q(1,-1)=0.04086$. In general, the value of $Q(i, j)$ can be found iteratively using the relation

$$Q(i, j) = \sum_{j^*=j-2}^{j+2} Q(i-1, j^*)q(j^*, j)e^{-r_{j^*}\Delta t}$$

where $q(j^*, j)$ is the probability of moving from node $(i-1, j^*)$ to node (i, j). Depending upon how the nodes $(i-1, j^*)$ (where $j^*=j-2$, j-1, j, j+1, j+2$) branch, there could be as many as five branches leading to node (i, j). However, for any given node $(i-1, j^*)$ there are only three values for which $q(j^*, j)$ is not equal to zero. Thus, the summation for $Q(i, j)$ could contain from one to five terms, depending upon the location of node (i, j) in the tree.

Consider a tree that has been constructed up to, and including, Time $n\Delta t$. The process of solving for $\theta(n\Delta t)$ will be similar to that presented above for finding $\theta(0)$. Two discount bonds will be used to infer the value of $\theta(n\Delta t)$. In this case, use one discount bond maturing at Time $(n+1)\Delta t$ and one discount bond maturing at Time $(n+2)\Delta t$. At Time $n\Delta t$, when $\theta(n\Delta t)$ is being estimated, the $Q(i, j)$'s for $i \le n$ are known. The value at Time 0 of a discount bond maturing at Time $(n+1)\Delta t$ is

$$\sum_j Q(n, j)e^{-r_j\Delta t}$$

The value at Time 0 of a discount bond maturing at Time $(n+2)\Delta t$ can be written in two equivalent ways. The left-side expression in the equation below is simply the present value of \$1 discounted at the $(n+2)\Delta t$-year yield. The right-side expression represents the value of \$1 obtained by holding a discount bond until Time $(n+1)\Delta t$ and then reinvesting the proceeds at that time at the prevailing short rate, r_{n+1}. The assumption of no arbitrage dictates that these two expressions must be equal. Therefore,

$$e^{-(n+2)R(n+2)\Delta t} = \sum_j Q(n, j)e^{-r_j\Delta t}$$
$$\times \mathrm{E}(e^{-r_{n+1}\Delta t}|r_n = r_j)$$

Again, the expectation can be approximated by

$$\mathrm{E}(e^{r_{n+1}\Delta t}|r_n = r_j) \cong e^{-r_j\Delta t}(1 - \mu_{n, j}\Delta t^2)$$

Substituting the approximation for the expectation and recalling that $\mu_{i, j}=\theta(i\Delta t)-ar_j$, $\theta(n\Delta t)$ is given by

$$\theta n\Delta t = \frac{\sum_j Q(n, j)e^{-2r_j\Delta t}(1 + ar_j\Delta t^2)}{\sum_j Q(n, j)e^{-2r_j\Delta t}\Delta t^2}$$
$$- \frac{e^{-(n+2)R(n+2)\Delta t}}{\sum_j Q(n, j)e^{-2r_j\Delta t}\Delta t^2}$$

This estimate is an approximation that in practice leads to a tree where discount bond prices calculated from the tree at Time 0 replicate market prices to four significant figures. Errors in the estimates are self-correcting in the sense that if the estimate for $\theta(n\Delta t)$ is slightly low, then the estimate for $\theta[(n+1)\Delta t]$ will tend to compensate by being slightly high. In the case of the extended-Vasicek model there is no need for an approximation because the expectation is known analytically to be

$$E(e^{-r_{n+1}\Delta t}|r_n = r_j)$$

$$= e^{-r_j\Delta t} e^{[-\theta(n\Delta t) + ar_j + \sigma^2\Delta t/2]\Delta t^2}$$

Using this result, then $\theta(n\Delta t)$ is given by

$$\theta(n\Delta t) = \frac{1}{\Delta t}(n+2)R(n+2) + \frac{\sigma^2\Delta t}{2}$$

$$+ \frac{1}{\Delta t^2}\ln\sum_j Q(n, j)e^{-2r_j\Delta t + ar_j\Delta t^2}$$

Use of this formula leads to a tree that will generate discount bond prices at Time 0 that are accurate to eight significant digits.

Now we can calculate the value of $\theta(1)=0.0213$. This, in turn, allows the drift for each of the nodes (1,1), (1,0), and (1, −1) to be calculated as $\mu_{1, 1}=0.00888$, $\mu_{1, 0}=0.0113$, and $\mu_{1, -1}=0.01372$. Therefore, the branches emanating from nodes (1, 1) and (1, 0) will be as illustrated in panel (B) of Figure 3.14. However, the branches emanating from node (1, −1) will be as illustrated in panel (A) of Figure 3.14. The probabilities for the short rate following each of these branches can now be calculated and the process repeated for the next time step. Figure 3.16 shows the interest rate tree for 4 periods and the $Q(i, j)$'s that correspond to each node of the interest rate tree. These $Q(i, j)$'s will prove useful in the next section on valuing interest rate

contingent claims using the extended-Vasicek model.

4.2 Valuing Interest Rate Contingent Claims

As in the simple illustrative example in Section 2 of this chapter, interest rate contingent claims can be valued by constructing a cash flow tree and then discounting back through the tree. However, the approach described in Section 4.1 allows discount bond and European-style[27] derivative securities to be valued quite simply. Consider an n-period discount bond that pays $100 at maturity. The value of the bond is

$$\sum_j Q(n, j)\$100$$

Since the $Q(n,j)$'s represent the value of a security that pays $1 if and only if node $Q(n,j)$ is reached, the sum of these is the value of a security that pays $1 no matter which node is reached at Time n. Multiplying each of the $Q(n, j)$'s by $100 gives the value of a security that pays $100 no matter which node is reached at Time n. This security is a discount bond with a face value of $100.

Interest rate contingent securities can be valued in a similar manner. Consider a European-style interest rate contingent security that matures at Time n and pays $F(n, j)$ if node (n, j) is reached. The value of this security is

$$\sum_j Q(n, j)F(n, j)$$

This method can be extended to value interest rate contingent securities with multiple cash flows if the security can be decomposed into a portfolio of European-style derivative securities. As an example, consider an interest rate cap. An interest rate cap generates potential cash flows periodically until it matures. However, a cap can be decomposed into a portfolio of caps, each maturing on a payment date of the original cap, that pay only once at maturity. We will illustrate this with an example.

Consider a four-year cap with an 11% strike rate, a notional amount of $100,000 and one payment per year. This cap would pay

$$C(i, j) = \text{Max}\{[(r_0 + j\Delta r - 11\%)(\$100{,}000)], 0\}$$

*Figure 3.16. A Four-Period Illustration of Short Rates
Generated by the Extended-Vasicek Trinomial Lattice Model*

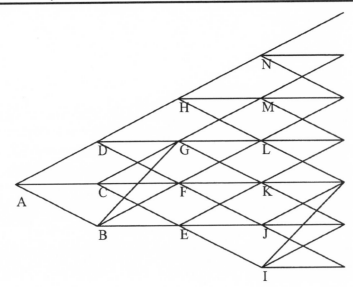

Each node (i,j) represents a short rate and a corresponding $Q(i,j)$ which is the value of a security that pays one dollar if and only if node (i,j) is reached and zero otherwise. For example, the node identified by the label G in this figure represents a short rate of 12.42% and $Q(2,1) = \$0.403$.

	A	B	C	D	E	F	G
Rate (%)	10.00	7.58	10.00	12.42	7.58	10.00	12.42
p_1	0.462	0.044	0.507	0.415	0.286	0.221	0.166
p_2	0.493	0.477	0.451	0.534	0.627	0.657	0.667
p_3	0.045	0.479	0.042	0.051	0.087	0.122	0.167
$Q(i,j)$	1.000	0.041	0.446	0.418	0.035	0.219	0.403
	H	I	J	K	L	M	N
Rate (%)	14.85	5.15	7.58	10.00	12.42	14.85	17.27
p_1	0.121	0.042	0.455	0.370	0.293	0.228	0.171
p_2	0.657	0.426	0.499	0.570	0.623	0.654	0.667
p_3	0.222	0.532	0.046	0.060	0.084	0.118	0.162
$Q(i,j)$	0.153	0.003	0.045	0.199	0.311	0.146	0.016

if node (i, j) is reached for each $i \leq 4$. An equivalent cash flow stream can be generated by purchasing four caps with the same 11% strike rate and \$100,000 notional amount but with cash flows occurring at only one point in time. These caps would have cash flows as follows

$C_1(1, j)$=Max$\{[(r_0+j\Delta r-11\%)(\$100,000)], 0\}$ if node $(1, j)$ is reached,

$C_2(2, j)$=Max$\{[(r_0+j\Delta r-11\%)(\$100,000)], 0\}$ if node $(2, j)$ is reached,

$C_3(3, j)$=Max$\{[(r_0+j\Delta r-11\%)(\$100,000)], 0\}$ if node $(3, j)$ is reached,

$C_4(4, j)$=Max$\{[(r_0+j\Delta r-11\%)(\$100,000)], 0\}$ if node $(4, j)$ is reached.

The values of these individual caps are given by

$$\sum_j Q(i, j) C_i(i, j); i = 1, 2, 3, 4$$

In order to preclude arbitrage opportunities, a portfolio of the four caps that replicates the original cap, C, must have the same value as $C(i, j)$, therefore,

$$C(i, j) = \sum_{i=1}^{4} \sum_j Q(i, j) C_i(i, j)$$

The cash flows of this cap are shown in Figure 3.17 and the value of the cap is \$4115.42. The same value for the cap would be obtained by discounting the cash flows through the tree as we did in the simple illustrative example, but this method is computationally more efficient.

5. Conclusion

In this chapter we have seen that the uncertainty about future interest rate movements can be captured in a simple lattice model of the short rate. In this model, movements in the short rate capture all relevant information contained in the term structure of interest rates. In other words, all spot interest rates for maturities

longer than the short rate are deterministically linked to the model of the evolution of the short rate and the current value of the short rate. We considered a simple illustrative example that served to highlight the issues involved in this modeling process and served to give insight into the conditions imposed by an assumption of no arbitrage. We then presented a more robust model of the term structure from Hull and White.[28] This model is one that creates a richer scenario set. It also is a member of the class of arbitrage-free models that provide an exact fit to the current term structure.

In subsequent chapters, we will enrich the scenario set further by introducing continuous-time models and multi-factor models of the evolution of the term structure. Continuous-time models usually have a discrete-time analog which gives rise to the continuous-time model in the limit as Δt goes to zero. Multi-factor models allow for more flexibility in the evolution of the term structure as more fundamental factors are added. In both cases, though, the increased richness of the scenario sets that can be generated will come at the cost of computational complexity.

End Notes

1. The strike price is a value selected by the investor. If at expiration the value of the underlying bond is higher than the strike price, the option holder receives a cash flow.

2. As will be shown later, in some cases an adjustment for risk is needed prior to discounting the cash flows.

3. Many caps are actually sold on a deferred basis, wherein any payment at the end of a period is determined by the difference between the index level and strike level at the end of the previous period. Some writers have shown that such an interest rate cap is equivalent to a put option on a Treasury bill (see, e.g., Stuart M. Turnbull and Frank Milne, "A Simple Approach to Interest-Rate Option Pricing," *The Review of Financial Studies*, Vol. 4, No. 1, 1991, pp. 87-120, or Phelim P. Boyle and Stuart M. Turnbull,

Figure 3.17. Cash Flows for a Four-Year Cap with an 11% Strike Rate, $100,000 Notional Amount and Annual Payments Generated by the Extended-Vasicek Trinomial Lattice Model

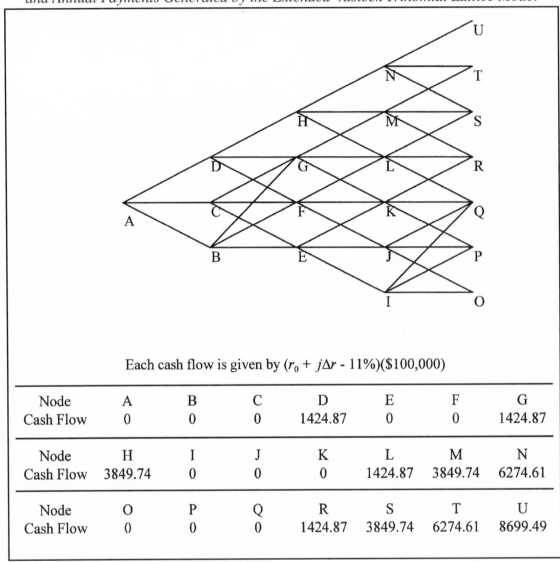

Each cash flow is given by $(r_0 + j\Delta r - 11\%)(\$100,000)$

Node	A	B	C	D	E	F	G
Cash Flow	0	0	0	1424.87	0	0	1424.87

Node	H	I	J	K	L	M	N
Cash Flow	3849.74	0	0	0	1424.87	3849.74	6274.61

Node	O	P	Q	R	S	T	U
Cash Flow	0	0	0	1424.87	3849.74	6274.61	8699.49

"Pricing and Hedging Capped Options," *The Journal of Futures Markets*, Vol. 9, No. 1, 1989, pp. 41-54). However, when the payment is based on contemporaneous interest rates, the payoff pattern on a cap is linearly related to interest rates, whereas the payoff pattern on a put is nonlinear in relation to interest rates. Our presentation here assumes payments based on contemporaneous interest rates.

4. It should be noted that there will be some rounding error in this example. Replicating these calculations, including

the values of the zero-coupon bond, using the multiplicative binomial model from Figure 3.5 will lead to exact results and would be a useful exercise for the reader.

5. Note that $[1+0.118034]^2=(1+0.25)$. Note also that the per period interest rates in Figure 3.10 are stated in annual terms by doubling the semiannual rate, rather than stating them in their effective annual rate equivalents, which would take compounding into account. Thus, the interest rates in Figure 3.10 do not correspond precisely with those in Figure 3.5.

6. Notice that π is used here as a variable and not as the universal constant (3.14159) from geometry. We adopt this notation because it is prevalent in the finance literature.

7. Oldrich Vasicek, "An Equilibrium Characterization of the Term Structure," *Journal of Financial Economics* 5 (1977), pp. 177-188.

8. M. Dothan, "On the Term Structure of Interest Rates," *Journal of Financial Economics*, Vol 7 (1978), pp. 229-264.

9. Georges Courtadon, "A More Accurate Finite Difference Approximation for the Valuation of Options," *Journal of Financial and Quantitative Analysis*, 17 (December 1982), pp. 697-703.

10. John C. Cox, Jonathan E. Ingersoll, Jr. and Stephen A. Ross, "An Intertemporal General Equilibrium Model of Asset Prices," *Econometrica* 53, No. 2 (March 1985), pp. 363-384.

11. Thomas Ho and S. Lee, "Term Structure Movements and Pricing Interest Rate Contingent Claims," *Journal of Finance* 41, 5 (1986), pp. 1011-1029.

12. Ho and Lee, "Term Structure Movements and Pricing Interest Rate Contingent Claims."

13. Fischer Black, Emanuel Derman, and William Toy, "A One-Factor Model of Interest Rates and its Application to Treasury Bond Options," *Financial Analysts Journal*, 46 (January-February 1990), pp. 33-39.

14. John C. Hull and Alan White, "Valuing Derivative Securities Using the Explicit Finite Difference Method," *Journal of Financial and Quantitative Analysis*, 25 (March 1990), pp. 87-100; "Pricing Interest Rate Derivative Securities," *Review of Financial Studies* 3, 4 (1990), pp. 573-592; "Numerical Procedures for Implementing Term Structure Models I & II," *Journal of Derivatives* (1994).

15. David Heath, Robert A. Jarrow, and Andrew J. Morton, "Bond Pricing and the Term Structure of Interest Rates: A New Methodology for Contingent Claim Valuation," *Econometrica* 60, 1 (1992), pp. 77-105.

16. Ho and Lee, "Term Structure Movements and Pricing Interest Rate Contingent Claims."

17. John C. Hull and Alan White, "One-Factor Interest Rate Models and the Valuation of Interest Rate Derivative Securities," *Journal of Financial and Quantitative Analysis*, 28, 2 (1993), pp. 235-254.

18. Black, Derman, and Toy, "A One-Factor Model of Interest Rates and its Application to Treasury Bond Options."

19. Hull and White, "Valuing Derivative Securities Using the Explicit finite Difference Method" and "Pricing Interest Rate Derivative Securities."

20. F. Black and P. Karasinski, "Bonds and Option Pricing when Short Rates are Log-normal," *Financial Analysts Journal* (May/June 1992), pp. 52-59.

21. Heath, Jarrow, and Morton, "Bond Pricing and the Term Structure of Interest Rates: A New Methodology for Contingent Claim Valuation."

22. Hull and White, "One-Factor Interest Rate Models and the Valuation of Interest Rate Derivative Securities" and "Numerical Procedures for Implementing Term Structure Models I & II."

23. Hull and White, "One-Factor Interest Rate Models and the Valuation of Interest Rate Derivative Securities."

24. Hull and White, "Valuing Derivative Securities Using the Explicit finite Difference Method."

25. Hull and White, "One-Factor Interest Rate Models and the Valuation of Interest Rate Derivative Securities."

26. This result is based on the exact representation of the expectation for the extended-Vasicek model given on page 49. In Figures 3.15 and 3.16 $M_{0,0} = 0.0101$ is used. If the approximation to the expectation is used then $M_{0,0} = 0.00995$.

27. In general, a derivative security is any security that derives its value from some other fundamental security. For example, the cash flows of a call option are determined by the relationship between the stock price and the strike price. European-style derivative securities are those that can be exercised, or generate potential cash flows, only at expiration.

28. Hull and White, "One-Factor Interest Rate Models and the Valuation of Interest Rate Derivative Securities."

Practice Exercises

1. Extend the simple multiplicative binomial lattice presented in Figure 3.5 to five periods (Time t to time $t+5$) using the same values of the short rate (0.05) the volatility parameter (0.25) and the probability of an up movement (0.5).

2. Calculate the spot rates and the implied forward rates based on the lattice generated in question 1.

3. Assume that each period in the lattice from question 1 is one year. Calculate the price of an interest rate cap that pays at the end of each year, has a strike rate of 6% and a notional amount of $1,000,000.

4. Repeat questions 1 through 3 assuming the short rate is 3% and then again assuming it is 7%. Notice the impact of changes in the short rate on the spot rates, implied forward rates and on the cap price.

5. Repeat questions 1 through 3 assuming the volatility parameter is 0.05 and then again assuming it is 0.45. Notice the impact of changes in the short rate on the short rates, implied forward rates and on the cap price.

6. Repeat questions 1 through 3 assuming the probability of an up movement is 0.46 and then again assuming it is 0.4. Notice the impact of changes in the probability on the short rates, implied forward rates and on the cap price.

7. Replicate Figures 3.16 and 3.17 for the following parameter values:

$$
\begin{aligned}
\sigma &= 0.02 \\
a &= 0.4 \\
\Delta t &= 1 \\
R(1) &= 0.09 \\
R(2) &= 0.095 \\
R(3) &= 0.10 \\
R(4) &= 0.1025 \\
R(5) &= 0.10
\end{aligned}
$$

Continuous-Time One-Factor Models

1. Introduction

Traditionally, continuous-time models of the term structure of interest rates were the exclusive province of academic researchers seeking to develop economic models that could explain the relationship between the term of an investment and its yield. Recently, however, practitioners began to apply term structure models for the valuation of fixed income and interest-sensitive securities. For example, the Vasicek[1] and Cox, Ingersoll and Ross[2] models have been implemented in their discretized form by Hull and White,[3] among others, and are in common use today. Therefore, it is appropriate to devote some attention to this class of models. In this chapter we will explore the theoretical properties of these models. In Chapter 5 we will introduce issues relating to their implementation. Even when discrete-time models are used, it is well worth studying continuous-time models of the term structure, because they provide the economic intuition that has molded the development of most discrete-time approaches.

2. The Term Structure of Interest Rates

In order to facilitate discussion of this topic, it will be helpful to introduce some notation. We will begin with a discrete-time presentation of the notation (much of which has been used in earlier chapters) in order to illustrate the relationships. Then, we will move to continuous time. First, let today be Time t. Denote today's price of a bond that pays \$1 at Time T as $P(t,T)$. Often, $P(t,T)$ is referred to as the price of a pure discount, or zero-coupon, bond. Define $\tau \equiv T-t$ be the time to maturity. The τ-period spot rate of interest at Time t is $s(t,T)$. This spot rate is stated on a per period basis with compounding occurring once per period. Much of the term structure literature is stated in terms of bond pricing because of the relationship between $P(t,T)$ and $s(t,T)$. This relationship is expressed in the following equation:

$$P(t, T) \equiv [1 + s(t, T)]^{-\tau}, T \geq 0 \qquad (4.1)$$

The locus of prices defined by (4.1) over positive values of T contains information about implied forward interest rates. Define $f(t,T)$ to be the one-period forward rate of interest from time T to time $T+1$ implied by the discount bond prices at Time t. Therefore,

$$f(t, T) = \frac{P(t, T)}{P(t, T + 1)} - 1, T \geq 0 \qquad (4.2)$$

The derivation of equation (4.2), based on the assumption of no arbitrage, was presented in the previous chapter. The expression in (4.2) can be used recursively to give an explicit dependence of price on implied forward rates as in the spot price relationship of equation (4.1).

$$P(t, T)$$
$$= \frac{1}{[1+f(t, t)][1+f(t, t+1)]...[1+f(t, T-1)]} \quad (4.3)$$

The focus on zero-coupon bonds is justified by noting that more complex default-free instruments can be treated as portfolios of zero-coupon bonds. This is true for any security where the payments are certain. However, this simple concept breaks down when the payments become uncertain, as in the case of interest rate contingent claims such as Treasury bond options or interest rate caps. But, before dealing with these securities, the equilibrium term structure for valuing nonstochastic cash flows must be determined. This term structure will also provide a basis from which all interest rate contingent claims can be valued.

2.1 The Term Structure in a Certain Economy

The simple definitions from the previous section can be combined with an assumption of no arbitrage to find equilibrium bond prices in an economy with certain cash flows. Here, a certain economy is one where all cash flows are non-stochastic and all future interest rates are known with certainty. This will serve as a starting point for considering more complex equilibria.

In order to simplify the presentation, define $r_t \equiv s(t, t+1)$ to be the short rate. That is, the short rate, r_t, is defined to be the one-period spot rate of interest at Time t. The assumption

of no arbitrage in a certain economy can be stated as

$$f(t, T) = r_T \quad \text{for all } T \geq 0 \quad (4.4)$$

For a deterministic economy, this condition means that the forward rates must be equal to the known future spot rates of interest. In order to demonstrate this claim, consider the case where (4.4) is not satisfied. For example, if $f(t,T) > r_T$, then an investor at Time t could sell short one bond maturing at Time T, receiving proceeds from the sale of $P(t,T)$. With these proceeds the investor could buy $P(t,T)/P(t,T+1) \equiv 1+f(t,T)$ bonds maturing at Time $T+1$. From the definition given by (4.2), the net outflow of this portfolio is zero. At Time T the investor would owe \$1 on the maturing bond, but at Time T, the bond maturing in the next period would be worth $1/(1+r_T)$, so the net position would be worth $(1+f(t,T))/(1+r_T)-1 > 0$. This violates the no arbitrage principle because with no net outlay, a positive future value was created. An analogous argument would hold in reverse for $f(t,T) < r_T$.

The no arbitrage condition in (4.4) leads to a few simple results that will lend intuition for the discussion of the term structure under interest rate uncertainty. First, (4.3) can be rewritten as

$$P(t, T) = \frac{1}{(1+r_t)(1+r_{t+1})...(1+r_{T-1})} \quad (4.5)$$

Equation (4.5) states that in equilibrium, the certain return from holding a bond that matures at Time T is equal to the total return from holding a series of one-period bonds over the same period. Next, let $R_t = (1+r_t)$. Then the yield to maturity (spot rate) of a pure discount bond can be expressed as

$$s(t, T) = (R_t R_{t+1}...R_{T-1})^{1/(T-t)} - 1 \quad (4.6)$$

The realized single-period return on any bond will be

$$\frac{P(t+1,T)}{P(t,T)} = R_t \qquad (4.7)$$

or the prevailing single-period spot rate plus one.

2.2 The Term Structure in an Uncertain Economy

In the certain economy of the previous section it was straightforward to derive an equilibrium condition based on an assumption of no arbitrage. However, even the most casual reading of the financial section of the newspaper will indicate that future interest rates are not certain. When future interest rates are uncertain, the no arbitrage condition given in (4.4) will not necessarily hold. The term structure literature contains many theories regarding the relationship between the interest rates on bonds of different maturities. One of the earliest of these theories is known as the *expectations hypothesis*. In essence, the expectations hypothesis was derived from the different forms of the no arbitrage condition given above with an expectation taken over the uncertain future quantities. There are, in fact, four general forms of the expectations hypothesis. However, only the *local expectations hypothesis* (LEH) will be considered here.[4] The LEH is derived from (4.7) above. With uncertainty in the evolution of interest rates, $P(t+1,T)$ is a random variable from the point of view of Time t. By taking an expectation over the possible values of $P(t+1,T)$, we arrive at the statement that the expected rate of return on any default-free bond over the next single period is equal to the prevailing single-period spot rate of interest. Formally, the LEH is stated as an expression that is based on equation (4.7) with an expectation taken over possible values of $P(t+1,T)$.

$$P(t,T) = \frac{E[\tilde{P}(t+1,T)]}{R_t} \qquad (4.8a)$$

$$= \frac{1}{R_t}E\left[\frac{\tilde{P}(t+2,T)}{\tilde{R}_{t+1}}\right] \qquad (4.8b)$$

$$= \dots = E\left(\frac{1}{R_t\tilde{R}_{t+1}\dots\tilde{R}_{T-1}}\right)(4.8c)$$

where the ~ symbol denotes a random variable when viewed from Time t. Notice that (4.8b) is obtained by applying (4.8a) to the price in the numerator of (4.8a). Equation (4.8c) is obtained by iterating the application of equation (4.8a). The expression in (4.8c) is analogous to equation (4.5). However, here the price is determined by the series of expected short rates.

This particular version of the expectations hypothesis has the advantage of leading to an equilibrium with no arbitrage in a continuous-time framework. Other versions of the expectations hypothesis can lead to equilibria that appear reasonable but that may have arbitrage opportunities in a continuous-time setting.

Other theories of the relationship between interest rates and maturity include the *liquidity preference theory* and the *preferred habitat theory*. While these theories have at their center some sort of expectations hypothesis, each theory differs in the way it suggests that risk determines the variations in yields on bonds of different maturities. The preferred habitat theory suggests that the relative riskiness of a bond is in part determined by the investment horizons of the investors who hold the bonds. For example, an investor who has a known liability due in 5 years will treat a 5-year zero-coupon bond as less risky than a shorter or longer term bond. This theory predicts that an investor with an investment horizon will demand a higher yield on bonds that mature before or after the desired time.

The liquidity preference theory is actually older than the preferred habitat theory, but can be treated as a special case of the preferred habitat theory. This theory argues that investors demand a higher yield as compensation for holding long-term bonds. The demanded risk premium increases with the maturity of the bond because of the increased variability of long-term bond prices. Therefore, in this theory all investors can be thought of as having a preferred habitat of the shortest period. In either case, investor preferences and, where applicable, investment horizons must be fully specified in order to derive the term structure of interest rates.

In the following section, the concepts discussed above will be recast in a continuous-time framework. Then, using this framework, a continuous-time model of the term structure will be derived.

2.3 The Term Structure in Continuous Time

Continuous-time approaches to the term structure look at time differently than their discrete-time counterparts. For these models time is a continuum—things are always happening. Therefore during any moment in time interest rates may be moving—sometimes as expected but sometimes not. These approaches to the term structure employ sophisticated mathematical tools, such as stochastic differential equations, to model the behavior of interest rates. Like their discrete-time counterparts, the simplest continuous-time models are single-factor models and focus on movements in the short-term interest rate over time.

When time is divided into discrete increments, as in the previous section, there may be some question as to what the appropriate interpretation of the smallest increment represents. That is, should the short rate be interpreted as an overnight rate, a weekly rate or a monthly rate? Much of modern financial theory is stated in terms of trading taking place continuously. With continuous trading, the tools of continuous-time mathematics are directly applicable. Therefore, in a continuous-time representation of interest rates, a single period is an instant and interest rates are compounded continuously. The definitions given in equations (4.1), (4.2) and (4.3) are restated in continuous time as

$$P(t, T) \equiv e^{-s(t, T)(T-t)}, t \leq T \qquad (4.9)$$

$$f(t, T) = -\frac{\partial P(t, T)/\partial T}{P(t, T)}, t \leq T \qquad (4.10)$$

$$P(t, T) = \exp\left(-\int_t^T f(t, s)ds\right) \qquad (4.11)$$

The local expectations hypothesis of equation (4.8) can be restated in continuous time as well. The hypothesis that the expected instantaneous return is the short rate is given as

$$\frac{E[\tilde{P}(t + \Delta t, T)]}{P(t, T)} = e^{r_t \Delta t}, \text{ as } \Delta t \to 0 \qquad (4.12)$$

Then the local expectations hypothesis in continuous time is stated as

$$P(t, T) = E\left[\exp\left(-\int_t^T \tilde{r}_s ds\right)\right] \qquad (4.13)$$

where the expectation is taken at Time t. Notice that equation (4.13) is the continuous time analog of equation (4.8c). It can be derived by following a line of reasoning analogous to that contained in equations (4.8). As in the discrete case, this statement arises from the hypothesis that the expected instantaneous rate of return on all default-free bonds is equal to the riskless single-period, or instantaneous, spot rate. Further, equation (4.13) shows that under the LEH, the price of a discount bond is simply the expected value of $1 discounted by the possible paths of the short rate process.[5]

The next step in considering the various hypotheses of the term structure is to construct a model of the term structure of interest rates. A model could be anything from a statistical fit based on observed prices to a complete general equilibrium specification of the economy and the determination of interest rates. For example, in the previous chapter, single-factor discrete-time models were considered.

The various models of the term structure posit that a finite number of factors completely describe the entire term structure at any point in time. This is the approach taken by Brennan and Schwartz[6] in their two-factor model of the term structure. In that model the instantaneous spot rate and the interest rate on a consol, or long rate, are the two factors. The Brennan and Schwartz[7] model has been widely used and some of its properties are examined in Babbel.[8] A different approach is used by Heath, Jarrow, and Morton,[9] who develop an *n*-factor model of the forward rate curve. They take an initial forward rate curve as given and specify its stochastic evolution through time. More will be said of these models in subsequent chapters.

2.4 A Single-Factor Model of the Term Structure of Interest Rates

The simplest model of the term structure assumes that a single factor captures all relevant information in pricing pure discount bonds. In general, a *factor* is a fundamental variable that is relevant in determining the value of a security. The current value of each factor in a model is in some way determined as a function of some fundamental source of uncertainty in the market. In continuous-time models, the fundamental sources of uncertainty are often modeled by a Brownian motion. Thus, the number of factors in the model would be equivalent to the number of Brownian motions employed in the model. This notion of Brownian motions providing the fundamental uncertainty in a model will be illustrated below.

In discrete-time models, the riskless single-period spot rate (short rate) is typically enlisted as the single factor. In continuous-time models the instantaneous spot rate (short rate) is most often used as the single factor. In both discrete-time and continuous-time models, the remainder of the term structure is deterministically linked to the short rate. Examples of this approach in continuous time can be seen in Vasicek,[10] Cox, Ingersoll, and Ross[11] and Campbell.[12] Each of these models specifies the stochastic evolution of the instantaneous riskless rate, hereafter the short rate, through time.

In continuous time this modeling process is accomplished by assuming that movements in the short rate, r, follow a diffusion process, and then by specifying a stochastic differential equation that governs the movement of r through time.

$$dr = b(r, t)dt + a(r, t)dZ \qquad (4.14)$$

where $b(r,t)$ and $a^2(r,t)$ are the instantaneous drift and instantaneous variance of the process, respectively. Notice that $a(r,t)$ is the instantaneous standard deviation, or square root of the instantaneous variance, of the short rate process. The last term, dZ, is the increment to a standard Brownian motion, or Wiener process,

$\{Z_t\}$. Increments to the process, $\{Z_t\}$, have mean zero and standard deviation one.

Perhaps the best way to illustrate this rather curious looking mathematical expression is with an analogy. Suppose you were at your desk job and wanted to retreat to the water cooler, where an unofficial social gathering usually takes place during working hours. As you start toward the water cooler, you no sooner take a step than the boss spots your intention and kicks you in some random direction. You then recover your bearings and head again toward the water cooler, whereupon the boss again delivers a swift kick, strong enough to relocate you in a random direction. The kicks vary not only in direction but also in strength. Some of them may hardly budge you at all, while others cause a substantial relocation. If this process were to repeat itself continuously and *ad infinitum*, not only would you have a sore backside, but there is no telling where you might end up.

In the stochastic differential equation, the left-side *dr* term represents the movement in the short-term interest rate at each instant in time. Its movements are determined by the combination of two forces—a deterministic force and a stochastic force. The first right-hand-side expression, $b(r,t)dt$, is the deterministic component of the formula and represents the general direction in which the short rate tends to drift, analogous to your movement toward the water cooler. The second right-hand-side expression, $a(r,t)dZ$, is the stochastic component, analogous to the boss's kicks, producing continuous, random dislocations in the movements of the short-term interest rate as it attempts to drift in its desired direction. In this way, fundamental uncertainty is introduce into the model of our single factor, the short rate.

In a simple model of bond pricing, it is assumed that all bond prices are functions of the current short rate and time; therefore, the price of any default-free bond can be written as $P(r,t,T)$. Notice that the price now explicitly reflects the dependence on the current short rate, the current point in time and the time of maturity. We will use this notational convention throughout the remainder of the chapter. Using Ito's lemma,[13] the price of a zero-coupon bond will evolve according to

$$\frac{dP(r,t,T)}{P(r,t,T)} = \alpha(r,t,T)dt + \sigma(r,t,T)dZ \quad (4.15)$$

where

$$\alpha(r,t,T)P = \frac{1}{2}a^2(r,t)P_{rr} + b(r,t)P_r + P_t \quad (4.16)$$

$$\sigma(r,t,T)P = a(r,t)P_r \quad (4.17)$$

and where subscripts denote partial derivatives.

Equation (4.15) implies that, within this model, price changes for bonds of all maturities are perfectly correlated.[14] Further, it is straightforward to show that for any two bonds, $G(r,t,T)$ and $F(r,t,T)$, their risk premia will be proportional to their standard deviations of return.

Consider a zero net investment portfolio of w_G dollars of bond G, w_F dollars of bond F, and (w_G+w_F) dollars borrowed at the instantaneous riskless rate, r. The instantaneous return on this portfolio is

$$[w_G(\alpha_G - r) + w_F(\alpha_F - r)]dt$$

$$+ [w_G\sigma_G + w_F\sigma_F]dZ \quad (4.18)$$

Equation (4.18) must be equal to zero in order to preclude arbitrage opportunities. Careful choice of w_G and w_F will remove the stochastic term from (4.18) and then the drift can be set equal to zero to see that in equilibrium both bonds must, at any point in time, satisfy

$$\frac{\alpha_G - r}{\sigma_G} = \frac{\alpha_F - r}{\sigma_F} = \lambda(r, t) \qquad (4.19)$$

Equation (4.19) is the continuous-time equivalent of the result we derived in Chapter 3. For all interest rate contingent securities the reward-to-risk ratio must be constant. As before, this invariant quantity, referred to as the market price of risk, is a function of the current short rate and time period. Equation (4.19) can be used to find the value of a discount bond. Consider equation (4.19) restated for a generic security,

$$\frac{\alpha(r, t, T) - r}{\sigma(r, t, T)} = \lambda(r, t)$$

Next, the valuation equation for a generic bond can be derived. Solving for $\alpha(r,t,T)$ for a generic bond and substituting from (4.17) for $\sigma(r,t,T)$ yields

$$\alpha(r, t, T) = \lambda(r, t)a(r, t)\frac{P_r}{P} + r \qquad (4.20)$$

Substitute $\alpha(r,t,T)$ from (4.20) into (4.16) to get the valuation equation.

$$\frac{1}{2}a^2(r, t)P_{rr} + [b(r, t) - \lambda(r, t)a(r, t)]P_r$$
$$+ P_t - rP = 0 \qquad (4.21)$$

where subscripts on P denote partial derivatives, and a double subscript denotes second partial derivatives. The solution of this partial differential equation, together with appropriate boundary conditions, is the value of a discount bond of the form $P(r,t,T)$. The boundary condition at maturity is $P(r,T,T)=1$. Boundary conditions for r complete the specification of the problem to be solved. As r approaches infinity, the value of the discount bond will approach zero. This is due to the effect of discounting at

an infinite rate. The boundary value for $r=0$ depends on the form of (4.14).

If the interest rate process is time homogeneous, i.e., the coefficients $a(.)$ and $b(.)$ do not depend on time, then the expected rate of return on each bond will not depend on calendar time explicitly, but rather on time to maturity. In this case the function for the bond's value can be written as $P(r,\tau)$, where $\tau=T-t$, and the risk premium function will depend only on the interest rate. Also, when the LEH holds, the expected instantaneous return for the bond is the spot rate. From equation (4.19), when the LEH holds, $\lambda(r,t)=0$.[15]

Next, consider a specific example of a single-factor model of the term structure. The model, commonly referred to as the Cox, Ingersoll, Ross (CIR) model, specifies that the short rate, r, follows an Ornstein-Uhlenbeck mean reverting process. Specifically,

$$dr = \kappa(\mu - r)dt + \sigma\sqrt{r}dZ \qquad (4.22)$$

This corresponds to equation (4.14) with $b(r,t)=\kappa(\mu-r)$ and $a^2(r,t)=\sigma^2 r$.

Let us dissect the two right-hand-side expressions of (4.22) further to gain a better understanding of the nature of this interest rate process. The first, or *drift*, term has four components. The long-run equilibrium rate of interest, denoted by μ, is the rate toward which the short rate reverts (μ is analogous to the location of the water cooler in our illustration). The gap between its current and long-run equilibrium level is represented by $(\mu-r)$. (This is analogous to the distance between yourself and the water cooler in our illustration.) The term κ is a measure of the sense of urgency exhibited in financial markets to close the gap, and gives the speed at which the gap is reduced, where the speed is expressed in annual terms. The higher the κ, the greater the urgency, or speed. In our illustration, it is a measure of intensity of physical/social thirst. The term dt represents a tiny increment in time. Because μ is a "mean" interest rate, in a sense, this formulation is sometimes referred to as a "mean reversion model."

To be concrete, suppose the long-run equilibrium rate of interest, μ, is 5%, and that the current short-term rate, r, is 9%. This represents a gap of –4%. If κ is 0.5, that would indicate that the short rate is expected to drift downward, half of the way toward its long-run equilibrium level, within a year, thereby closing the remaining gap to 2%. If this deterministic process were to go on unimpeded, by the next year the short rate would be at 7% and the remaining gap of 2% would again be lessened by one half, or to 1%, by the end of the second year. The process would continue until the drift ultimately brings the two rates into convergence. Note that the wider the gap, the larger the expected movements in the short rate are toward closing the gap. If the gap is negative, the short rate should drift downward. If it is positive, the short rate should drift upward toward μ.

Except for one thing. Recall the random kicks. The second right-hand-side expression represents a stochastic, random element that also influences the trajectory of the short rate. You can think of the dZ term as a *diffusion process*, much like the one that would be followed by molecules from a drop of perfume diffusing around in a room until they permeate the entire room space. The increments to diffusion movements must be scaled upward so that they correspond to units appropriate for measuring interest rate movements. This is accomplished by multiplying dZ, which is defined as having a standard deviation of one, by $\sigma\sqrt{r}$. In essence, the randomness is introduced as if random

numbers were being drawn from a standard normal distribution and then scaled by a factor that makes the "kick" correspond to the standard deviation of the interest rate process. The term σ is a partial measure of interest rate volatility, and is assumed to be constant here. However, the full measure of volatility, $\sigma\sqrt{r}$, will depend upon the level of interest rates. For example, if r is high, then $\sigma\sqrt{r}$ will deliver a larger "kick" than if r is low. This is a useful feature in modeling interest rates and also accords with historical observations about their behavior. Interest rates tend to be more volatile when they are high than when they are low, as demonstrated in Figure 4.1.

A side benefit from employing this formulation is that as interest rates get very low, the size of the "kicks" to the interest rate tends to become extremely small. Indeed, if the short rate were ever to hit 0%, the $\sigma\sqrt{r}$ "kick" term also would be zero, and all of the movement in the short rate would be due to the first, or drift, component of the stochastic differential equation. This means that the CIR model will not allow interest rates to become negative, which is a very useful property of a system that purports to properly model interest rate behavior. As interest rates drift upward from zero, the stochastic "kick" term would again exert its influence. The influence could be substantial if interest rates get very high, because $\sigma\sqrt{r}$ would gain in value. However, at very high interest rates, the influence of the downward drift pressure would again begin to dominate the stochastic kick element, because the strength of the kick grows at $\sqrt{r}$, whereas the strength of the drift is related to r itself, which increases more rapidly than its square root. If this were not the case, the interest rates could eventually explode to levels without bounds. Thus, this concise model of interest rate behavior has another desirable property.

In general, the relative influence of the deterministic and stochastic components of the short-term interest rate depends on four parameters: the level of the instantaneous short rate (which enters into both the deterministic and the stochastic components), the long-run mean interest rate level (which enters only into the deterministic component), the speed of mean reversion (which also enters only into the deterministic component), and the volatility scaling factor (which enters only into the stochastic component).

In Figure 4.1, we illustrate three possible interest rate paths that are consistent with this type of process. The parameter values are stated in annualized terms. Initially r is set at 18%, 10% or 2%, but drifts toward μ, at 10%. The drift is continuously jarred by the stochastic term, and may thus never cause the short-term rate to reach its long-run average level. The path originating at 10% shows how the short

rate may remain below the long-run average of 10% for an extended time due to the stochastic term. On the other hand, the paths originating at 18% and 2% show how the interest rate may overshoot its mark and jump to the other side of μ, at which point the sign of the drift will be reversed. As r approaches μ, the drift term becomes very small, and its influence is easily overpowered by the stochastic term. The process creates an infinite number of these interest rate paths.

We turn our attention now to valuing discount bonds based on assuming a diffusion process of the form (4.22) for the short rate. The form of the valuation equation will be the same as equation (4.21). Assuming that the LEH holds, and substituting for appropriate terms from a diffusion of the form (4.22), the valuation equation is

$$\frac{1}{2}\sigma^2 r P_{rr} + \kappa(\mu - r)P_r - P_\tau - rP = 0 \quad (4.23)$$

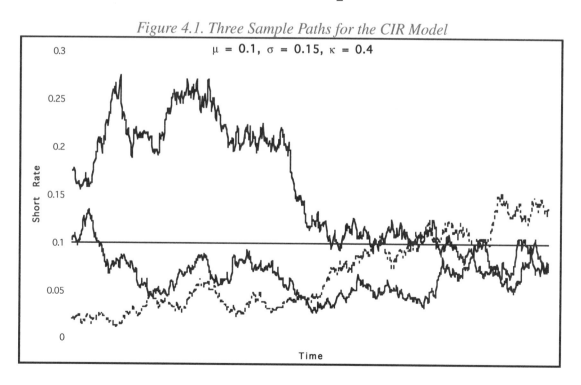

Figure 4.1. Three Sample Paths for the CIR Model

where subscripts on P denote partial derivatives and, because $\tau=T-t$, $P_\tau=-P_t$. The terminal condition is $P(r,0)=1$. This particular model of the term structure was solved in closed form by Cox, Ingersoll, and Ross (1985).[16] The price of a zero-coupon bond is given by

$$P(r,\tau) = A(\tau)e^{B(\tau)r} \qquad (4.24)$$

where

$$A(\tau) = \left(\frac{2\gamma e^{(\kappa-\gamma)\tau/2}}{g(\tau)}\right)^{2\kappa\mu/\sigma^2}$$

$$B(\tau) = \frac{-2(1-e^{-\gamma\tau})}{g(\tau)}$$

$$g(\tau) = 2\gamma + (\kappa-\gamma)(1-e^{-\gamma\tau})$$

$$\gamma = \sqrt{\kappa^2+2\sigma^2}$$

$$\tau = T-t$$

The spot rate and forward rate curves are given by

$$s(r,\tau) = \frac{-rB(\tau)-\ln A(\tau)}{\tau} \qquad (4.25)$$

$$f(r,\tau) = r + \kappa B(\tau)(r-\mu)$$
$$-\frac{1}{2}\sigma^2 B^2(\tau)r \qquad (4.26)$$

These two functions are graphed for three different values of the short rate, r, in Figure 4.2. This exhibit illustrates some of the characteristics of the CIR model of the term structure.

First, spot rate and forward rate curves can be either upward sloping, downward sloping or have a single hump. However, both the yield and forward rate curves converge to the same finite limit of $s_\infty=2\kappa\mu/(\gamma+\kappa)$ (Sinf in the exhibit legends). This value is likely to be different than the long run average of the short rate, μ. In the

examples illustrated in Figure 4.1, $s_\infty<\mu$. As shown in Figure 4.2, when the short rate is above μ, the yield curve will be uniformly decreasing. When the short rate is below s_∞, the yield curve will be uniformly increasing. For intermediate values the yield curve will have a single hump. Notice that while the short rate tends to revert toward the long-run average short rate as in Figure 4.1, the long-term spot rates do not. Increasing the value of μ or the short rate will increase yields for all maturities. However, while the impact of increasing μ will be larger for longer maturities, an increase in the short rate will have a greater impact on shorter maturities. The yields will decrease as σ^2 increases, but the impact of a change in κ depends on the current value of the short rate.

The CIR model of the term structure has been used in numerous works as a relatively simple way to introduce interest rate uncertainty into an economic model. Examples include Ramaswamy and Sundaresan,[17] and Kim, Ramaswamy, and Sundaresan,[18] and as a starting point for a two-factor model, Fong and Vasicek.[19]

The valuation equation for the CIR model, given in equation (4.23), is actually just a special case of a general valuation equation. There are two broad modeling methodologies that each end up with a valuation equation of the form of equation (4.23): equilibrium models and arbitrage valuation models. In the appendix to this chapter we present the assumptions used in each of the modeling methodologies and show how these each lead to a similar valuation equation.

With an understanding of the issues involved in modeling the term structure, we will now turn our attention to valuing interest rate contingent claims in a continuous-time setting.

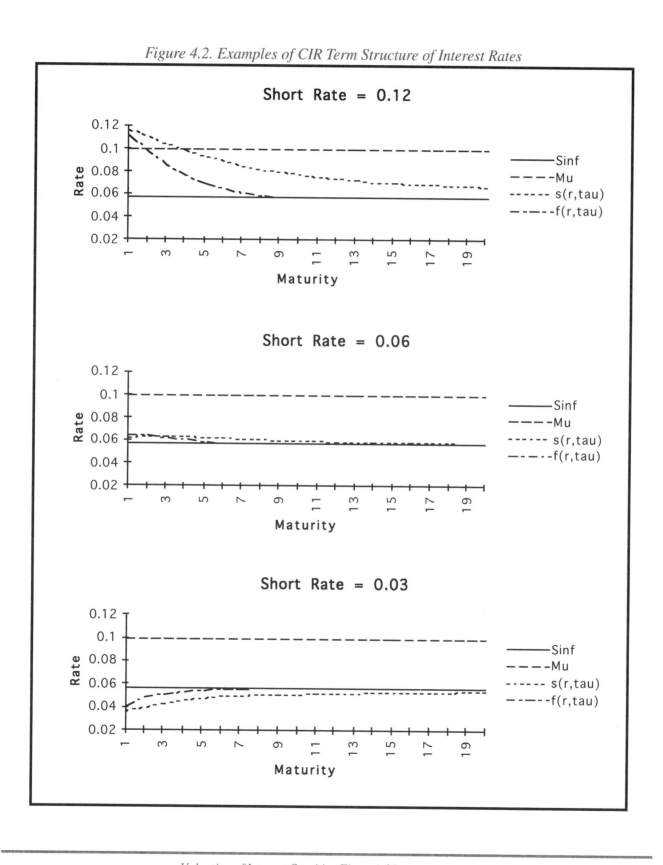

Figure 4.2. Examples of CIR Term Structure of Interest Rates

3. Interest Rate Contingent Securities

In the preceding sections we restricted our discussion to discount bonds and term structure modeling issues. However, much of that discussion can be extended to apply to the broader category of interest rate contingent securities. The conclusion that the reward to risk ratio is constant as stated in equation (4.19) applies to all interest rate contingent securities. Following that discussion through to equation (4.21) then gives us the general form of the valuation equation for all interest rate contingent securities. That is,

$$\frac{1}{2}a^2(r,t)P_{rr} + [b(r,t) - \lambda(r,t)]P_r$$

$$+ P_t - rP = 0 \qquad (4.27)$$

The differentiation between securities is accomplished through careful specification of the boundary conditions.

As an example, consider a one-year interest rate cap with a notional amount of $1 and a strike rate of x that pays once at maturity. This is essentially a European-style option on the short rate that pays $\text{Max}(r-x,0)$ dollars in one year. Let the value of the cap be denoted by $C(r,t)$ where $dr = b(r,t)dt + a(r,t)dZ$. Assuming that the LEH holds, the value of this cap will be determined by the solution to the following partial differential equation subject to appropriate boundary conditions.

$$\frac{1}{2}a^2(r,\tau)C_{rr} + b(r,t)C_r - C_\tau - rC = 0 \quad (4.28)$$

The boundary conditions are on the extreme values of r and the initial value of τ. The maturity condition, or equivalently, the initial condition on τ is

$$C(r,0) = \text{Max}(r-x,0) \qquad (4.29)$$

As before, at any time prior to maturity as the interest rate increases to infinity the value of the security goes to zero. This is stated formally as

$$\lim_{r \to \infty} C(r,\tau) = 0, \tau > 0 \qquad (4.30)$$

Finally, equation (4.28) evaluated at $r=0$ forms the lower boundary for r:

$$b(0,\tau)C_r - C_\tau = 0 \qquad (4.31)$$

Recall that $a(0,t)=0$ in order to preclude negative interest rates from being realized.

Taken together, equations (4.28)-(4.31) form a well-specified partial differential equation problem. The solution to this problem is the value of this simple interest rate cap. Notice that the difference between this problem and the one for the discount bond is in the maturity condition where $\tau=0$. It is this difference that uniquely identifies the security being valued as a cap rather than a STRIP.

We will leave a discussion of solutions to these P.D.E. type of problems for the next chapter. If a closed form solution is not readily obtainable, then some sort of approximate solution technique must be employed. In Chapter 5 we will introduce two numerical methods for obtaining approximate solutions. This will also allow us to show the relationships between the continuous-time and discreet-time single-factor models.

End Notes

1. Oldrich Vasicek, "An Equilibrium Characterization of the Term Structure," *Journal of Financial Economics* 5 (1977), pp. 177-188.

2. John C. Cox, Jonathan E. Ingersoll, Jr., and Stephen A. Ross, "An Intertemporal General Equilibrium Model of Asset Prices," *Econometrica* 53, No. 2 (March 1985), pp. 363-384.

3. John C. Hull and Alan White, "Valuing Derivative Securities Using the Explicit finite Difference Method," *Journal of Financial and Quantitative Analysis* 25 (March 1990), pp. 87-100; "Pricing Interest Rate Derivative Securities," *Review of Financial Studies* 3,4 (1990) pp. 573-592; and, "Numerical Procedures for Implementing Term Structure Models I & II," *Journal of Derivatives*, (1994).

4. See John C. Cox, Jonathan Ingersoll, Stephen Ross, "An Interpretational General Equilibrium Model of Asset Prices," *Econometrica* 53 no. 2 (March 1985), pp. 363-384, or John Y. Campbell, "A Defense of Traditional Hypotheses About the Term Structure of Interest Rates," *Journal of Finance* 41 (1986), pp. 183-193. for a detailed description of the various versions of the expectations hypothesis. For the purpose of this chapter it is sufficient to note that the local expectations hypothesis is consistent with a valid equilibrium.

5. While equation (4.13) looks similar to the valuation relationship that arises from pricing under the risk neutral probability measure [see Jonathan E. Ingersoll Jr., *Theory of Financial Decision Making*, (Totowa: Rowman and Littlefield, 1987) p. 395], it is actually derived from the condition that the interest rate risk premium is zero under the local expectations hypothesis.

6. Michael Brennan and Eduardo Schwartz, "A Continuous Time Approach to the Pricing of Bonds," *Journal of Banking and Finance*, Vol. 3 (1979), pp. 133-155.

7. Brennan and Schwartz, "A Continuous Time Approach to the Pricing of Bonds."

8. David F. Babbel, "Interest Rate Dynamics and the Term Structure," *Journal of Banking and Finance*, Vol. 12 (1988), pp. 401-407.

9. David Heath, Robert A. Jarrow, and Andrew J. Morton, "Bond Pricing and the Term Structure of Interest Rates: A New Methodology for Contingent Claim Valuation," *Econometrica* 60, 1 (1992), pp. 77-105.

10. Vasicek, "An Equilibrium Characterization of the Term Structure."

11. John C. Cox, Jonathan E. Ingersoll, and Stephen A. Ross, "A Re-examination of Traditional Hypotheses about the Term Structure of Interest Rates," *Journal of Finance*, Vol. 63 (1981), pp. 769-799.

12. John Y. Campbell, "A Defense of Traditional Hypotheses About the Term Structure of Interest Rates," *Journal of Finance* 41 (1986), pp. 183-193.

13. See John C. Hull, *Options, Futures and Other Derivative Securities, 2nd Edition*, (Englewood Cliffs, NJ: Prentice Hall, 1993), Appendix 10A, pp. 243-244 for a good discussion of Ito's Lemma.

14. This is true because dr is defined with only one Brownian motion. However, it is not true if dr depends on several Brownian motions, i.e., the right-hand side of equation (4.15) is of the form

$$... + \sigma_1 dZ_1 + \sigma_2 dZ_2 + ...$$

15. For other issues regarding the case where $\lambda(r,t) = 0$, refer to Arnold Barnett, "Optimal Control of the B/B/C Queue," *Interfaces* (August 1978), pp 49-52.

16. It is not necessary to assume the LEH holds to obtain (4.23). Alternatively, any specification of b(.) and λ(.) from (4.21) such that $b(r,t) - \lambda(r,t)a(r,t) = \kappa(\mu - r)$ would also lead to (4.23). See Cox, Ingersoll, and Ross, "An Intertemporal General Equilibrium Model of Asset Prices."

17. K. Ramaswamy and S. Sundaresan, "The Valuation of Floating Rate Instruments: Theory and Evidence," *Journal of Financial Economics* (June 1986), pp. 175-219.

18. I. J. Kim, K. Ramaswamy, and S. Sundaresan, "Does Default Risk in Coupons Affect the Valuation of Corporate Bonds?: A Contingent Claims Model," *Financial Management*, Vol. 22, No. 3 (1992), pp. 117-131.

19. H. Gifford Fong and Oldrich A. Vasicek, "Fixed-Income Volatility Management: A New Approach to Return and Risk Analyses in Fixed-Income Management," *Journal of Portfolio Management*, Summer 1991, pp. 41-46.

Practice Exercises

1. What is the valuation equation of the form (4.21) for the short rate process

$$dr = \kappa(\mu - r)dt + \sigma dZ$$

sometimes referred to as the Vasicek short rate process?

Questions 2-5 are based on the following information:

The spot rate and the forward rate curves are given by equations (4.25) and (4.26) for the CIR model. Use a spreadsheet to graph these as curves for maturities from 1 year to 20 years based on $\kappa=0.2$, $\mu = 0.1$, $\sigma=0.327$, and $r_t=0.03$. Notice that these are the parameters used in the lower panel of Figure 4.2.

2. Vary κ from 0.1 to 1.0 and notice the impact on the curves.

3. Vary μ from 0.01 to 0.1 and notice the impact on the curves.

4. Vary σ from 0.05 to 0.5 and notice the impact on the curves.

5. Vary ρ from 0.03 to 0.14 and notice the impact on the curves.

6. Equation (4.28) is the valuation equation for an interest rate cap. Equations (4.29), (4.30), and (4.31) are the boundary conditions that complete the specification of the problem that must be solved for the value of an interest rate cap. If $P(r,\tau)$ denotes the price of an interest rate floor, write the valuation equation and the boundary conditions that would comprise the P.D.E. problem that must be solved to find the value of an interest rate floor.

Appendix. The Approaches to Valuation

There are two broad approaches to valuation models: equilibrium models and arbitrage valuation models that are sometimes referred to as contingent claims models. Equilibrium valuation models fall into two general categories: partial and general equilibrium. In a partial equilibrium valuation model some fundamental value is taken as given in order to derive an equilibrium. For example, in a CAPM-type pricing model an individual's assessments of assets' price dynamics or probability distributions are given exogenously. In a general equilibrium framework, these things would be endogenously determined. These two approaches to equilibrium modeling will be presented in order to show that they can lead to the same results using different sets of assumptions. As a specific example, the CIR model will be derived using both approaches. Finally, a contingent claims model will be presented.

In the basic equilibrium model employed in finance, intertemporal uncertainty is captured by a vector of possible future states of the world. Consider a world with two periods, today and tomorrow. There are S possible states of the world tomorrow. A security which pays \$1 in state s tomorrow has a price p_s today and is referred to as an Arrow-Debreu security or a state-contingent claim. In this world there are N assets. Let $\mathbf{n}_j$ be an N-vector and $\mathbf{y}_j$ be an S-vector with each element, n_{ij} and y_{ij}, representing the number of shares of asset i held in portfolio j and the value tomorrow of asset j in state i, respectively. Define the matrices $\mathbf{N}=(\mathbf{n}_1, \mathbf{n}_2, \dots , \mathbf{n}_S)$ and $\mathbf{Y}=(\mathbf{y}_1, \mathbf{y}_2, \dots , \mathbf{y}_N)$. The market is said to be complete if there is a solution to the equation

$$\mathbf{YN} = \mathbf{I}_N$$

where $\mathbf{I}_N$ is an N by N identity matrix. Here a complete market refers to the ability to combine the N primitive assets into S portfolios that act as state-contingent claims. If there are fewer than S primitive assets, then it is clear that no nontrivial solution to this equation will exist. If there are S primitive assets whose payoffs are linearly independent then there will be a solution. If there are more than S assets, then there can be no more than S linearly independent assets. In this case the $N–S$ additional assets are redundant. More will be said regarding the pricing of redundant securities later.

If the payoff schedule of the N assets in the S states is given by Y, then the vector of today's values for the primitive assets is given by

$$\mathbf{v} = \mathbf{Y'p}$$

where $\mathbf{p}$ is the vector of state prices. Finally, if markets are complete, then a riskless asset can be constructed by holding one of each of the state-contingent claim securities. The riskless rate is given by $r=(\mathbf{1'p})^{-1}-1$.

In this framework, a partial equilibrium model would take the state-contingent claim prices as given and would then value the primitive assets. A general equilibrium model would have the state contingent prices determined endogenously. An example of each from the bond pricing literature will be presented. First, the general equilibrium model used by Cox, Ingersoll and Ross[1] (hereafter CIR) to derive the term structure model described above will be presented. Next, the single-factor model of Brennan and Schwartz[2] will provide an example of partial equilibrium modeling techniques.

A General Equilibrium Bond Pricing Model

CIR[3] present a general equilibrium model of an economy with stochastic production. It is a complete intertemporal description of a continuous-time competitive economy. A k-dimensional vector, $\mathbf{Y}(t)$, determines the production opportunities at Time t that will be available to the economy in the future. The vector of expected changes in $\mathbf{Y}$ is $\boldsymbol{\mu}$ and the covariance matrix of the changes in $\mathbf{Y}$ is $\mathbf{SS'}$. The economy comprises individuals who seek to maximize their Von Neumann-Morgenstern expected utility as a function of consumption at Time t, $C(t)$, production opportunities at Time t, $\mathbf{Y}(t)$, and time, t. This objective takes the functional form

$$\underset{C, a, b}{Max} \int_t^T U(C(s), Y(s), s)ds \qquad \text{(A.1)}$$

where C^* is the optimal consumption level, a^* is the optimal proportion of wealth, W, to be invested in each of the production processes, and b^* is the optimal proportion of wealth to be invested in each of the contingent claims. These contingent claims are endogenously created securities whose payoffs are functions of W and Y. The remaining wealth is invested in borrowing or lending at the interest rate r which is determined by a budget constraint.

In equilibrium the interest rate and the expected rates of return on the contingent claims must adjust until all wealth is invested in the physical production processes. This investment can be done either directly, by individuals, or indirectly by firms. This allows CIR to determine the value of the indirect utility function as if they were solving a planning problem with only the physical production processes available. With this solution, they can then determine the optimal values of contingent claims and levels of borrowing and lending, and thus the interest rate and rates of return on contingent claims.

This is an example of endogenous determination of the prices for the fundamental securities in the economy. The solution of the individual's utility maximization problem subject to production opportunities and a budget constraint lead to state-contingent prices. It is in this sense that this is considered a general equilibrium model. Once the primitive asset values, in this case the production processes, are determined, the interest rate and other prices can be determined as functions of the state-contingent claims.

In deriving the single-factor model of the term structure, CIR present a special case of the more general model wherein the change in production opportunities over time is described by a single state variable, Y. They next assume that the means and variances of the rates of return on the production processes are proportional to Y. They formalize these assumptions by using the following form for the stochastic differential equation that describes the evolution of Y through time:

$$dY(t) = (\xi Y + \zeta)dt + \nu\sqrt{Y(t)}dw(t) \quad (A.2)$$

where ξ, ζ and n are constants, with $\zeta \geq 0$. This allows them to invoke the results derived in the more general model and write the interest rate dynamics as

$$dr = \kappa(\mu - r)dt + \sigma\sqrt{r}dZ \quad (A.3)$$

This is equation (4.22) from the term structure material presented above. The closed-form solution for zero-coupon bond pricing model was also presented in Equation (4.24) above.

A Partial Equilibrium Bond Pricing Model

As stated above, in a partial equilibrium model the state prices, or distribution of returns, are given exogenously. The model focuses on the specific sector of interest within the economy.

An example of this approach is the zero-coupon bond valuation model used by Brennan and Schwartz[4] (hereafter BrS) as a starting point to valuing default-free savings, retractable and callable bonds. The zero-coupon bond portion of the model will be reviewed here.

The focus of the paper is to value instruments whose values depend strongly on interest rates. Therefore the stochastic nature of interest rates must be incorporated in the form of a term structure model. Lacking any clear best choice of term structure model, BrS choose a simple assumption about equilibrium that leads to a valuation function for pure discount bonds. They assume that in equilibrium the LEH holds so that the instantaneous expected rate of return on default-free securities of all maturities is equal to the instantaneously risk-free interest rate. They assume that the instantaneous risk-free rate follows the stochastic process,

$$dr = \mu(r)dt + \sigma(r)dZ \quad (A.4)$$

where dZ is a Wiener process. In the absence of a general equilibrium model, the only restriction BrS place on (A.4) is to avoid the dominance of money. This is accomplished by assuring that the nominal interest rate remains non-negative. Assuming that $\mu(r) \geq 0$ and $\sigma(0) = 0$ is sufficient to create a reflecting barrier at zero and assure that the short rate will never be negative. Also, the economy is assumed to be complete with no frictions on exchange.

The value of the pure discount bond promising \$1 at maturity is expressed as $B(r,\tau)$ where t is the time to maturity. Using Ito's lemma, the dynamics for the bond are given by

$$dB = B_r dr + \frac{1}{2}B_{rr}(dr)^2 + B_t dt \quad (A.5)$$

where the subscripts denote partial derivatives. Then, substituting $\sigma^2(r)dt=(dr)^2$ and noting that $dt=-d\tau$,

$$\frac{dB}{B} = \frac{-B_\tau + \mu(r)B_\tau + \frac{1}{2}\sigma^2(r)B_{rr}}{B}dt$$

$$+ \frac{\sigma(r)B_r}{B}dZ \qquad (A.6)$$

The LEH requires that in equilibrium the expected instantaneous return on the bond be equal to the instantaneous risk-free rate, r, so that

$$\frac{1}{2}\sigma^2(r)B_{rr} + \mu(r)B_r - rB - B_\tau = 0 \quad (A.7)$$

Note that if the process on r in equation (A.4) is a mean-reverting, square root process of the form in equation (A.3), then this is the same valuation equation as that obtained in the CIR model. However, in the partial equilibrium framework of the BrS model the LEH was a necessary condition to derive this equation. As discussed above, in the general equilibrium framework of CIR, LEH was not necessary to derive their valuation equation (A.23). In either case, the LEH implies a valuation equation of the form of (A.7) in a model with the short rate as the single state variable.

In order to complete the specification of the solution, BrS impose boundary conditions for the extreme values of the interest rate process and the terminal value of the bond. First, at maturity the bond pays \$1 with no default risk. Therefore,

$$B(r,0) = 1 \qquad (A.8)$$

This can be considered as a terminal value condition in t or an initial condition in τ. Prior to maturity, if the interest rate reaches zero, then the partial differential equation evaluated at zero yields a natural boundary condition at the origin. The valuation equation evaluated at zero itself becomes the boundary:

$$\mu(0)B_r(0, \tau) - B_\tau(0, \tau) = 0 \qquad (A.9)$$

And finally, as the interest rate becomes very large the value of the bond tends toward zero. Formally, this is stated as

$$\lim_{r \to \infty} B(r, \tau) = 0, \text{ for } \tau > 0 \qquad (A.10)$$

Taken together, (A.7)-(A.10) form a well posed partial differential equation problem. Because the focus of the paper was to value more complex instruments using this pure discount bond as a fundamental, they do not present a solution of this particular model. However, this model serves to illustrate the differences between general and partial equilibrium modeling techniques. For the CIR and Vasicek models there are known closed form solutions, but in general, numerical methods must be used to solve for the value of interest rate contingent claims in this framework.

Arbitrage Valuation Models

Arbitrage valuation models, often referred to as contingent claim valuation models, are really a type of partial equilibrium model. They take the state-contingent claim prices as given and then value other securities relative to the primitive securities that span the state space. This is possible because the payoffs to any security that is not used in forming the spanning set of assets can be replicated by a combination of the spanning assets. Consider the following simple extension to the state space economy presented in the equilibrium valuation model section above.

In complete markets, redundant securities are priced using an assumption that there will be no arbitrage opportunities in equilibrium. Consider a market with $S+1$ assets and S possible states. If this market is complete, then asset $S+1$ with payoffs $\mathbf{y}_{S+1}$ is redundant. It is redundant in the sense that its payoffs can be replicated by a linear combination of the first S assets that span the state space. Let $\mathbf{Y}_S=(\mathbf{y}_1, \mathbf{y}_2,..., \mathbf{y}_S)$ be a matrix with columns of the S payoff vectors of the spanning assets. Let $\mathbf{x}$ be the vector of weights that when multiplied by $\mathbf{Y}_S$ replicates $\mathbf{y}_{S+1}$ such that

$$\mathbf{y}_{S+1} = \mathbf{Y}_S\mathbf{x} \qquad (A.11)$$

Transpose and postmultiply both sides of (A.11) by $\mathbf{p}$ to get

$$\mathbf{y}'_{s+1}\mathbf{p} = (\mathbf{Y}_S\mathbf{x})'\mathbf{p} \qquad (A.12)$$

The right-hand side of (A.12) is the value of the replicating portfolio. The left-hand side of (A.12) is, by assumption of no arbitrage, the value of the redundant security. Equation (A.11) is the condition that assures no arbitrage in a complete market. If this condition is not satisfied, then individuals could make costless and riskless profit. Competition is given as the motive force that removes any such arbitrage opportunities.

This simple concept lies at the heart of most of modern financial theory. For example, the common stock option is a redundant security, or contingent claim, in the sense presented above. Its value depends on the value of the stock that the option is written on. The stock's value, or price distribution, is taken as given in order to value the option based on the assumption of no arbitrage. Corporate debt has also been cast as a contingent claim, or option, on the total value of the firm. Indeed, common stock itself may be construed as an option, or residual claim on the value of the firm. Similarly, an interest rate cap is a redundant security in the sense illustrated in Chapter 3. The cash flows, and therefore, the value of an interest rate cap can be synthesized using two discount bonds. In this case the discount bonds are members of the spanning set of securities and the interest rate cap is redundant.

Appendix Notes

1. John C. Cox, Jonathan E. Ingersoll, Jr., and Stephen A. Ross, "An Intertemporal General Equilibrium Model of Asset Prices," *Econometrica* 53, No. 2 (March 1985), pp. 363-384.

2. Michael J. Brennan and Eduardo S. Schwartz, "Savings Bonds, Retractable Bonds and Callable Bonds," *Journal of Financial Economics* 5 (1977), pp. 67-88.

3. Cox, Ingersoll, and Ross, "An Intertemporal General Equilibrium Model of Asset Prices."

4. Brennan and Schwartz, "Savings Bonds, Retractable Bonds and Callable Bonds."

Solution Approaches to Single-Factor Models

1. Introduction

In Chapters 3 and 4, we discussed single-factor models of the term structure of interest rates. While the setting changed from simple discrete-time models to a rather complex discrete-time model and then to continuous-time models, the fundamental ideas remained the same. Our goal throughout has been to construct a scenario set of future term structures of interest rates that is consistent with a definition of equilibrium. The usual definition of equilibrium is the absence of arbitrage opportunities. Based upon that scenario set we can price interest rate contingent claims. We concluded Chapter 4 without going into detail on the solution for the price of interest rate contingent claims in a continuous-time setting. It is to that topic that we turn our attention in this chapter.

In this chapter, we will explore the relationships between discrete-time and continuous-time models. We will also consider some of the available methods for solving the partial differential equations that emerge from the continuous-time models. In fact, we will show that there are discrete-time approximations to continuous-time models when analytic solutions are not available.

In the next section we will present two different derivations of the well-known Black and Scholes[1] option pricing formula. While this is a slight departure from interest-rate contingent claims, it will show the relationship between a simple discrete-time binomial model and its continuous-time counterpart. Further, once the Black and Scholes model is derived, we can present a closed-form solution for a call option on a Treasury security.

2. The Black and Scholes Option Valuation Model

In the original presentation of the model, Black and Scholes (hereafter denoted BS) derived their results in a general equilibrium framework. However, as demonstrated in the appendix to Chapter 4, the same valuation result can often be obtained through either a general or a partial equilibrium approach. In fact, several alternative derivations of the basic option pricing formula of BS have been presented. Two variations will be presented here. First, a simple binomial branching model will illustrate the risk-neutral, or preference-free, valuation methodology introduced by BS. This approach makes the intuition clear without the added complexity of the continuous-time mathematics. Second, the continuous-time hedging approach to security valuation will be illustrated based on Merton's derivation of the BS model.[2]

2.1 Discrete-Time Equity Option Valuation

For the binomial branching approach, consider a stock with a price, S, that can either go up, with subjective probability p, or go down, with subjective probability $1-p$, over the next period. In this simple model the two possible outcomes, up or down, represent the entire state space. Repeated branching generates the scenario set for stock price movement over time. The stock price increases from S to $S_u=(1+z_u)S$ or decreases to $S_d=(1+z_d)S$, where z_u and z_d are the realized rates of return on the stock in the two states, and $z_u>r>z_d$, where $R=(1+r)$ and r is the riskless rate. Notice that in this case we are assuming a non-stochastic, flat term structure of interest rates. The inequality condition on rates of return assures that there will not be arbitrage. Denote a call option on this stock with exercise price K and τ periods until maturity by $C(S, \tau, K)$.

In order to value the option, construct a portfolio of the option and stock that is not subject to the risk inherent in the up or down movement of the stock price. This is accomplished by finding the portfolio that has the same value the next period no matter which state is realized. For this portfolio, the outcome next period is certain. Further, in order to avoid arbitrage, the next period value of the portfolio must be equal to the sum of one plus the riskless rate, multiplied by the current value of the portfolio. This relationship allows the value of the option to be derived.

Consider the portfolio formed by going short one call option and buying m shares of the stock. The value of this portfolio next period is $mS_u-C(S_u,\tau-1;K)$ or $mS_d-C(S_d,\tau-1;K)$ with probabilities p and $1-p$, respectively. The portfolio outcomes in the two states can be equated by choosing

$$m = \frac{C(S_u, \tau-1;K) - C(S_d, \tau-1;K)}{S_u - S_d} \quad (5.1)$$

Computing the outcomes the next period using the value of m in equation (5.1), the portfolio is worth

$$\frac{(1+z_d)C(S_u, \tau-1;K)}{z_u - z_d}$$

$$-\frac{(1+z_u)C(S_d, \tau-1;K)}{z_u - z_d} \quad (5.2)$$

in either state. The outcome becomes certain because the outcome is the same regardless of which state of the world is realized the next period. However, the absence of arbitrage requires that this quantity be equal to R times the current value of the portfolio. Formally, the no arbitrage condition is

$$R[mS - C(S, \tau;K)]$$
$$= \frac{(1+z_d)C(S_u, (\tau-1);K)}{z_u - z_d}$$
$$-\frac{(1+z_u)C(S_d, (\tau-1);K)}{z_u - z_d} \quad (5.3)$$

Then, solving for $C(S,\tau;K)$, the value of the option is

$$C(S, \tau;K) = \frac{1}{R}\left[\frac{r-z_d}{z_u-z_d}C(S_u, \tau-1;K)\right.$$
$$\left. + \frac{z_u-r}{z_u-z_d}C(S_d, \tau-1;K)\right]$$
$$\equiv \frac{1}{R}[\pi C(S_u, \tau-1;K)$$
$$+ (1-\pi)C(S_d, \tau-1;K)] \quad (5.4)$$

Note that $\pi \equiv (r-z_d)/(z_u-z_d)$ satisfies the definition of a probability. That is, the "probabilities" of the two mutually exclusive states sum to one and $0<\pi<1$. Equation (5.4) shows that the current value of the option can be expressed as an expected value of the possible next period values of the option discounted at the riskless rate. However, the probabilities used in this expected value have nothing to do with subjective beliefs of what the probability may be of each state occurring. These are the risk-neutral probabilities and are analogous to the risk-neutral probability introduced in Chapter 3. They are unique and are not affected by the introduction of a derivative asset, such as the option, because the two states of the state space are completely spanned by the stock and the riskless asset.[3]

The valuation equation (5.4) can also be stated in terms of state prices. To facilitate comparison to the discussion of derivative assets presented in the previous chapter, consider the following system of equations that govern the prices of the stock and bond in terms of state prices. The state prices, p_i, are the price of a security that pays \$1 if and only if state i is reached. The sum of the state prices is, by definition, \$1.

$$p_u R + p_d R = 1 \qquad (5.5a)$$

$$p_u(1 + z_u) + p_d(1 + z_d) = 1 \qquad (5.5b)$$

These equations are sometimes referred to as the supporting equations for the spanning securities. Solving system (5.5) for the state prices yields

$$p_u = \frac{r - z_d}{R(z_u - z_d)}, \; p_d = \frac{z_u - r}{R(z_u - z_d)} \qquad (5.6)$$

In terms of these state prices, the value of the option is

$$C(S, \tau;K) = p_u C(S_u, \tau - 1;K)$$
$$+ p_d C(S_d, \tau - 1;K) \qquad (5.7)$$

which is just a restatement of equation (5.4). The risk-neutralized probabilities defined in equation (5.4) are, in fact, just a restatement of the idea that in a complete market the absence of arbitrage allows redundant securities to be valued in terms of state prices, regardless of investor preferences.

One way to implement equation (5.4) for valuing an option is to observe that $C(S,0;K)$ is a known function. It takes the value $\text{Max}(S-K,0)$ for the finite number of possible values of S when $\tau=0$. Using this observation and equation (5.4), the value of $C(S,1;K)$ can be determined for each possible value of S. This process can be used recursively to find the value of $C(S,\tau;K)$. However, if z_u and z_d are constant over time, it is possible to use the risk-neutralized probabilities to simplify the calculation of the option's value. In this case, the risk-neutralized probability distribution at time t for the value of the stock at time T, S_T, is

$$\Pr[S_T = S(1 + z_u)^i(1 + z_d)^{\tau-i}]$$
$$= \frac{\tau!}{i!(\tau-i)!}\pi^i(1 - \pi)^{\tau-i} \qquad (5.8)$$

which is the binomial density function and $\tau=T-t$. Applying this to the option price,

$$C(S, \tau;K) = SB\left(\tau - I, \tau;\frac{(1 + z_d)(1 - \pi)}{R}\right)$$
$$- K\frac{1}{R^\tau}B(\tau - I, \tau;1 - \pi) \qquad (5.9)$$

where I is the smallest integer satisfying $(1+z_u)^i(1+z_d)^{\tau-i}S>K$ and $B(.)$ is the cumulative binomial distribution function. In the limit, as the time increment goes to zero, equation (5.9) is the BS option pricing model. The result depends on the observation that, in the limit, the binomial distribution converges to the normal distribution. However, rather than present that limiting result in detail, it is sufficient to note the insights gained to this point.[4]

First, for a stock and a riskless bond that span the state space, taking the riskless rate and the probability distribution for the stock price as given, it is possible to derive the value of the option as a redundant security. Second, in the absence of arbitrage, the value of the option does not depend on investor preferences. Finally, it is possible to define a risk-neutralized probability measure that can be used in valuing redundant securities. This probability measure is not based on the subjective probability of an event. Rather, it is a construct that behaves as a probability and allows derivative securities to be valued as expected values of cash flows, under the risk-neutralized probability measure, discounted at the riskless rate.

2.2 Continuous-Time Equity Option Valuation

These same ideas apply in continuous-time as well. In this case the key assumption regarding the distribution of the stock price is that the price evolves according to the following stochastic differential equation:

$$dS = \alpha S dt + \sigma S dZ \qquad (5.10)$$

where α is the instantaneous rate of return on the stock, σ^2 is the instantaneous variance of return on the stock, and $\{Z_t\}$ is a standard Brownian motion, or Wiener process. Assume for now that α and σ are constants. As before, the bond is assumed to be riskless with a constant instantaneous rate of return, r. (Note that

in the previous section, r was defined as a one-period spot rate.)

Notice that equation (5.10) is the continuous-time analog to the multiplicative binomial branching process presented above. In the limit, as the time increment goes to zero, the distribution of the stock return for the multiplicative binomial branching process is normal. Equation (5.10) implies that the instantaneous return on the stock price is normal. Therefore, in the limit, equation (5.10) represents the same distributional assumption on the changes in the stock price as we made earlier.

Consider a security, such as an option, whose value is a function of the stock price and time, $F(S,t)$. Using Ito's Lemma, the diffusion process governing the movement of F through time is

$$dF = \left(\frac{1}{2}\sigma^2 S^2 F_{SS} + \alpha S F_S + F_t \right) dt + \sigma S F_S dZ$$

$$\equiv \alpha_F dt + \sigma_F dZ$$

where the subscripts on F denote partial derivatives.

As in the binomial case, we will form a portfolio, $X = mS - F - (m-1)$, of m dollars of the stock and selling \$1 of the security, F. The portfolio will be funded by borrowing at the riskless rate, r. The diffusion process governing the return on the portfolio is

$$\frac{dX}{X} = \left[m(\alpha - r) - \frac{\alpha_F}{F} + r \right] dt + \left(m\sigma - \frac{\sigma_F}{F} \right) dZ$$

Setting $m = \sigma_F/(\sigma F)$ will cause the term multiplying dZ to be equal to zero and, therefore, create a risk-free security out of the portfolio. Because this is a zero net investment portfolio, funded by borrowing at the riskless rate, r, the expected return, or drift, must be equal to zero in order to avoid arbitrage. That is,

$$m(\alpha - r) - \frac{\alpha_F}{F} + r = 0$$

Substituting for m, σ_F and α_F, and simplifying yields the Black and Scholes valuation equation,

$$\frac{1}{2}\sigma^2 S^2 F_{SS} + rSF_S - rF + F_t = 0 \quad (5.11)$$

For a call option on the stock, the Black and Scholes call option formula is the solution to (5.11) subject to the boundary conditions that uniquely identify the call option. For a call option that matures at time T with a strike price K the form of this solution at time t is

$$F(S, t) = SN(d_1) - Ke^{-r(T-t)}N(d_2) \quad (5.12)$$

where

$$d_1 = \frac{\ln\left(\frac{S}{K}\right) + \left(r + \frac{1}{2}\sigma^2\right)(T-t)}{\sigma\sqrt{T-t}}$$

$$d_2 = d_1 - \sigma\sqrt{T-t}$$

For simplicity, α is assumed to be constant. However, the analysis will not change if α is stochastic or an arbitrary function of S and t. On the other hand, the complete derivation will only go through if σ is constant. If σ is a known function of S and t, then the PDE derived above will still apply, but the Black and Scholes call option formula would no longer be valid.

2.3 Call Option on a Treasury Bill

Occasionally, people attempt to value a call option on a Treasury bill in a manner similar to the equity option presented above. The crucial assumption, as before, is on the distribution of future prices for the underlying

security. In the previous section, we took equation (5.10) as given and then valued the call option as a function of the stock price. If we are willing to make the same distributional assumption about the movement of the T-bill's price through time, then we can apply the BS model to a call option on the T-bill.

Assume that the stochastic process governing movement of the T-bill's price through time is

$$dB = \alpha B dt + \gamma B dZ \quad (5.13)$$

where

B is the current price of the T-bill,

T_c is the maturity date of the call option,

α is the instantaneous expected return of the T-bill,

γ is the instantaneous volatility of the rate of return on the T-bill,

K is the strike price of the call option, and

r is the current instantaneous risk-free interest rate.

Then, direct application of the Black and Scholes call option formula leads to the following price for the call option on the T-bill.

$$F(B, t) = BN(d_1) - Ke^{-r(T_c-t)}N(d_2) \quad (5.14)$$

where

$$d_1 = \frac{\ln\left(\frac{B}{K}\right) + \left(r + \frac{1}{2}\gamma^2\right)(T_c-t)}{\gamma\sqrt{T_c-t}}$$

$$d_2 = d_1 - \gamma\sqrt{T_c-t}$$

However, there are problems with this sort of direct application of an equity option pricing model to fixed income securities. One problem relates to the volatility parameter of the underlying security's price process, denoted by γ for the T-bill. As with almost all fixed income securities, a T-bill has a fixed maturity. As the T-bill approaches maturity, its price approaches par and the volatility of price movements decreases. In fact, at maturity, the volatility of the T-bill's price process is zero. For options that are very short-lived relative to the T-bill they are written on, the changing volatility is not of major importance. However, as the maturity of the option increases, the changing volatility becomes more important.

There are adjustments that are used in practice to deal with the changing volatility of the T-bill.[5] However, there is a more fundamental problem relating to the volatility of the T-bill's price process. Recall from the previous section that the Black and Scholes model is derived based on the assumption of a flat, non-stochastic term structure of interest rates. This assumption can be seen in either equation (5.4) or equation (5.6) where the risk-free rate is r for every time step in the lattice. Therefore, there is no volatility of interest rates within this model. This leads to an internal inconsistency in applying the BS model to a call option on a T-bill. Consider equation (5.13). If interest rates never change, then the T-bill price will change only in a deterministic manner as it approaches maturity. There will be no volatility in the T-bill price process. Therefore, $\gamma=0$ and equation (5.14) is invalid.

The problem arises from the interest rate sensitivity of the cash flows on the call option. Recall from Chapter 3 that when cash flows depend on the level of interest rates, then valuing the cash flows requires discounting by paths. In order to correctly value a call option on a T-bill, the T-bill must first be valued. Then, the value of the call option is computed as a "T-bill contingent" security.

Consider the Vasicek model that was implemented in its extended form in discrete time using a trinomial lattice in Chapter 3. Recall that at each time step the direction of the middle branch emanating from each node was determined by the drift, or expected change, in the short rate. The drift used there was the discrete-time analog of the continuous-time extended Vasicek model

$$dr = [\theta(t) - ar]dt + \sigma dZ \qquad (5.15)$$

Equation (5.15) embodies the assumption that the short rate follows a mean reverting process through time where $\theta(t)$ is related to the time-varying level toward which interest rates revert and a is the rate of reversion. Further, the distribution of future short rates, conditional on today's rate and the process (5.15), is normal. There is a closed form solution for a call option on a T-bill based on a special case of (5.15),

$$dr = \kappa(\mu - r)dt + \sigma dZ$$

A discount bond, like a T-bill, can be valued based on this special case of (5.15) and some equilibrium condition. Following a procedure similar to what we did for the CIR model in equation (4.22), the extended Vasicek model implies that the Time t price of a discount bond that pays \$1 at Time T will have the form

$$P(r, t, T) = A(t, T)e^{-B(t, T)r} \qquad (5.16)$$

where $A(t,T)$ and $B(t,T)$ are functions of time but not of the interest rate. Notice that while equation (5.16) has the same form as equation (4.24), the $A(t,T)$ and $B(t,T)$ expressions are different than for the CIR model. For the Vasicek model they are

$$B(t, T) = \frac{1}{\kappa}\left(1 - e^{-\kappa(T-t)}\right)$$

$$A(t, T)$$

$$= \exp\left((B(t, T) - (T - t))R(\infty) - \frac{\sigma^2}{4\kappa}B^2(t, T)\right)$$

where

$$R(\infty) = \mu - \frac{\sigma^2}{2\kappa^2}$$

Equation (5.16) is used in determining the cash flows to the call option on the T-bill. The stochastic process for the price of the T-bill, as a function of the short rate, is found using Ito's Lemma. The stochastic process for the T-bill price is of the form

$$dP = \alpha(P, t)dt + \gamma(t)PdZ \qquad (5.17)$$

Notice that (5.17) implies that the distribution of T-bill returns given today's price is normal.

The normality of the T-bill return leads to a price function that is a variation of the Black and Scholes model. The call option price is given by

$$C(r, t, T_c) = P(r, t, T)N(h)$$
$$- KP(r, t, T_c)N(h - \sigma_P) \qquad (5.18)$$

where T_c is the maturity of the call option and T is the maturity of the underlying T-bill,

$$h = \frac{1}{\sigma_P}\log\frac{P(r, t, T)}{P(r, t, T_c)K} + \frac{\sigma_P}{2}$$

and

$$\sigma_P^2 = \sigma^2 B(T - T_c)^2 \frac{1 - e^{-2\kappa(T_c - t)}}{2\kappa}.$$

Notice the similarity between the form of the call option price in (5.18) to that in (5.14). The differences are all attributable to the fact that the model of stochastic interest rates is being used in discounting the potential cash flows to the option. For example, in the second term of (5.14), the strike price is discounted by $e^{-r(T_c - t)}$. This is the Time t price of one dollar paid at Time T_c if the term structure of interest rates is flat and nonstochastic. However, in equation (5.18) the discount factor multiplying the strike price is the model-based price of a discount bond that pays \$1 at Time T_c, the maturity of the call option.

Similarly, the simultaneous valuation problem is illustrated by the first term. Notice that the price of the underlying T-bill, $P(r,t,T)$, must be calculated, based on the model, in order to compute the model-based value of the call option. The important point that this problem illustrates is that the underlying instrument is the interest rate, not the T-bill. Both the T-bill and the call option on the T-bill derive their value from interest rates. This points out the care that must be taken when applying equity option pricing methodologies to fixed income securities.

3. Numerical Solution Techniques

As we have seen in the previous chapter, the problem of valuing an interest rate contingent security often results in a partial differential equation with a set of boundary conditions that must be solved. In the previous section we went a step further and wrote down a closed-form solution, equation (5.12), to the partial differential equation (5.11) for an equity option. Then we discussed how to extend the equity option methodology to a fixed-income option. However, with many interest rate contingent securities, a nice closed-form solution may not be obtainable. It these cases we turn to numerical solution techniques. In this section we will introduce an alternative to the trinomial lattice method of numerical valuation, the *finite difference* method. The finite difference method is a numerical technique for approximating the solution to a partial differential equation. Following that we will show the relationship between the trinomial lattice valuation methodology introduced in Chapter 3 and the finite difference method. We will show that under certain conditions they are, in fact, identical.

3.1 The Finite Difference Method

To introduce the finite difference method we will draw on the work of Brennan and Schwartz (BrS).[6] We will begin with the simple problem of valuing a zero-coupon bond as a function of stochastic interest rates. Assume that the bond is sold at a discount and pays $1 at maturity. The stochastic interest rates are modeled by assuming that the instantaneous risk-free rate follows a stochastic process of the form

$$dr = \mu(r)dt + \sigma(r)dZ \qquad (5.19)$$

where dZ is a Wiener process. Equation (5.19) is a general specification that covers several of the stochastic processes we have considered to this point. We must restrict (5.19) slightly in order to avoid the dominance of money. This is accomplished by assuring that the nominal interest rate remains non-negative. Assuming that $\mu(r) \geq 0$ and $\sigma(0) = 0$ is sufficient to create a reflecting barrier at zero and assure that the short rate will never be negative. Also, the economy is assumed to be complete with no frictions on exchange.

The value of the pure discount bond promising $1 at maturity is expressed as $B(r, \tau)$ where τ is the time to maturity. Using Ito's lemma, the dynamics for the bond price are given by

$$dB = B_r dr + \frac{1}{2}B_{rr}(dr)^2 + B_t dt \qquad (5.20)$$

where the subscripts denote partial derivatives. Then, substituting $\sigma^2(r)dt = (dr)^2$ and noting that $dt = -d\tau$,

$$\frac{dB}{B} = \frac{-B_\tau + \mu(r)B_r + \frac{1}{2}\sigma^2(r)B_{rr}}{B}dt$$
$$+ \frac{\sigma(r)B_r}{B}dZ \qquad (5.21)$$

The LEH requires that in equilibrium the expected instantaneous return on the bond be equal to the instantaneous risk-free rate, r, so that

$$\frac{1}{2}\sigma^2(r)B_{rr} + \mu(r)B_r - rB - B_\tau = 0 \qquad (5.22)$$

The expectation that is taken over the expected return, $E(dB/B)$, often leads to some confusion. The confusion stems from the distinction between risk-neutralized, or martingale, probabilities and the objective probabilities.[7] If the market price of interest rate risk is positive, i.e., $\lambda(r) > 0$, then the expectation taken over the expected return that leads to (5.22) is based on the subjective probability distribution. If the drift of the interest rate process (5.19) is modified to be $\mu^*(r) = \mu(r) - \lambda(r)\sigma(r)$, then the derivation of (5.22) is based on the modified drift and the risk-neutral probability measure. However, if the LEH holds, then the subjective probability measure and the risk-neutral probability measure are identical.

In order to complete the specification of the solution, we must impose boundary conditions for the extreme values of the interest rate process and the terminal value of the bond. First, at maturity the bond pays $1 with no default risk. Therefore,

$$B(r, 0) = 1 \qquad (5.23)$$

This can be considered as a terminal value condition in t or an initial condition in τ. Prior to maturity, if the interest rate reaches zero, then the partial differential equation evaluated at zero yields a natural boundary condition at the origin. The valuation equation evaluated at zero itself becomes the boundary:

$$\mu(0)B_r(0, \tau) - B_\tau(0, \tau) = 0 \qquad (5.24)$$

And finally, as the interest rate becomes very large the value of the bond tends toward zero. Formally, this is stated as

$$\lim_{r \to \infty} B(r, \tau) = 0, \text{ for } \tau > 0 \qquad (5.25)$$

Taken together, (5.22)-(5.25) form a well-posed partial differential equation problem. This problem must be solved. The solution could be either a closed form expression or a numerical approximation. Where a closed form solution is not feasible, numerical solutions are used.

The basic idea of the finite difference method is to approximate the derivatives of a partial differential equation with discrete difference equations. This will generate a system of linear equations that can be solved using the tools of linear algebra. The logic of this approach is the reverse of the logic used to define a derivative. Recall that for a continuous function $f(x)$, the derivative of f with respect to x is defined as

$$\frac{df}{dx} = \lim_{h \to 0} \frac{f(x + h) - f(x)}{h} \qquad (5.26)$$

When this limit exists, a function is said to be differentiable. With a partial differential equation we have an expression that includes derivatives of a differentiable function. Rather than consider the derivatives, we consider the finite differences for some sufficiently small value of h.

In order to present the discretization of the PDE, we will use the following notation

$$f(r, \tau) = f(r_i, \tau_j) = f(ih, jk) = f_{i,j}$$

This notation anticipates that the discretization will have us considering a function, $f(r,t)$, and its derivatives at a finite number of discrete points. The points, referred to as mesh points, will form a grid in two dimensions, r and τ. The mesh points on the grid will be non-negative integer multiples of h in the r dimension and non-negative integer multiples of k in the τ dimension. A generic grid is depicted in Table 5.1. Note that the vertical dimension represents r and the horizontal dimension represents τ.

Table 5.1. Generic Grid for Finite Difference Method

	$0k$	$1k$	$...$	$(m-1)k$	mk
$0h$	$f_{0,0}$	$f_{0,0}$	$...$	$f_{m-1,0}$	$f_{m,0}$
$1h$	$f_{1,0}$	$f_{0,0}$			
.	.				.
.	.		$f_{i,j}$		.
.	.				.
$(n-1)h$	$f_{n-1,0}$				
nh	$f_{n,0}$		$...$		$f_{n,m}$

We will use the following derivative approximations:

$$\frac{\partial f}{\partial \tau} \approx \frac{f_{i,j} - f_{i,j-1}}{k}$$

$$\frac{\partial f}{\partial x} \approx \frac{f_{i+1,j} - f_{i,j}}{h}$$

$$\frac{\partial^2 f}{\partial x^2} \approx \frac{f_{i+1,j} - 2f_{i,j} + f_{i-1,j}}{h^2}$$

Substituting the discrete approximations for the derivatives in (5.22) yields the difference equation

$$\frac{1}{2}\sigma^2(r)\left[\frac{B_{i+1,j}-2B_{i,j}+B_{i-1,j}}{h^2}\right]$$

$$+\mu(r)\left[\frac{B_{i+1,j}-B_{i,j}}{h}\right]-r[B_{i,j}]$$

$$-\left[\frac{B_{i,j}-B_{i,j-1}}{k}\right]=0 \qquad (5.27)$$

This differencing scheme is referred to as the *implicit finite difference* method. Rearranging (5.27) shows that we have the following system of equations to solve

$$B_{i,j-1} = U_i B_{i-1,j} + V_i B_{i,j} + W_i B_{i+1,j}$$
$$i = 1, 2, ..., n-1$$
$$j = 1, 2, ..., m \qquad (5.28)$$

where

$$U_i = -\sigma^2(ih)\frac{k}{2h^2}$$

$$V_i = 1 + ihk + \mu(ih)\frac{k}{h} + \sigma^2(ih)\frac{k}{h^2}$$

$$W_i = -\mu(ih)\frac{k}{h} - \sigma^2(ih)\frac{k}{2h^2}$$

are the coefficients that correspond to each value of i and where we have $n+1$ mesh points in the r dimension and $m+1$ mesh points in the τ dimension in our grid. Therefore, system (5.28) represents the discretized problem on the interior of the grid. We will use the boundary conditions to complete the problem. Notice that the boundary condition (5.24), where $r=0$, constrains $U_0=0$ and that the

boundary condition (5.25), where r goes to infinity, constrains $B_{n,j}=0$. With these two observations, the system of equations (5.28) can be represented as a tridiagonal system of n linear equations in n unknowns.

$$\begin{bmatrix} V_0 & W_0 & 0 & . & . & . & . & 0 \\ U_1 & V_1 & W_1 & . & & & & . \\ 0 & . & . & . & . & & & . \\ . & . & . & . & . & . & & . \\ . & . & . & . & . & . & . & . \\ . & & & . & . & . & . & 0 \\ . & & & & . & U_{n-2} & V_{n-2} & W_{n-2} \\ 0 & . & . & . & . & 0 & U_{n-1} & V_{n-1} \end{bmatrix} \begin{bmatrix} B_{0,j} \\ B_{1,j} \\ . \\ . \\ . \\ . \\ . \\ B_{n-1,j} \end{bmatrix}$$

$$= \begin{bmatrix} B_{0,j-1} \\ B_{1,j-1} \\ . \\ . \\ . \\ . \\ . \\ B_{n-1,j-1} \end{bmatrix}$$

for $j=1, 2, ... , m$. \qquad (5.29)

Given the terminal value condition that $B_{i,0}=1$ for $i=1, 2, ... , n$, the unknown $B_{i,j}$ terms can be found by solving system (5.29) recursively. Starting with $j=1$, solving (5.29) will determine the $B_{i,1}$ terms. Then, for $j=2$, solving (5.29) again will determine the $B_{i,2}$ terms. By repeating this process until $j=m$, we find the value of the security. A by-product of this numerical method is that we solve not only for the value of the security at one interest rate, but for a whole spectrum of interest rates.

One problem with the approach as outlined is that the short rate can be any real value from zero to infinity. It would require an infinite number of mesh points in the r dimension to represent all possible values of r. However, in practice (in the U.S.) interest rates above 30% or 40% are extreme. So, we can include a limited range of values of the short rate in our grid with the boundary (5.25) imposed along the appropriate edge of the grid and still achieve satisfactory results. Also, it is not unusual to use the assumption that

$$\lim_{r \to \infty} B_{rr} = 0$$

in order to implement the boundary where r goes to infinity.

A more sophisticated way to deal with the semi-infinite domain in the short rate is presented by Brennan and Schwartz. They show how a change of variable can be used to transform the problem into a finite domain. Consider the transformation

$$x = \frac{1}{1+r} \qquad (5.30)$$

For the transformed problem, x will range between zero and one. Using Ito's lemma, we can derive the stochastic process governing movements in x as a function of r. The valuation problem is then recast in terms of x with an isomorphic relation to the problem stated in terms of r. Therefore, the grid will cover the full range of possible values of x. Once the problem is solved as a function of x, the appropriate answer for the current short rate will be determined by the relationship between x and r.

We will demonstrate the use of the finite difference method using the transformed state variable x. First, we need to derive the sto-chastic process that governs movements in x. Using Ito's Lemma, the stochastic process for x can be derived as a function of r,

$$dx = x_r dr + \frac{1}{2}x_{rr}(dr)^2 \qquad (5.31)$$

Using equation (5.30), $x_r = -x^2$, $x_{rr} = 2x^3$, and

$$dx = [-x^2 \mu_*(x) + x^3 \sigma_*^2(x)]dt$$
$$- x^2 \sigma_*(x)dz \qquad (5.32)$$

where

$$\mu_*(x) \equiv \mu(r) \text{ and } \sigma_*(x) \equiv \sigma(r)$$

Let $b(x,\tau) \equiv B(r,\tau)$ and note that $r=(1-x)/x$. Using the same approach as we used to derive equation (5.22) above, we can derive the following valuation equation as a function of x and τ.

$$\frac{1}{2}x^4 \sigma_*^2(x)b_{xx} + \left[-x^2\mu_*(x) + x^3\sigma_*^2(x)\right]b_x$$
$$- \left(\frac{1-x}{x}\right)b - b_\tau = 0 \qquad (5.33)$$

The boundary conditions must also be restated in terms of $b(x,\tau)$. The boundary conditions that correspond to the limiting interest rate condition (5.25), the zero interest rate condition (5.24) and the terminal value condition (5.23) are

$$b(0, \tau) = 0; \tau > 0 \qquad (5.34)$$

$$\mu_*(1)b_x(1, \tau) + b_\tau(1, \tau) = 0 \qquad (5.35)$$

$$b(x, 0) = 1. \qquad (5.36)$$

The P.D.E. problem represented by (5.33)-(5.36) can be solved using the finite difference method presented above. The discretized version of (5.33) is

$$\frac{1}{2}x^4\sigma_*^2(x)\left[\frac{B_{i+1,j}-2B_{i,j}+B_{i-1,j}}{h^2}\right]$$

$$+\left[-x^2\mu_*(x)+x^3\sigma_*^2(x)\right]\left[\frac{B_{i+1,j}-B_{i,j}}{h}\right]$$

$$+\left[\frac{1-x}{x}\right]\left[B_{i,j}\right]+\left[\frac{B_{i,j}-B_{i,j-1}}{k}\right]=0 \quad (5.37)$$

Rearranging (5.37) yields

$$b_{i,j-1}=u_ib_{i-1,j}+v_ib_{i,j}+w_ib_{i+1,j}$$
$$i=1,2,\ldots,n-1 \quad (5.38)$$
$$j=1,2,\ldots,m$$

where

$$u_i=-(ih)^4\sigma_*^2(ih)\frac{k}{2h^2}-(ih)^2\mu_*(ih)\frac{k}{h}$$

$$+(ih)^3\sigma_*^2(ih)\frac{k}{h}$$

$$v_i=1+\frac{1-ih}{ih}k+(ih)^2\mu_*(ih)\frac{k}{h}$$

$$-(ih)^3\sigma_*^2(ih)\frac{k}{h}+x^4\sigma_*^2(ih)\frac{k}{h^2}$$

$$w_i=-(ih)^4\sigma_*^2(ih)\frac{k}{2h^2}$$

and where ih, $i=0,1,\ldots,n$ are the values of x at the $n+1$ mesh points in the x dimension.

As before, the system of equations (5.38) applies to the interior of the grid. We can make a couple of observations about the behavior of the problem on the boundaries and then state the problem in matrix form. Notice that the boundary condition (5.35), where $x=1$, is analogous to the boundary where $r=0$, (5.24) and thus, $u_n=0$.

The boundary condition (5.34), where $x=0$ (r goes to infinity) constrains $B_{0,j}=0$. With these two observations, the system of equations (5.38) can be represented as a tridiagonal system of n linear equations in n unknowns.

$$\begin{bmatrix} v_1 & w_1 & 0 & . & . & . & . & 0 \\ u_2 & v_2 & w_2 & . & & & & . \\ 0 & . & . & . & . & & & . \\ . & . & . & . & . & . & & . \\ . & & . & . & . & . & & . \\ . & & & . & . & . & . & 0 \\ . & & & & . & u_{n-1} & v_{n-1} & w_{n-1} \\ 0 & . & . & . & . & 0 & u_n & v_n \end{bmatrix}\begin{bmatrix} b_{1,j} \\ b_{2,j} \\ . \\ . \\ . \\ . \\ . \\ b_{n,j} \end{bmatrix}$$

$$=\begin{bmatrix} b_{1,j-1} \\ b_{2,j-1} \\ . \\ . \\ . \\ . \\ . \\ b_{n,j-1} \end{bmatrix}$$

for $j=1,2,\ldots,m$. $\qquad(5.39)$

Consider the CIR model where (5.19) has the form

$$dr=\kappa(\mu-r)dt+\sigma\sqrt{r}dZ \quad (5.40)$$

The CIR model has a known closed-form solution for the price of a zero-coupon bond. We presented that solution in Chapter 4 as equation (4.24). Because the CIR model has an exact solution, it will serve as a good example of the finite difference method so that we may validate our results. First, we will walk through a finite difference approximation to the CIR model with a limited grid size in order to illustrate the technique. Then, we will show calculated results for larger grid sizes and compare them to the closed-form solution.

For the interest rate process (5.40) assume $\kappa=0.2$, $\mu=0.06$, $\sigma=0.22$ and the current short rate is 25%, i.e., $r=0.25$. While a short rate of 25% may seem unreasonable, it will be convenient for our first example because it falls right on one of the mesh points. The bond to be valued is a discount bond that pays one dollar at maturity.

The stochastic process for x is fully defined by noting that

$$\mu_*(x) = \kappa\left(\mu - \frac{1-x}{x}\right)$$

$$\sigma_*(s) = \sigma\sqrt{\frac{1-x}{x}}$$

in equation (5.32). For $h=0.2$ and $k=0.1$, the coefficients u_i, v_i, and w_i can be computed and the matrix equation becomes

$$\begin{bmatrix} 1.3842 & -0.0004 & 0 & 0 & 0 \\ 0.0230 & 1.1293 & -0.0023 & 0 & 0 \\ 0 & 0.0201 & 1.0518 & -0.0052 & 0 \\ 0 & 0 & 0.0091 & 1.0221 & -0.0062 \\ 0 & 0 & 0 & -0.0060 & 1.0060 \end{bmatrix}$$

$$\times \begin{bmatrix} b_{1,j} \\ b_{2,j} \\ b_{3,j} \\ b_{4,j} \\ b_{5,j} \end{bmatrix} = \begin{bmatrix} b_{1,j-1} \\ b_{2,j-1} \\ b_{3,j-1} \\ b_{4,j-1} \\ b_{5,j-1} \end{bmatrix} \quad (5.41)$$

By inverting the coefficient matrix, the $b_{i,j}$ can be solved for iteratively. The values of $b_{i,j}$ for $j=0, 1, ..., 4$ are presented in Table 5.2. We pause here to underscore the importance of the coefficient matrix in (5.41). This simple example will allow the reader to recreate this exercise and validate any routines written in the process. Similarly, Table 5.2 provides a check on the $b_{i,j}$'s generated by the matrix in (5.41).

A grid with 6 mesh points in the x dimension will not lead to great accuracy in the approximated solutions. However, there is no hard and fast rule on how many mesh points are sufficient. For the purpose of illustration, Table 5.3 shows the approximated value of a one-year zero coupon bond for various values of h and k. The current short rate is assumed to be 11.11%.[8] Again, this value was selected because it falls on a mesh point for each of the cells of Table 5.3. In general, when the current value of r does not fall on a mesh point, an interpolation between the two nearest mesh points must be

Table 5.2. Calculated Values Using the Finite Difference Approximation

					j		
i	x	r	0	1	2	3	4
5	1.0	0.000	1	0.9998	0.9996	0.9992	0.9986
4	0.8	0.250	1	0.9761	0.9532	0.9312	0.9102
3	0.6	0.667	1	0.9389	0.8828	0.8312	0.7835
2	0.4	1.500	1	0.8727	0.7639	0.6705	0.5898
1	0.2	4.000	1	0.7227	0.5223	0.3775	0.2729
0	0	∞	1	0	0	0	0

made. The value of the discount bond according the closed-form solution (4.24) is 0.899807. Notice that even for the roughest grid where $h=k=0.1$, the error is only 0.0014. For the finest grid where $h=k=0.005$, the approximation is accurate to four decimal places.

Table 5.3. Approximated Solutions
for a One-Year Discount Bond

	k			
h	0.1	0.02	0.01	0.005
0.1	0.901220	0.900456	0.900359	0.900310
0.05	0.900996	0.900224	0.900126	0.900077
0.01	0.900825	0.900047	0.899949	0.899900
0.005	0.900804	0.900026	0.899927	0.899878

As we discussed in Chapter 4, valuing other interest rate contingent securities involves specifying the boundary conditions appropriate for the features of the instrument. Brennan and Schwartz[9] discuss the boundary conditions for a variety of embedded bond option features. In Chapter 4, we presented an interest rate cap in equations (4.28)-(4.31). The cap can be valued just as we did the discount bond using the finite difference method. The only difference is in the terminal value condition. Once the terminal cash flows for the cap are determined, then solving the problem is simply a matter of iteration.

3.2 The Trinomial Lattice Method

In Chapter 3 we presented the trinomial lattice method for approximating the value of an interest rate contingent security. In that chapter, the trinomial lattice was presented simply as a means of modeling stochastic future interest rates. It turns out that there is a tight linkage between the trinomial lattice approach and the continuous-time economic models described in Chapter 4.

Consider an interest rate contingent security, with price $f(r,\tau)$, that depends on the short rate and its maturity for its value. Note that $\tau=T-t$ where T is the maturity date and today is Time t. The short rate follows a stochastic process of the form

$$dr = \mu(r, t)dt + \sigma(r, t)dZ \qquad (5.42)$$

As Cox, Ingersoll and Ross[10] showed, and as we demonstrated in equation (4.21), any interest rate contingent security must satisfy

$$\frac{1}{2}\sigma^2(r, t)f_{rr} + [\mu(r, t) - \lambda(r, t)\sigma(r, t)]f_r$$
$$- f_\tau - rf = 0 \qquad (5.43)$$

where $\lambda(r,t)$ is the market price of interest rate risk.

We will discretize equation (5.43) using the approximations

$$\frac{\partial f}{\partial \tau} \approx \frac{f_{i, j+1} - f_{i, j}}{k}$$

$$\frac{\partial f}{\partial x} \approx \frac{f_{i+1, j} - f_{i-1, j}}{2h}$$

$$\frac{\partial^2 f}{\partial x^2} \approx \frac{f_{i+1, j} - 2f_{i, j} + f_{i-1, j}}{h^2}$$

Substituting the approximations to the derivatives transforms the valuation equation (5.43) into the difference equation

$$a_i f_{i-1, j} + b_i f_{i, j} + c_i f_{i+1, j} = f_{i, j+1} \qquad (5.44)$$

where

$$a_i = \frac{\sigma^2(r, t)\frac{k}{2h^2} - [\mu(r, t) - \lambda(r, t)\sigma(r, t)]\frac{k}{2h}}{1 + rk}$$

$$b_i = \frac{1}{1+rk}\left[1 - \sigma^2(r,t)\frac{k}{h^2}\right]$$

$$c_i = \frac{\sigma^2(r,t)\dfrac{k}{2h^2} + [\mu(r,t)-\lambda(r,t)\sigma(r,t)]\dfrac{k}{2h}}{1+rk}$$

This approximation scheme is called the *explicit finite difference* method. This scheme relates three values of f at $\tau=j$ to one value of f at $\tau=j+1$. Therefore, this scheme involves multiplying known values of f at $\tau=j$ by known coefficients to get a value of f at $\tau=j+1$. This explicit computation of the $f_{i,j}$ values motivates the name of the method.

The relationship between the explicit finite difference method and the trinomial lattice method can be seen by defining the following terms:

$$p_{i,i-1} = \sigma^2(r,t)\frac{k}{2h^2}$$

$$-[\mu(r,t)-\lambda(r,t)\sigma(r,t)]\frac{k}{2h}$$

$$p_{i,i} = 1 - \sigma^2(r,t)\frac{k}{h^2}$$

$$p_{i,i+1} = \sigma^2(r,t)\frac{k}{2h^2}$$

$$+[\mu(r,t)-\lambda(r,t)\sigma(r,t)]\frac{k}{2h}$$

so that equation (5.44) becomes

$$f_{i,j+1} = \frac{1}{1+rk}$$

$$\times [p_{i,i-1}f_{i-1,j}+p_{i,i}f_{i,j}+p_{i,i+1}f_{i+1,j}] \quad (5.45)$$

The terms $p_{i,i-1}$, $p_{i,i}$, and $p_{i,i+1}$ can be interpreted as the probability of moving from r_i to r_{i-1}, r_i, or r_{i+1}, respectively at time j over an interval of time of length k. In fact, it can be shown that $p_{i,i-1}$, $p_{i,i}$, and $p_{i,i+1}$ sum to one and that they imply a drift rate in r of $\mu(r,t)-\lambda(r,t)\sigma(r,t)$. Therefore, equation (5.45) can be interpreted as the statement that $f_{i,j+1}$ is the expected value of future $f_{i,j}$'s within a trinomial lattice framework.

The version of the trinomial lattice method that we presented in Chapter 3 had a modified branching process that implemented a mean reverting process for the short rate. In their 1990 paper in the *Journal of Financial and Quantitative Analysis* and also in their 1994 paper in the *Journal of Derivatives*, Hull and White[11] extend the trinomial lattice methods in other ways to enhance the speed of convergence or the computational efficiency of the models. However, at its heart, the trinomial lattice method is identical to the explicit finite difference method. In fact, models that are implemented in discrete-time lattice techniques are discretized versions of the continuous-time models discussed in Chapter 4 and in this chapter. This relationship allows the elegant theoretical models that are derived in a continuous-time framework to be implemented in a practical setting. This close tie between theory and practice is almost unique among economic models.

4. Comparison of Models for Term Structure Fitting

Up to this point, we have discussed a variety of issues surrounding interest rate contingent claim valuation. However, at the core of this topic is term structure modeling. As we have shown, once a model of the term structure is constructed, valuing an interest rate contingent security simply involves calculation of appropriately discounted cash flows. Therefore, it is reasonable to ask which model of the term structure is best. The answer is: it depends. There are a variety of single-factor term structure models that assume that the short rate is the stochastic state variable of interest. Many of these models have the form

$$dr = \mu(r, t)dt + \sigma r^\gamma dZ \qquad (5.46)$$

Two that we have considered in some detail are the Vasicek model, where $\gamma=0$, and the CIR model, where $\gamma=0.5$.

Recall that in the derivation of valuation equation (5.22) we made the assumption that $\sigma(0)=0$ in order to avoid negative interest rates and therefore the dominance of money over bonds. Notice that the Vasicek model does not satisfy the requirement that $\sigma(0)=0$. This is a known shortcoming of the model. However, the extended Vasicek model has enough advantages in implementation that the admission of the possibility of negative interest rates, and therefore the dominance of money, is often overlooked.

The advantage of the extended Vasicek model stems from one major distinction between it and the continuous-time Vasicek model presented in equation (5.16). The extended Vasicek model has a time dependent function, $\theta(t)$, in its drift term. It is natural to ask what impact the extension to a time dependent drift will have. Recall that the goal of arbitrage free models, such as the extended Vasicek and others, is to provide an exact fit to the current term structure. An equilibrium model with constant parameters in the drift and volatility terms will not be able to provide an exact fit to the current term structure except by extraordinary luck.

Figure 5.1 shows a term structure with an unusual shape traced by a solid line and labeled as "Actual" in the legend. The continuous-time Vasicek model, when fit to this actual term structure results in the line with the small dashes labeled as "Vasicek" in the legend. The extended Vasicek model provides the fit illustrated by the thick dashed line that is labeled "Extended" in the legend. Notice that the best that the model with no time-varying parameters can do is to trace the general slope of the actual term structure. On the other hand, the extended Vasicek model with the time-varying drift is able to provide an exact fit to the actual term structure.

The exact fit to the current term structure is desirable because there will be no model-induced arbitrage when pricing interest rate contingent securities. If the Vasicek model were used to reprice the zero-coupon bonds that correspond to the spot rates of the actual term structure, the model would misprice most of them and seem to indicate arbitrage opportunities. However, we must operate under the assumption that the market is correct and the model is in error. Thus, the advantage of the models with time-varying parameters is that they can provide an exact fit to both the current term structure of interest rates and of volatilities. This removes any difference between model-based and market-based zero-coupon bond prices.

Notice that while we used the extended Vasicek model to illustrate lattice building, it is possible to implement other forms of (5.46) with $\gamma>0$ as well. However, a transformation of the state variable is required in order to have a constant volatility term for the state variable. Herein lies the other advantage of the extended Vasicek model. It has a constant volatility and is, therefore, much easier to implement.

Figure 5.1. Comparison of Term Structure Fitting Ability for Vasiek and Extended Models

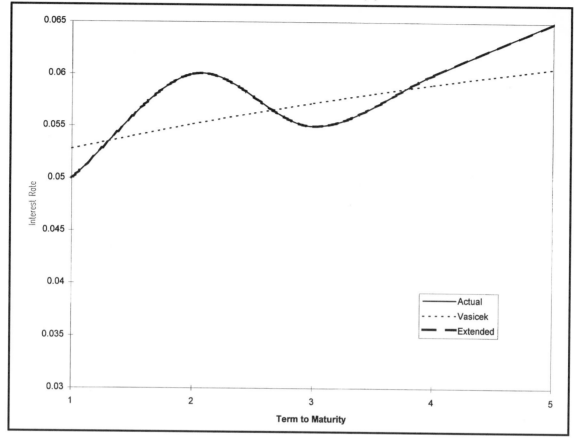

We should also note that there are other models of the term structure that take the forward rates as the state variables. The most prominent of these is the model presented by Heath, Jarrow and Morton.[12] They take the current forward rate curve as given and model its movement through time as an n-factor stochastic process. There are also models that treat one of the parameters of a short rate process as stochastic. These multi-factor models assume a stochastic process that governs the movements of one or more parameters of the short rate process. It is to these multi-factor models that we turn our attention in the next chapter.

End Notes

1. Fischer Black and Myron Scholes, "Pricing of Options and Corporate Liabilities," *Journal of Political Economy* 81 (1973), pp. 637-659.

2. Because the results are well known and are being presented here only as background for the model developed later in this paper, neither derivation will be completely rigorous. However, complete details of the following material can be found in most any advanced text on finance. The binomial model will draw on Jonathan Ingersoll, *Theory of Financial Decision Making*, while the continuous-time model will draw on Robert C. Merton, "The Relationship Between Put and Call Prices: As Comment," *Journal of Finance* 28 (1973), pp. 181-184, and "Theory Of Rational Option Pricing," *Bell Journal of Economics and Management Science* 4

(1973), pp. 141-183, and Jonathan E. Ingersoll Jr., *Theory of Financial Decision Making*, Totowa, Rowman and Littlefield (1987).

3. The appendix to Chapter 4 gave a brief introduction to the concept of spanning a state space in order to value derivative securities.

4. For the complete derivation, see Jonathan Ingersoll, *Theory of Financial Decision Making*, pp. 322-323.

5. See for example John C. Hull, *Introduction to Futures and Options Markets*, 2nd Ed., p. 398.

6. See Michael J. Brennan and Eduardo S. Schwartz, "Retractable Bonds and Callable Bonds," *Journal of Financial Economics* 5 (1977), pp. 67-88.

7. In Chapter 3 we described in some detail the relationship between the objective probabilities and the risk-neutral probabilities. The relationship in continuous time is analogous to the discrete-time relationship described there.

8. We would have selected 11.11% in the previous example except it did not fall on one of the mesh points illustrated in Table 5.2.

9. Brennan and Schwartz, "Retractable Bonds and Callable Bonds."

10. John C. Cox, Jonathan E. Ingersoll, Jr., and Stephen A. Ross, "An Intertemporal General Equilibrium Model of Asset Prices," *Econometrica* 53, No. 2 (March 1985), pp. 363-384.

11. John Hull and Alan White, "Numerical Procedures for Implementing Term Structure Models," *Journal of Derivatives*, Vol. 1, No. 3 (1994), pp. 64-76.

12. See David Heath, Robert Jarrow, and Andrew Morton, "Bond Pricing and the Term Structure of Interest Rates: a New Methodology," *Econometrica*, 60, 1 (1992), pp. 77-105.

Practice Exercises

1. Calculate European-style T-bill call option prices based on the Black-Scholes model in equation (5.14) assuming that $\alpha=0.05$, $\gamma=0.118$, $K=95$, $T-t=0.5$ years, and $r=0.05$.

2. Calculate European-style T-bill call option prices based on the Vasicek model in equation (5.18) assuming $\kappa=0.5$, $\mu=0.06$, $\sigma=0.15$, $T-t=1$, and $T_c-t=0.5$. Notice that these interest rate parameters are consistent with the α and γ given for the T-bill in problem 1.

3. Compare the results from questions 1 and 2 for a variety of parameter values.

4. In order to understand the finite difference method, recreate Table 5.1 assuming that $\kappa=0.5$, $\mu=0.05$, and $\sigma=0.2$.

6

Multi-Factor Continuous-Time Models

1. Introduction

Up to this point we have considered single-factor models of the term structure of interest rates. These single-factor models have given us insight into the economics and the techniques involved in pricing interest rate contingent claims. However, it has long been understood that single-factor models of the term structure lack the flexibility necessary to perform adequately in some applications. In this chapter we will introduce some multi-factor models that have been tried. It will quickly become apparent that the introduction of multiple factors greatly complicates the implementation of term structure models. Therefore, in practice, the added flexibility of the multi-factor model must be weighed against the computational overhead in choosing which model to use.

In our discussion of single-factor models we began with discrete time and showed how uncertainty about future interest rates could be modeled using a lattice. After establishing the intuition in discrete time in Chapter 3, we discussed the economics of term structure modeling in Chapter 4. In our discussion of multi-factor models, we will begin with the economics. The

intuition is the same as the intuition that we established in Chapter 3: define a model of interest rate movements and then price cash flows based on the interest rate model. After this chapter establishes the economic issues in multi-factor models, we will devote Chapter 7 to implementation issues.

In the single-factor models the stochastic factor is almost always assumed to be the short rate. In the extension to multi-factor models, a variety of stochastic factors are used. For example, the long-run average interest rate level in a mean reverting model could be treated as a stochastic factor. Alternatively, the volatility parameter could be treated as a stochastic factor. We will also consider a model that describes the evolution of the forward rate curve as a multi-factor stochastic process.

Notice that in the previous chapters we introduced the idea that a single-factor model can be used to fit not only the spot rate term structure but also the volatilities of the spot rates as well. This was accomplished by having two arbitrary functions of time in the drift of the short rate process. The inclusion of multiple parameters that are functions of time differs from including multiple stochastic factors. Recall that a factor is a stochastic variable that represents a distinct source of uncertainty in the model. A parameter that is a function of time allows more flexibility, but is not representative of a source of uncertainty.

In this chapter we will introduce these approaches along with their advantages and weaknesses. We will not be able to offer an exhaustive treatment in this chapter. However, we will be able to offer a jumping-off point for the reader that desires to enter the literature regarding the use of these models.

2. Multi-Factor Term Structure Models

In this section we will introduce five multi-factor term structure models that have been presented in the literature. First, we will consider the Cox, Ingersoll and Ross (CIR) two-factor model with the short real rate and the inflation rate as factors. Second, we will discuss the Brennan and Schwartz (BrS) two-factor model that takes the short rate and the consol rate as stochastic factors. Third, we will examine the Fong and Vasicek (FV) model that takes the short rate and the volatility parameter of the short rate process as stochastic factors. Fourth, we will present an extension to the Hull and White (HW) model where the mean-reverting drift of the short rate process incorporates a stochastic term. Finally, we will introduce the Heath, Jarrow and Morton (HJM) model that models the forward rate curve as a multi-factor process.

2.1 The Cox, Ingersoll and Ross Model
Recall from Chapter 4 that the Cox, Ingersoll and Ross (CIR) model used the short rate as the single stochastic state variable. Here we will consider an extension of the single-factor CIR model where contracts are stated in nominal

terms and the price level, $p(t)$, is a second stochastic state variable, or factor. CIR introduced this extension themselves, and further research suggests that it is a useful extension. There is some evidence that the single-factor model lacks sufficient flexibility to adequately model nominal interest rates.

Consider a contract that will with certainty at time T pay $1/p(T)$. We will call this contract a nominal unit discount bond and denote its value in real terms by $N(r,p,t,T)$. Assume that the stochastic process that governs movements in p is

$$dp = \mu(p)dt + \sigma(p)dZ_2 \qquad (6.1)$$

where dZ_2 is the increment to a Brownian motion that is uncorrelated with dZ in the interest rate process given in equation (4.22). Using Ito's Lemma and the same line of reasoning that led to the valuation equation in (4.23), the valuation equation for this two-factor model is

$$\frac{1}{2}\sigma^2 r N_{rr} + \frac{1}{2}\sigma^2(p)N_{pp} + \kappa(\mu - r)N_r$$
$$+ \mu(p)N_p + N_t - rN = 0 \qquad (6.2)$$

with terminal condition $N(r,p,T,T)=1/p(T)$. The solution to (6.2) is

$$N(r, p, t, T) = P(r, t, T)E[1/p(T)] \qquad (6.3)$$

where $P(r,t,T)$ is the value of the real discount bond given in (4.24).

In this formulation, the expected inflation rate is the drift component, $\mu(p)$, in (6.1). Notice that the drift depends only on the current price level. Consider the common case where prices are lognormally distributed so that $\mu(p)=\mu_p p$ and $\sigma(p)=\sigma_p p$ and

$$N(r, p, t, T) = e^{-(\mu_p - \sigma_p^2)(T-t)} \frac{P(r, t, T)}{p(t)} \quad (6.4)$$

Notice that in the case of lognormally distributed prices the price of the nominal bond in nominal terms, $N^* = p(t)N$, is independent of the current price level. However, the price is a function of the distribution of possible future price levels.

While this model is intuitively appealing in the way it deals with the influence of inflation on interest rates, it has not been used much in practice. In reality, all of the term structure models we have discussed up to this point are subject to the same criticism—they are not explicitly models of either real or nominal interest rates. As such, if uncertain inflation is an important component of future interest rates, it should be included explicitly in a term structure model. At the least, a model of nominal interest rates should be sufficiently flexible so that the impact of uncertain inflation rates will not render the model less useful.

As we discussed in Section 3 of Chapter 4, valuation of interest rate contingent claims would involve deriving a valuation equation, specifying appropriate boundary conditions and then solving the partial differential equation problem. While this model has a closed form solution for discount bonds, valuation of most interest rate contingent securities would require numerical methods. We will discuss numerical methods for multi-factor models in Chapter 7.

2.2 The Brennan and Schwartz Model

One of the criticisms of single-factor models is that they imply that price movements of all bonds are perfectly correlated. Consider the CIR or the Vasicek one-factor models. The uncertainty about future interest rates is modeled by a single stochastic factor, dZ. The same random shock drives price movements for all bonds in the same direction at the same time. Even though the magnitude of a price movement will vary from one bond to another depending on maturity and coupon rate, the direction of price changes will be the same for all bonds; hence, the perfect correlation of bond price movements.

In order to allow for the imperfect correlation in price movements that is actually observed in the market, a second stochastic factor may be introduced. If movements in the second stochastic factor are not perfectly correlated with movements in the first stochastic factor, then there will not be perfect correlation between bond price movements. Brennan and Schwartz[1] (BrS) propose a continuous-time model that uses the instantaneous spot rate, r, and the consol rate, l, as the two factors. Note that the consol rate is the yield on an instrument that pays a continuous coupon of l. This short-rate and long-rate pair are assumed to contain all information about default-free securities contained in the term structure at any point in time. They are assumed to follow a joint stochastic process of the general type:

$$dr = \beta_1(r, l, t)dt + \eta_1(r, l, t)dZ_1 \quad (6.5)$$

$$dl = \beta_2(r, l, t)dt + \eta_2(r, l, t)dZ_2 \quad (6.6)$$

where t is calendar time, dZ_1 and dZ_2 are Wiener processes with $dZ_1 dZ_2 = \rho dt$.

Given that these two factors summarize all information in the term structure, then the value of any generic zero-coupon bond can be expressed as a function of the short rate, long rate, and time and is written $G(r, l, t)$. More complex securities may also be expressed as a function of r, l, t and other parameters that uniquely identify the contract. However, the derivation of the valuation equation will be identical to the derivation for the zero-coupon bond.

The intuition behind the selection of these two factors is that short rate carries information about the current status of the economy or current supply and demand conditions for loanable funds, while the consol rate carries information about the market's beliefs about future short rates or long run inflation. By applying Ito's lemma to $G(r,l,t)$ and substituting from (6.5) and (6.6) for dr and dl, respectively, the stochastic process that governs movements in the bond price may be written as

$$\frac{dG}{G} = \mu(r, l, t)dt + \sigma_1(r, l, t)dZ_1$$

$$+ \sigma_2(r, l, t)dZ_2 \quad (6.7)$$

where

$$\mu(r, l, t) = (G_r\beta_1 + G_l\beta_2 + \frac{1}{2}G_{rr}\eta_1$$

$$+ \frac{1}{2}G_{ll}\eta_2 + G_{rl}\rho\eta_1\eta_2 + G_t)/G$$

$$\sigma_1(r, l, t) = (G_r\eta_1)/G$$

$$\sigma_2(r, l, t) = (G_l\eta_2)/G$$

Note that subscripts on G denote partial derivatives.

Equation (6.7) shows that the instantaneous returns of all bonds are linear functions of the two stochastic increments dZ_1 and dZ_2. The absence of arbitrage implies a condition on expected returns that depends on the market prices of risk for short rate and consol risk, denoted by $\lambda_1(r,l,t)$ and $\lambda_2(r,l,t)$ respectively, such that for any bond

$$\mu(r, l, t) = r + \lambda_1(r, l, t)\sigma_1(r, l, t)$$

$$+ \lambda_2(r, l, t)\sigma_2(r, l, t) \quad (6.8)$$

Equation (6.8) is the equilibrium condition for this model of the term structure.

Substituting for $\mu(r,l,t)$ in the equilibrium condition in equation (6.8) yields the valuation equation. Suppressing dependence on r, l and t for the sake of notational convenience, the valuation equation is

$$\frac{1}{2}G_{rr}\eta_1 + G_{rl}\rho\eta_1\eta_2 + \frac{1}{2}G_{ll}\eta_2 + G_r(\beta_1 - \lambda_1\eta_1)$$

$$+ G_l(\beta_2 - \lambda_2\eta_2) + G_t - rG = 0 \quad (6.9)$$

In order to complete the valuation problem, appropriate boundary conditions must be added. The maturity condition, $G(r,l,t=T)=1$, leads to the value of a discount bond that pays \$1 at maturity. This value can then be scaled up to calculate the value of bonds with a larger face value. Similarly, portfolios of scaled discount bonds can be used to value any default-free coupon bond. The boundary conditions on the extreme values of the state variables must also be specified. They are similar to those given in previous chapters. As before, the boundary conditions uniquely determine the instrument being valued. Thus, general interest rate contingent securities can be valued using equation (6.9) and appropriate boundary conditions.

Brennan and Schwartz also show how equation (6.9) can be restated with λ_2 stated in terms of λ_1 so that only the market price of short rate risk enters the valuation problem.[2] Therefore, when the LEH holds, the market prices of interest rate risk will not enter into the valuation problem.

The BrS model advances the single-factor models of the term structure by adding flexibility and bringing the model in line with the empirical observation that price movements on bonds are not perfectly correlated. While there are no traded consols in the United States, the model has been implemented with a long Treasury bond yield as proxy for the consol rate. The model has been tested and shown to be a significant improvement over single-factor models. It is used frequently in theoretical as well as practical applications.

The BrS model has also been criticized for one potential internal inconsistency. The price of a consol is the inverse of its yield. In the case of the BrS model, the second stochastic state variable is the consol rate. However, if one were to price a consol using the BrS model there is no reason to expect that the price will necessarily equal the inverse of the state variable, l.[3]

Variations of the BrS model have been proposed where the second stochastic factor is a fixed maturity spot rate or the spread between the short and long rate. While these, as well as the original BrS model, have been used successfully in practice, they are subject to the same internal inconsistency problem. A different choice of the second stochastic factor can lead to a model that is internally consistent yet still allows for bond price movements to be less than perfectly correlated. For example, the volatility parameter in the short rate process could be stochastic. The Fong and Vasicek model is an example of this approach.

2.3 The Fong and Vasicek Model

The Fong and Vasicek (FV) model is based on the observation that the volatility of interest rates is not necessarily constant. They derive a model that has the attractive quality that it yields measures of exposure to interest rate risk and to volatility risk. Like the CIR model, it also has a closed-form solution. However, also like the CIR

model, valuation of most interest rate contingent claims would require numerical procedures.

The FV model uses the same assumption on interest rate movements as the Vasicek model of equation (5.15),

$$dr = \kappa(\mu - r)dt + \sigma dZ_1 \qquad (6.10)$$

where $\sigma = \sqrt{v}$.

Next, they model the uncertainty about future volatility levels by specifying a stochastic process for the instantaneous variance of the interest rate process, v,

$$dv = \gamma(\alpha - v)dt + \xi\sqrt{v}dZ_2 \qquad (6.11)$$

where γ is the intensity of mean reversion, α is the long-run average level of v, and ξ is the volatility parameter for the process. The correlation between the two random components, dZ_1 and dZ_2, may be non-zero.

Notice that the stochastic process for v has the form of the CIR interest rate process. While it is similar to the interest rate process in having a mean reverting drift term, the instantaneous variance of dv is proportional to v. This means that very quiet markets are not likely to become suddenly volatile and that unstable markets have the potential to become suddenly stable or even more volatile.

Using Ito's Lemma, we derive a partial differential equation to which the Time t price of a discount bond that pays \$1 at Time T, $P(r,v,t,T)$, must be subject:

$$\frac{dP}{P} = a(r, v)dt - \sigma P_r dZ_1 - \xi\sqrt{v}P_v dZ_2 \quad (6.12)$$

where $a(r,v)$ is the expected return on the discount bond. Using the no-arbitrage equilibrium condition we can derive a valuation equation of the form

$$a(r, v) = r + \lambda_r \sigma P_r / P + \lambda_v \xi \sqrt{v} P_v / P \quad (6.13)$$

where λ_r and λ_v are the market prices of interest rate and interest rate volatility risk, respectively. Equation (6.13) is of the same form as equation (6.2) with the addition of the market price of risk terms. We have purposefully hidden the details of the valuation equation here in order to illustrate the economic intuition of the valuation equation. Equation (6.13) states mathematically that the instantaneous expected return on the discount bond must be the risk-free rate plus a risk premium for each source of risk in this market.

The solution to (6.13) with boundary conditions appropriate to a discount bond has the form

$$P(r, v, t, T) = \exp[-rD(t, T) + vF(t, T)$$

$$+ G(t, T)] \quad (6.14)$$

The exact specification of $D(t,T)$, $F(t,T)$, and $G(t,T)$ will not be given here.[4] However, the pricing relationship in equation (6.14) allows for some insight into the strengths of the FV model.

First, this model is more flexible than the Vasicek model that FV extend. The FV model is capable of generating term structures that are monotonically increasing, decreasing, or that have one or two humps. Second, the FV model also leads to a nice interpretation of two of the terms in equation (6.14). Using (6.14) the following relations can be derived

$$D(t, T) = -\frac{1}{P} \frac{\partial P}{\partial r} \quad (6.15)$$

$$F(t, T) = \frac{1}{P} \frac{\partial P}{\partial v} \quad (6.16)$$

According to equation (6.15), $D(t, T)$ is a measure of interest rate risk exposure, or duration, for the discount bond. Similarly, (6.16) establishes $F(t, T)$ as a measure of volatility risk exposure.

While the FV model offers straightforward measures of exposure to interest rate or volatility risk, it is also subject to some weaknesses. The use of the Vasicek interest rate process allows for the possibility of negative interest rates. We discussed this issue in Chapter 5 in some detail. Despite this theoretical flaw in the FV model, the flexibility and straightforward interpretation that it offers make it a popular model in practice.

2.4 The Hull and White Model

Hull and White (HW) have provided a two-factor version of their extended-Vasicek model of the term structure. The need for this model is based on the observation that the term structure of volatility often displays a "hump" in the cap markets. The single-factor models are not rich enough to fit this hump in the volatility structure. The inclusion of a stochastic reversion level generates a term structure model which is able to fit a single hump in the volatility structure.

As with the extended Vasicek model discussed in Chapters 3 and 5, the short rate is assumed to follow a stochastic process of the form

$$dr = [\theta(t) + u - ar]dt + \sigma_1 dZ_1 \quad (6.17)$$

where the parameter u has been added as a stochastic parameter of the drift specification. The parameter u is assumed to follow the stochastic process

$$du = -bu\, dt + \sigma_2 dZ_2$$

where the initial value of u is zero, u reverts to zero at rate b, and the stochastic components, dZ_1 and dZ_2, have instantaneous correlation ρ.

Hull and White provide a closed-form solution for the value of a discount bond as a function of the short rate and time to maturity, $P(r,t,T)$.[5] The solution has the form

$P(r, t, T)$

$$= A(t, T)\exp[-B(t, T)r - C(t, T)u] \quad (6.18)$$

In addition to the price of a discount bond, there is a closed-form solution for the value of a European call option on a discount bond. The call option price is

$$C(r, t, T; K) = P(r, t, s)N(h)$$

$$- KP(r, t, T)N(h - \sigma_p) \quad (6.19)$$

where K is the strike price, $N(\ )$ is the cumulative normal distribution,

$$h = \frac{1}{\sigma_P}\log\frac{P(r, t, s)}{P(r, t, T)K} + \frac{\sigma_P}{2},$$

s is the maturity of the bond, T is the maturity of the option, and σ_P is the volatility of the bond's price process.

As with the Fong and Vasicek model, the Vasicek model, and the extended Vasicek model, this model allows negative interest rates to be obtained. However, as with the others, this model is relatively straightforward to implement and has the flexibility to fit observed term structures. The practical virtues often outweigh the theoretical shortcomings.

2.5 The Heath, Jarrow and Morton Model

Up to this point, every model we have considered uses the short rate as a stochastic factor in valuation. However, as we pointed out in Chapter 3, there are really three possibilities for the choice of fundamental factor: bond prices, spot rates, or forward rates. Once one of these three is modeled, the other two are uniquely determined by arbitrage arguments. Heath, Jarrow and Morton (HJM) choose to use forward rates as the fundamental factors in their model. Their contribution, though, is not their choice of forward rates to be modeled but the use of equivalent martingale pricing.

As HJM discuss, with respect to interest rate contingent securities, there are two goals of arbitrage pricing theory. The first is to price all zero-coupon bonds as functions of a finite number of stochastic state variables. The second is to price all interest rate contingent claims, taking as given the prices of the zero-coupon bonds. As we saw in our discussion of the BrS or the FV model, the market price of risk for the various stochastic factors enter in to the zero-coupon bond prices.[6] The difficulty in implementation stems from the need to specify a functional form for the market prices of the fundamental risks. HJM provide a methodology that removes all market price of risk terms from the pricing of interest rate contingent securities.

The fundamental assumption of HJM is an assumption that forward rate movements are driven by n stochastic factors. Within a finite time horizon denoted by $[0,\tau]$, they take the initial, Time 0, forward rate curve, denoted by $f(0,T)$, $T \in [0,\tau]$, as given. For an arbitrary fixed value of T, forward rate movements are governed by a stochastic process of the form

$$df(t, T) = \alpha(f, T)dt + \sum_{i=1}^{n} \sigma_i(f, T)dZ_i$$

$$\text{for all } 0 \leq t \leq T \quad (6.20)$$

By adding restrictions that preclude the dominance of money and that ensure the existence of the necessary expectations operators, HJM establish a unique equivalent martingale measure. They then show that under the equivalent martingale measure, the prices of interest rate contingent securities do not depend on the market prices of the fundamental risk factors. This finding is analogous to the risk-neutralized probability framework we derived in Chapter 3. In the HJM framework, prices of interest rate contingent claims are dependent on the short rate and the volatility parameters, $\sigma_i(f,T)$, $i=1, 2, \ldots, n$. This is not surprising given our exposure to the Black and Scholes option pricing formula. Recall that the price of the option depends on the risk-free rate and the volatility of the underlying price process. The price of the option is independent of the drift of the underlying price process. Since the market prices of risk enter only into the drift, HJM are able to price interest rate contingent securities independent of the market prices of risk under the equivalent martingale measure.

3. Conclusion

In this chapter we have introduced some of the reasons for using multi-factor models. In order to illustrate the approaches that have been taken, we briefly described five different models that range from theoretical interest to mainstream practice. These models illustrate the issues involved in constructing a multi-factor model of the term structure. In the next chapter, we will discuss issues surrounding implementation of multi-factor models for interest rate contingent claims pricing.

End Notes

1. Michael J. Brennan and Eduardo S. Schwartz, "Savings bonds, Retractable Bonds and Callable Bonds," *Journal of Financial Economics* 5 (1977), pp. 67-88.

2. See Michael J. Brennan and Eduardo S. Schwartz, "An Equilibrium Model of Bond Pricing and a Test of Market Efficiency," *Journal of Financial and Quantitative Analysis* 17, 3 (1982), pp. 301-329.

3. This inconsistency has been pointed out by Duffie and Kan "A Yield-Factor Model of Interest Rates" working paper, Graduate School of Business, Stanford University (1995). D. Duffie, J. Ma, and J. Young, "Black's Consol Rate Conjecture," Working Paper, Graduate School of Business, Stanford University (1995), forthcoming, *Annals of Applied Probability*, gives purely technical regularity conditions for the stochastic differential equation defining the short rate and consol rate so that the model is internally consistent.

4. For the complete derivation of the pricing model the reader is referred to H. Gifford Fong and Oldrich A. Vasicek, "Fixed-Income Volatility Management: A New Approach to Return and Risk Analyses in Fixed-Income Management," *Journal of Portfolio Management* (Summer 1991), pp. 41-46.

5. See John Hull and Alan White, "Numerical Procedures for Implementing Term Structure Models: Two-Factor Models," *Journal of Derivatives* (Winter 1994).

6. Assuming the LEH holds sets the market price of short rate risk to zero. This does not necessarily remove the market price of other risks from the bond price.

Practice Exercises

1. When would a term structure model of nominal interest rates that does not include inflation as one of its factors be likely to be adequate?

2. There is potential for internal inconsistency in the Brennan and Schwartz two-factor model. How can this model be implemented with an assurance of no internal inconsistency?

3. The Fong and Vasicek model of section 2.3 and the Hull and White model of section 2.4 both use a stochastic process of similar form

for the short rate. However, while Fong and Vasicek choose the volatility parameter to be the second stochastic factor, Hull and White choose the level that rates revert to as the second stochastic factor. Why not make both parameters stochastic and use a three factor model?

Multi-Factor Discrete-Time Models

1. Introduction

In the previous chapter we discussed several of the approaches that have been devised for extending single-factor models to multiple factors. As we saw in Chapter 5, there is a clear relationship between continuous-time and discrete-time models. In each case, the discrete-time model had a continuous-time analog. In fact, the discrete-time models are numerical approximations to the continuous-time models. The same is true for multi-factor models. While the models in the previous chapter were all stated in continuous time, they too are implemented in discrete time. Indeed, due to the almost complete lack of closed-form solutions for interest rate contingent security prices in a multi-factor framework, these models are almost always implemented using discrete-time numerical techniques. However, due to the complex nature of these numerical techniques, we will devote this chapter to an introductory discussion of implementation issues. This introduction will serve as a jumping off point into the literature. As in Chapter 5, there are two basic types of numerical techniques that are used in solving for interest rate contingent claim prices: lattices and numerical solutions to partial differential equations (PDE). We will discuss

each in turn and then make some concluding comments.

2. Multi-Factor Lattices

The most basic multi-factor model of term-structure dynamics would be a straightforward extension to two factors of the binomial model presented in Chapter 3. In a binomial model where the short rate is taken as the single factor, the short rate moves either up or down over the next time period. In a two-factor model, each of the two factors is assumed to move either up or down over the next time period. The lattice that is generated is three dimensional, as opposed to the two dimensional lattice generated by the single-factor binomial model.

2.1 Path Independent Models

A three dimensional lattice is illustrated in Figure 7.1. The initial node represents the current values of the two factors, denoted by r and γ. The up or down movement of each of these factors is represented by u or d, respectively. For example, over the first time period, the case where r goes up and γ goes down is denoted by u,d. Conversely, the case where r goes down and γ goes up is denoted by d,u. As illustrated in Figure 7.1, when Time *t* is the current point in time, at Time *t*+1 there are four possible values that the pair of factors could assume. Iterating this branching process for a second time period leads to nine possible pairs of values for the two factors at Time *t*+2. In general, there will be $(n+1)^2$ nodes at Time *t*+*n*, *n*=0, 1, 2... for a recombining lattice. Notice that this lattice is based on the same assumption of path independence as the binomial models of Chapter 3. Therefore, as in Chapter 3, we have a recombining lattice. An example of recombination is shown in the figure by having two up movements in *r* accompanied by an up and down movement in γ (denoted by *uu,ud*) lead to the same node as two up movements in *r* accompanied by a

down and up movement in γ (denoted by *uu,du*).

The process of implementing a two-factor lattice is logically identical to the process for single-factor lattices introduced in Chapter 3. First, generate a lattice of values that the factors can attain. Second, generate a corresponding lattice of cash flows that would occur if those values of the two factors are attained. Finally, discount the cash flows by their associated short-rate paths to get the value of the interest rate contingent claim. In fact, for cases where the model is path independent, that is, cases where the model generates a recombining lattice such as the one in Figure 7.1, we can discount iteratively through the lattice just as we did in Chapter 3.

Figure 7.1. A Recombining Lattice for a Two-Factor Binomial Model

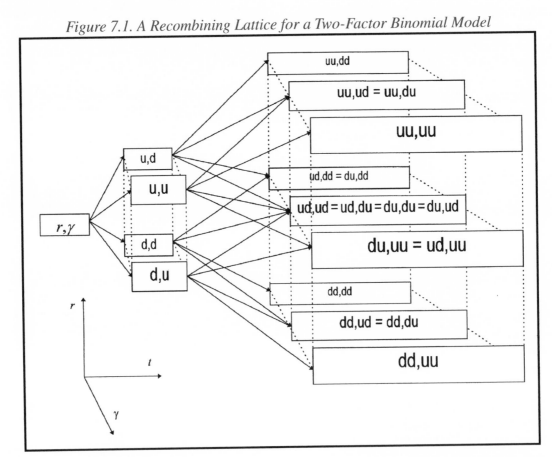

Chapter 7

Examples of a second factor in a term structure model were given in Chapter 6 and include the inflation rate, volatility of movements in the short rate, the long-run average level of the short rate, or a spot rate of longer maturity than the short rate. Also, we saw that the two factors could be two forward rates of different maturities. However, the implementation in a lattice framework will be quite different depending upon which of these is selected as the second stochastic factor. We will illustrate this by extending the simple multiplicative binomial model from Chapter 3 using the inflation rate and then later the volatility parameter as a second stochastic factor.

Consider, as an example of a path-independent model, a variation of the CIR model of nominal interest rates introduced in Chapter 6. In that model, CIR assume that movements in the real short rate and in the price level for the economy each follow stochastic processes. For this example, we will make simplifying assumptions for illustration purposes. Specifically, the simple multiplicative model is used to represent the dynamics of the real short rate.[1] The dynamics of the expected inflation rate, i_t, will be represented by a simple additive model where

$$i_t = \begin{cases} i_{t-1} + \Delta, & \text{with probability } \pi \\ i_{t-1} - \Delta, & \text{with probability } (1-\pi) \end{cases}$$

and Δ is a constant. In the limit, as we saw in Chapter 5, the real short rate follows a lognormal distribution. The inflation rate has the normal as its limiting distribution. This allows for the possibility of negative expected inflation. The nominal rate, x_t, will be determined using the Fisher Equation:

$$x_t = (1 + r_t)(1 + i_t) - 1 \qquad (7.1)$$

Notice that this expression represents a model of nominal interest rates that are a function of real rates and expectations about future inflation.

The expression in (7.1) is actually an approximation that ignores any interaction between inflation rates and real rates. Equation (7.1) would hold with equality in either of two cases. First, if the correlation between the two factors is found to be zero through empirical study then there will be no interaction terms. Second, if the true stochastic processes for the real short rate and the inflation rate are orthogonalized yielding transformed state variables r_t and i_t that are uncorrelated, then equation (7.1) will hold.[2]

An example of this orthogonalization process is in a typical implementation of the Brennan and Schwartz two-factor model discussed in Chapter 6. Recall that their two factors were the short and long interest rates. Because the short and long rates are roughly 60 percent correlated with each other, to facilitate implementation they are orthogonalized by transforming the long-rate factor to a spread between the long and short rates. These two factors, the short rate and the spread, are virtually uncorrelated.

The first two periods of the lattice generated by this model are shown in Figure 7.2. Panel A shows the evolution of the state variables. Notice that each node has the value of the short real rate followed be the value of the expected inflation rate, separated by a comma. Panel B shows the lattice for the nominal rate, as determined by equation (7.1), that corresponds to the state variables shown in Panel A.

Figure 7.2. Nominal Interest Rate Model
Panel A

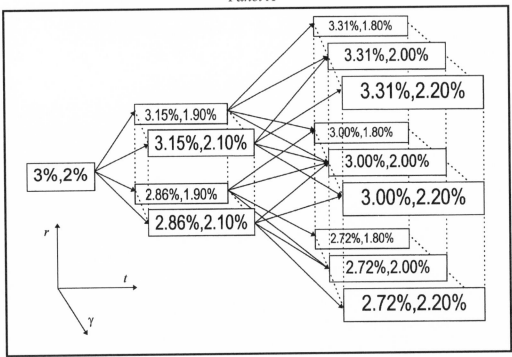

Panel B

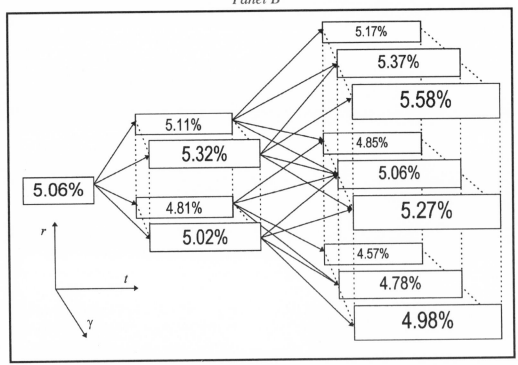

Chapter 7

In order to value an interest rate contingent security, a lattice of cash flows must be constructed and then discounted by interest rates and probabilities. For example, consider an interest rate cap with annual reset, a 5.1% strike rate and one dollar notional amount. The cash flows for this cap are shown in Figure 7.3. As before, we can discount iteratively through the lattice. We will illustrate this process by considering the calculations for the node at Time $t+1$ where both state variables have increased from their Time t values, labeled as node A.

Figure 7.4 shows node A from Figure 7.3. The probabilities are shown for each branch. Because the two state variables are completely uncorrelated, either by assumption or by construction, the probabilities are simply the product of the probabilities for the individual state variables. The value of node A is given by

$$0.0046 = \frac{p\pi(0.0048) + p(1-\pi)(0.0027)}{(1+0.0532)}$$

$$+ \frac{(1-p)\pi(0.0017) + (1-p)(1-\pi)(0.0000)}{(1+0.0532)}$$

where $p=0.6$ and $\pi=0.5$. Notice that the discount rate is the nominal rate that corresponds to node A. This calculation is carried out for nodes B, C, and D. Then, the value of the cap is

$$0.0017 = \frac{p\pi(0.0046) + p(1-\pi)(0.0011)}{(1+0.0506)}$$

$$+ \frac{(1-p)\pi(0.0005) + (1-p)(1-\pi)(0.0000)}{(1+0.0506)}$$

per dollar of notional amount at Time t.

A further discussion of the issues involved in implementing two-factor lattices is given by Hull and White.[3] In that paper they discuss the issues of mean reversion and building correlation

Figure 7.3. Cap Cash Flows as a Percent of Notional Amount (5.1% Strike Rate)

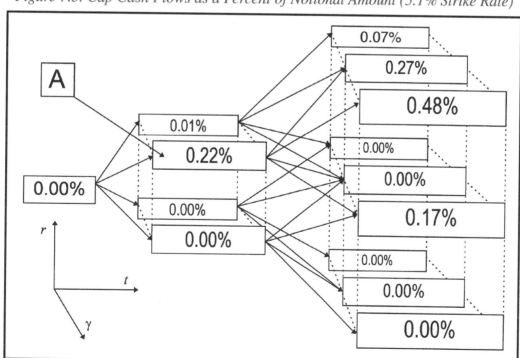

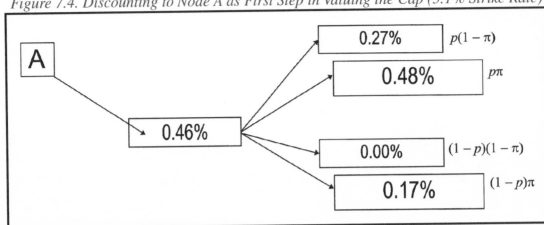

Figure 7.4. Discounting to Node A as First Step in Valuing the Cap (5.1% Strike Rate)

between the variables into the lattice. Another example of implementing a two-factor model is given by Heath, Jarrow and Morton.[4] They show how a model with two forward rates as the stochastic factors may be implemented in a discrete-time approximation to their own continuous time model.

2.2 Path Dependent Models

Figure 7.5 shows the more common case where the lattice is not recombining. An example of a model that is path dependent would be the simple multiplicative model extended to have the volatility parameter, σ, be the second stochastic factor. In this case, evolution of the short rate is governed by

$$r_t = \begin{cases} r_{t-1}(1+\sigma_t^u), & \text{with probability } p\pi \\ r_{t-1}(1+\sigma_t^d), & \text{with probability } p(1-\pi) \\ \dfrac{r_{t-1}}{(1+\sigma_t^u)}, & \text{with probability } (1-p)\pi \\ \dfrac{r_{t-1}}{(1+\sigma_t^d)}, & \text{with probability } (1-p)(1-\pi) \end{cases}$$

where p is the probability of an up movement in the short rate, π is the probability of an up

movement in the volatility parameter, and σ^u and σ^d are the values of the volatility parameter in an up state or a down state, respectively. The movements in the volatility parameter are given by

$$\sigma_t = \begin{cases} \sigma_t^u = \sigma_{t-1}(1+\xi), & \text{with probability } \pi \\ \sigma_t^d = \dfrac{\sigma_{t-1}}{(1+\xi)}, & \text{with probability } (1-\pi) \end{cases}$$

where ξ is the volatility parameter of σ_t and π is the probability of an up movement σ_t. In the limit, the volatility parameter has a lognormal distribution.

Notice that in this model, at Time t the Time $t-1$ level of the interest rate and the volatility parameter are known, the new level of the volatility parameter is revealed to be either σ_t^u or σ_t^d and the short rate moves either up or down by an amount determined by the revealed volatility level. Notice also that the value of the volatility parameter is path independent. However, because the value of the short rate depends on the value of the volatility parameter, which varies over time, the short rate is path dependent. This can be seen in Figure 7.5.

Figure 7.5. Path Dependent Lattice

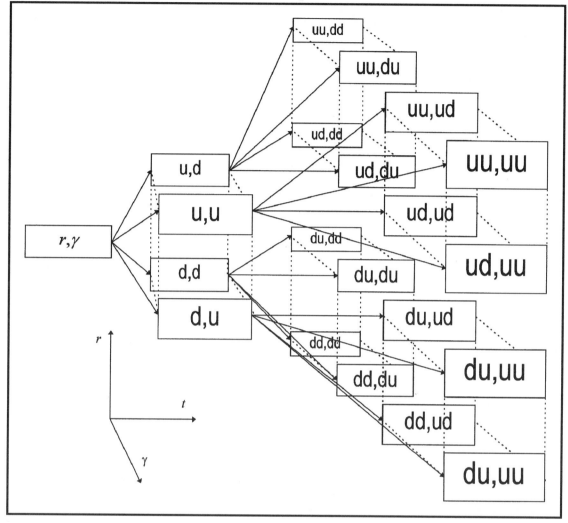

Calculating interest rate contingent claim values is much more computationally intensive in this case. Because of the path dependence of the values of the state variables, and therefore the values of the interest rate contingent cash flows, each potential cash flow must be discounted by its own unique path. There are 4^n nodes at Time $t+n$, n=0, 1, 2, ... for this path dependent example.

In order to limit the number of computations used in path dependent models, valuation is often done through simulation. Paths are randomly generated based on the underlying stochastic processes and the present values of cash flows along those paths are weighted by their probability of occurrence. As the number of generated paths increases, the accuracy of the simulation increases. With simulations, valuation models can be extended to more than two-factors without unreasonable computational costs. We will discuss simulations in greater detail in Chapter 8.

3. Numerical Solutions to Partial Differential Equations

As we saw in Chapter 5, there is a well-defined relationship between lattice-based approximations to the value of an interest rate contingent claim and numerical solutions to the partial differential equation (PDE) problem that defines the value of an interest rate contingent claim. The same holds true for multi-factor models. When derived in continuous time, the value of an interest rate contingent claim is found by solving a PDE similar to equations (6.2) and (6.9) subject to appropriate boundary conditions. However, it is extremely rare to be able to find a closed-form solution to these multi-factor models. Therefore, in most cases we resort to numerical techniques to find solutions for specific values of the parameters and state variables.

An entire text would be needed to adequately cover the numerical analysis involved in solving a PDE. However, the intuition is fairly straightforward. The most common numerical approach employed in the finance literature for two-factor models is an extension of the finite difference implicit method called the alternating direction implicit (ADI) method. Recall that in the finite difference methods employed for single-factor models, the continuous state space was discretized in two dimensions: time and the single state variable. In the case of a two-factor model, the ADI method would discretize the state space in three dimensions: time and the two state variables. Just as with the finite difference methods, the initial condition must be specified in order to start the iteration process. For example, in the case of a discount bond, the initial condition in the time-to-maturity dimension would be the face value of the bond, that is, the amount to be paid at maturity. In the case of a single-pay interest rate cap, the initial condition in the time-to-maturity dimension would be the payment to the cap as a function of the two state variables at maturity. (Of course, a coupon bond or a multi-period cap would be valued as a portfolio of their respective single-pay instruments.) Further, boundary conditions for the extreme values of both state variables must be imposed.

Recall that for the finite difference methods a vector was specified as an initial condition in the time-to-maturity dimension. That vector was iterated with the end points given by the boundary conditions on the state variable and the interior governed by the difference equation approximation to the PDE. In the case of the two-factor model a plane is specified as the initial condition for the time-to-maturity dimension. The edges of the plane are determined by the boundary conditions on the two state variables. The interior of the plane is determined using a difference equation approximation to the PDE. The plane is then calculated iteratively to find the current value of the security.

The number of calculations involved in these discrete approximation schemes can quickly become massive. In fact, the computational costs limit us in practice to two factor models. For this reason, it is more common to see multi-factor models implemented using lattice schemes or Monte Carlo simulations.

4. Conclusion

The literature on multi-factor models is relatively young and incomplete. We have attempted to introduce the ideas that underlie these approaches to valuation. We found that the strategies used for multi-factor models are the same as for single-factor models. A lattice of state variables is generated. Based on the values of the state variables a lattice of cash flows is constructed. The cash flows are discounted by paths back to the initial time and a value for the interest rate security is found.

The difficulty is not in understanding the logic of these approaches. Rather, it is the details of programming these models into a computer, the computational expense, issues of orthogonalizing stochastic factors or building correlation into the approximation that make implementing these models difficult. However, as we will discuss in Chapter 8, there are reasons that it may be worth the cost involved in implementing a multi-factor model.

End Notes

1. Recall that in the simple multiplicative binomial lattice model the entire term structure of interest rates is implicitly modeled. In the case of this example, the entire term structure of real interest rates is implicit in the model of the real short rate.

2. There are a variety of reasons that equation (7.1) may be questioned beyond the assertion that it is an approximation that ignores interaction terms. A thorough review of this topic can be found in *Financial Markets, Instruments, and Institutions* by David Babbel and Anthony Santomero (Burr Ridge, IL, Irwin Press, 1996). However, this simple model will be used for pedagogical purposes. Any actual implementation would, of necessity, be more complex.

3. John C. Hull and Alan White, "Numerical Procedures for Implementing Term Structure Models I & II," *Journal of Derivatives* (1994).

4. D. Heath, R. Jarrow, and A. Morton, "Bond Pricing and the term Structure of Interest Rates: A Discrete Time Approximation," *Journal of Financial and Quantitative Analysis*, 25 (1990), pp. 64-76.

Practice Exercises

1. In comparing the discrete-time implementations of the CIR two-factor model and the Fong and Vasicek two-factor model, what is one factor that determines whether a model will be implemented with a recombining lattice or a non-recombining lattice?

2. In the single-factor CIR and Vasicek models mean reversion tends to attenuate, or narrow, the distribution of short rates that can be obtained around the long-run average level, μ. The BrS two-factor model has been implemented in discrete form using the following equations

$$\frac{r_t - r_{t-1}}{r_t} = \frac{a_1}{r_{t-1}} + b_1\left(\frac{l_{t-1}}{r_{t-1}} - 1\right) + \varepsilon_{1t}$$

$$\frac{l_t - l_{t-1}}{l_t} = a_2 + b_2 r_{t-1} + c_2 l_{t-1} + \varepsilon_{2t}$$

The rate of reversion parameter, b_1, was estimated to be about 0.2. The reversion parameter for the CIR and Vasicek models, κ, is often estimated to be about 0.4. Which of these models would you expect to generate the widest distribution of possible short rates?

Simulation Approaches

1. Introduction

To this point most of our attention has been directed toward valuation of interest rate contingent cash flows using lattice methods. Continuous-time valuation models were heralded more for the economic intuition they bring than for their practical use. More often than not, they provide no closed-form solutions to the values of financial instruments, and numerical methods, or discrete-time approximations, must be used to value these instruments. Mentioned briefly in passing was an alternative method of valuation—Monte Carlo simulation. The simulation method is generally well understood by actuaries and financial analysts. Therefore, in this chapter we will review only briefly the simulation methods and then focus most of our comments on the benefits and drawbacks of this alternative.

2. Structure of Simulation Models

Perhaps the best way to describe the structure of a simulation model is to give an example of one. We will therefore begin by describing the two-factor simulation model proposed by Fong and Vasicek, discussed in Section 2.3 of Chapter 6. Recall that the two stochastic factors in their model were the short rate and volatility. They modeled the movement in these factors in equations (6.10) and (6.11) as follows:

$$dr = \kappa(\mu - r)dt + \sqrt{v}\,dZ_1$$
$$dv = \gamma(\alpha - v)dt + \xi\sqrt{v}\,dZ_2 \qquad (8.1)$$

We will assume here that these two processes are the *risk neutralized* processes; i.e., they have already been transformed to reflect the market prices of interest rate risk and variance risk.[1] Recall that Z_1 and Z_2 are Wiener processes with unit variance, $E(dZ_1)^2 = E(dZ_2)^2 = dt$; μ is the central value toward which the short rate r has a tendency to revert, with the reverting force $\kappa(\mu - r)$ proportional to its current deviation from the mean; instantaneous variance is v. In the second equation, α is the long-term average value of v; $\gamma > 0$ is the proportionality constant of the mean reverting force; $\xi^2 v$ is the instantaneous variance of the volatility process, proportional to the level of v. The Wiener processes Z_1 and Z_2 are assumed to exhibit instantaneous correlation of ρ with each other. The variance v of the short rate possesses a stationary distribution concentrated on strictly positive values whenever

$$\gamma\alpha \geq \frac{1}{2}\xi^2.$$

The stationary mean and variance of v are α and

$$\left(\frac{1}{2}\xi^2\alpha\right)\Big/\gamma, \text{ respectively.}$$

Now in order to simulate these processes, we must first transform the continuous-time equations into their discrete-time counterparts, for simulations must be conducted in discrete-time intervals. The discretized versions of the processes, which are generated by applying the Euler rule,[2] are given below:

$$r_t - r_{t-1} = \kappa(\mu - r_{t-1})\Delta t + \sqrt{v_{t-1}}\varepsilon_1 \sqrt{\Delta t}$$
$$v_t - v_{t-1} = \gamma(\alpha - v_{t-1})\Delta t + \xi\sqrt{v_{t-1}}\varepsilon_2\sqrt{\Delta t} \qquad (8.2)$$

In these discretized versions of the processes, ε_1 and ε_2 are random samples from a standardized bivariate normal distribution. A simple procedure for obtaining such samples with the appropriate correlation is as follows.[3] First, draw two independent samples ϕ_1 and ϕ_2 from a univariate standardized normal distribution. Then create the required samples ε_1 and ε_2 as follows:

$$\varepsilon_1 = \phi_1$$
$$\varepsilon_2 = \rho_{1,2}\phi_1 + \sqrt{1 - \rho_{1,2}^2}\phi_2 \qquad (8.3)$$

A single simulation run involves obtaining $2 \times N$ independent samples of ϕ from a univariate standardized normal distribution, so that N samples of ε_1 and ε_2 can be constructed. These are then substituted into the discretized equations above to produce simulated paths for each factor, thereby permitting a sample value for the interest-sensitive instrument to be calculated.

The next step in a simulation is to model the cash flows, assigning appropriate levels to the various time points and paths. This can be a very complex process and an entire book could be written on the intricacies involved for some financial instruments, such as mort-gage-backed securities and collateralized mortgage obligations.[4]

The point to make here is that these cash flows can be dependent on the levels and/or paths of either or both of the two stochastic factors. Indeed, sufficient information exists at each node in time for any pair of factors to generate the entire term structure of interest, so the cash flow could also depend on any reference rate or combination of reference rates in the term structure. Because the term structure of interest in this model at a point in time is completely specified by a knowledge of the positions of these two factors, along with the parameters given in the two equations, the entire term structure of interest need not be computed, but the cash flow can be specified as a (perhaps complicated) function of the two factors, and their history.

The final step is to discount the cash flows by the short rate paths that would give rise to them, obtaining a present value for each path in the simulation. Then, by summing the present values and dividing by the number of paths, we arrive at an estimate of the value of the financial instrument. The structure of this simulation process is depicted in Table 8.1. The first column gives the time period under consideration. The ensuing columns provide the values of the various factors and parameters, such as interest rate volatility, short rates, and cash flows, for each of the simulation paths over time.

3. A Numerical Example

Below we have provided the first two runs of a simulation example based on the Fong-Vasicek two-factor model described above. We have assumed that each period is one year in length. The instrument to be valued provides

Table 8.1. Structure of a Simulation

Period	Simulated Paths of Interest Rate Volatility					Simulated Paths of "Short Rates"					Simulated Paths of Cash Flows				
	Simulated Paths					Simulated Paths					Simulated Paths				
	1	2	3	...n...	N	1	2	3	...n...	N	1	2	3	...n...	N
1	σ_{11}	σ_{12}	σ_{13}	$...\sigma_{1n}...$	σ_{1N}	r_{11}	r_{12}	r_{13}	$...r_{1n}...$	r_{1N}	CF_{11}	CF_{12}	CF_{13}	$...CF_{1n}...$	CF_{1N}
2	σ_{21}	σ_{22}	σ_{23}	$...\sigma_{2n}...$	σ_{2N}	r_{21}	r_{22}	r_{23}	$...r_{2n}...$	r_{2N}	CF_{21}	CF_{22}	CF_{23}	$...CF_{2n}...$	CF_{2N}
3	σ_{31}	σ_{32}	σ_{33}	$...\sigma_{3n}...$	σ_{3N}	r_{31}	r_{32}	r_{33}	$...r_{3n}...$	r_{3N}	CF_{31}	CF_{32}	CF_{33}	$...CF_{3n}...$	CF_{3N}
⋮	⋮	⋮	⋮	⋮	⋮	⋮	⋮	⋮	⋮	⋮	⋮	⋮	⋮	⋮	⋮
t	σ_{t1}	σ_{t2}	σ_{t3}	$...\sigma_{tm}...$	σ_{tN}	r_{t1}	r_{t2}	r_{t3}	$...r_{tm}...$	r_{tN}	CF_{t1}	CF_{t2}	CF_{t3}	$...CF_{tm}...$	CF_{tN}
⋮	⋮	⋮	⋮	⋮	⋮	⋮	⋮	⋮	⋮	⋮	⋮	⋮	⋮	⋮	⋮
T	σ_{T1}	σ_{T2}	σ_{T3}	$...\sigma_{Tn}...$	σ_{TN}	r_{T1}	r_{T2}	r_{T3}	$...r_{Tn}...$	r_{TN}	CF_{T1}	CF_{T2}	CF_{T3}	$...CF_{Tn}...$	CF_{TN}

two cash flows of \$1 at Time 3 and again at Time 4. It also provides a cap-like interest-sensitive cash flow at Time 5, amounting to the maximum of $[100\times(r_5-0.06), 0]$, where r_5 is the short rate prevailing at Time 5. The parameter values used in the simulation are as follows: $r_0=0.07$; $\mu=0.06$; $v_0=0.00009800$; $\alpha=0.00007056$; $\kappa=0.4$; $\gamma=0.8$; $\xi=0.0025$; $\rho=0.5$; $dt=1.0$. In each simulation run, the random draws from our univariate standardized normal distribution are labeled $N(0,1)$, and are shown in the shaded rows of Table 8.2. Note that we needed two fully independent series of these random draws for each run to avoid violating the model's Markovian assumption. In general, $2\times N$ random draws are needed in this two-factor model for a simulation with N runs.

We have provided a comprehensive list of all of the values resulting from the simulation runs to allow readers to confirm their understanding of this technique. All values were computed in an Excel spreadsheet using the two pairs of equations denoted above as (8.2) and (8.3). The coefficient for diffusion in volatility was computed as $\xi\sqrt{v_{t-1}}$, which scales the random shock to volatility,

$$\varepsilon_2 = \rho_{1,2}\phi_1 + \sqrt{1-\rho_{1,2}^2}\,\phi_2,$$

to appropriate levels. The product of these two terms is then be multiplied by $\sqrt{\Delta t}$ to produce the discretized approximation of $\xi\sqrt{v}dz_2$. To be concrete, using values of $\rho=0.5$, $v_0=0.000098$, $\xi=0.0025$, $\phi_1=-0.36366373$ and $\phi_2=-1.00629904$, we obtained values at Time 1 of:

Coefficient of diffusion in volatility

$$= 0.0025 \times \sqrt{0.00009800} = 0.00002475$$

$$\varepsilon_2 = 0.5 \times (-0.36366373) + \sqrt{1-0.5^2}$$

$$\times (-1.00629904) = -1.05331240$$

These two values are shown in the table for Simulation Run Number 1 of Table 8.2. The numbers in this table translate into the figures in Table 8.1 as follows. The 13th row of Simulation Run Number 1 (shown in Panel A), labeled v, becomes the second column in Table 8.1; the 13th row of Simulation Run Number 2 (shown in Panel B) becomes the third column in Table 8.1. The 12th rows in Panels A and B, labeled r, become the first two columns in the Simulated Paths of "Short Rates" section of Table 8.1. The cash flows associated with these interest rate paths, shown in the 16th rows of Panels A and B, become the first two columns in the "Cash Flows" section of Table 8.1. Note that only one of them, the cash flow occurring at Time 5, is contingent on interest rate levels prevailing at that time. (In this example, there is no path dependency for any of the cash flows.)

If two runs of the simulation were sufficient—and they aren't—to engender confidence in the valuation, our estimated value of this security would be \$1.84825 (=[\$1.6287+\$2.0678]÷2), because the two simulation runs were equally probable. While our example has not been elegant in technique, it is useful for pedagogical purposes. Numerous techniques have been developed to simplify the computational aspects of a simulation and achieve greater efficiency.[5]

Table 8.2. First Two Runs of a Simulation[6]

Panel A

Simulation Run Number 1

Time:	0	1	2	3	4	5
$N(0,1)$		-0.36366373	0.42693955	-2.37127097	-0.64720098	-0.24931296
$N(0,1)$		-1.00629904	-0.14735861	-0.14355351	-0.87075023	-0.50809831
ε_1		-0.36366373	0.42693955	-2.37127097	-0.64720098	-0.24931296
ε_2		-1.05331240	0.08585348	-1.30995647	-1.07769231	-0.56468252
drift r		-0.00400000	-0.00095997	-0.00178330	0.00674940	0.00574807
diffusion r		0.00989949	0.00706964	0.00824387	0.00656068	0.00688335
drift v		-0.00002195	0.00001646	2.08E-06	0.00002201	0.00001854
diffusion v		0.00002475	0.00001767	0.00002061	0.00001640	0.00001721
Δr		-0.00760009	0.00205834	-0.02133175	0.00250332	0.00403196
Δv		-0.00004802	0.00001798	-0.00002492	4.34E-06	8.83E-06
r	0.07000000	0.06239991	0.06445826	0.04312651	0.04562983	0.04966179
v	0.00009800	0.00004998	0.00006796	0.00004304	0.00004738	0.00005621
std. dev. (v)	0.00989949	0.00706964	0.00824387	0.00656068	0.00688335	0.00749712
$exp(-\int r\, dt)$	1.0000	0.93594370	0.87842123	0.83241728	0.79628382	0.75923388
Payoff(t)	0.0000	0.0000	0.0000	1.0000	1.0000	0.0000
PV(Payoff)	0.0000	0.0000	0.0000	0.8324	0.7963	0.0000
$\sum PV$(Payoff)	**1.6287**					

Panel B

Simulation Run Number 2

Time:	0	1	2	3	4	5
$N(0,1)$		1.44917976	1.71121883	0.83334044	-0.98192231	0.55726559
$N(0,1)$		-0.22042855	-2.19262802	-0.39461838	0.84903604	-0.42993179
ε_1		1.44917976	1.71121883	0.83334044	-0.98192231	0.55726559
ε_2		0.53369316	-1.04326215	0.07492067	0.24432562	-0.09369905
drift r		-0.00400000	-0.00813846	-0.01134981	-0.00915887	-0.00226363
diffusion r		0.00989949	0.00944755	0.00704688	0.00822798	0.00866104
drift v		-0.00002195	-0.00001496	0.00001672	0.00000229	-0.00000356
diffusion v		0.00002475	0.00002362	0.00001762	0.00002057	0.00002165
Δr		0.01034615	0.00802837	-0.00547735	-0.01723810	0.00256288
Δv		-0.00000874	-0.00003960	0.00001804	0.00000731	-0.00000559
r	0.07000000	0.08034615	0.08837452	0.08289716	0.06565906	0.06822194
v	0.00009800	0.00008926	0.00004966	0.00006770	0.00007501	0.00006942
std. dev. (v)	0.00989949	0.00944755	0.00704688	0.00822798	0.00866104	0.00833198
$exp(-\int r\, dt)$	1.0000	0.92758293	0.85254149	0.78257208	0.72655045	0.67950692
Payoff(t)	0.0000	0.0000	0.0000	1.0000	1.0000	0.8222
PV(Payoff)	0.0000	0.0000	0.0000	0.7826	0.7266	0.5587
$\sum PV$(Payoff)	**2.0678**					

4. Advantages and Disadvantages of Simulation

Generally, simulations are done for two or more factors. It is usually more cumbersome to run a simulation for a single-factor model than it is simply to generate an entire lattice and conduct a valuation that way. However, when more than one factor is involved, computations in a lattice grow far more rapidly in time than in a simulation, where they grow linearly in time. Accordingly, a valuation model with more than a single factor is usually implemented via simulation.

Perhaps the main advantage of the simulation approach is that it permits the inclusion of path dependency in the cash flows of the instrument being valued. This path dependency is important for many of the assets held by insurers, as well as most of their liabilities. Another advantage is that simulation allows for more realistic jumps in interest rates of varying amounts along a single path, whereas lattices tend to produce streams of similar jumps. Finally, the analyst does not need to worry about producing branches that rejoin at each node.

Along with these four advantages comes one disadvantage. The simulation approach is difficult for exact pricing of American options (which allow for early exercise) because the exercise decision at each point in time is dependent on prices at each node. An exact pricing model (such as a lattice) compares the computed value of the option at each node with its call price, and can imitate the investor's decision whether to exercise the option. (Even though the holders of such options may not exercise them at optimal times, the fact that they trade in a liquid market means that investors who are more alert to such opportunities are likely to buy and exercise them when deviations from proper pricing are noticed, driving prices toward their theoretical levels.) To determine the price at a given node in time using simulation methodology, a new set of simulation runs would need to be performed branching from that node. Then the future state price could be calculated and a prudent exercise decision could be made. But it would take only a few nodes before the entire simulation approach would become completely unwieldy, running into billions of calculations! Thus, for instruments that feature American-style options, the standard simulation approach will not guarantee rational pricing.[7]

5. Simulation through Lattices

We have seen that simulations possess one attribute that is important in the valuation of many interest-sensitive securities—they allow for path dependence. Financial instruments that exhibit path dependence in their cash flows require a valuation model that accommodates this dependency.[8] Lattices that recombine do not feature this attribute, and as shown in Chapter 7, lattices that do not recombine pose curious theoretical questions, and quickly become computationally unwieldy as the number of periods grows. However, lattices have one attribute that is very helpful in valuations—at each node the price of the instrument being valued is known. For instruments whose payoffs (e.g., call, prepayment, lapse) depend on the state prices at each node, lattices provide a natural valuation approach.

But what about those financial instruments, such as mortgage-backed securities or life insurance policies, whose payoffs may depend not only on the state contingent prices at each node, but also upon how interest rates evolved in getting to that point? Simulation through lattices is the technique most often employed to value such securities. This technique combines the property of path dependence along with the virtue of having an entire term structure of interest and state prices fully determined at each node.

To simulate through a lattice, the first step is to set up and initialize the parameters of the lattice so that it is consistent with observed prices of Treasury securities, and options on Treasury futures. Then we can simulate through the lattice in a simple way. For example, if a trinomial lattice is being used, with probabilities of jumping upward, sideways, and downward of 40%, 35%, and 25%, respectively, then we could refer to a random number table and assign upward jumps to all two-digit numbers selected from 00-39, sideways moves to numbers between 40-74, and downward jumps to numbers between 75-99. At each node the exercise is repeated before moving rightward to the next node. If the probabilities for directional movements change over time, then the random number ranges are modified accordingly.

In this way, the computer can track the precise sequence it followed to arrive at a given node, and the cash flow at that node can be made dependent not only on the entire term structure of interest and contingent price at that node, and all of the interest-sensitive contingencies after that node, but also on the evolution of the term structure prior to reaching that node. Therefore, simulating through lattices overcomes the limitation of pure simulation, because it is able to obtain exact pricing for securities with American-style options, as well as any other interest rate contingent cash flows. Moreover, the models can capture any path dependencies in the cash flows.

Once the cash flows are assigned to the nodes, the valuation proceeds in the usual manner of simulations, discounting each cash flow by the sequence of short rates that gives rise to it, and weighing all of the path-dependent present values generated by the probabilities of occurrence of the paths. If the method for simulating the jumps described in the previous paragraph is used, the path-dependent present values need only be summed and divided by the total number of paths, because the probabilities of directional jumps have already been incorporated into the number of paths generated.

While our discussion of simulations has been straightforward, it is actually a rather complex task to perform in practice. It is often more painstaking to artfully model the path-dependent cash flows than it is to simulate the evolution of the random behavior of economic factors on which the valuation is based.[9] In modeling an insurance policy, it is particularly difficult to model the cash flows because often, available data permit little more than an educated guess. However, as the modeling technology becomes more widespread, we expect that data will be collected in a form that is directed toward the requirements of the valuation models.

6. Implementational Issues
6.1 How Many Paths?
Most early Wall Street applications of Monte Carlo simulations for valuing interest-sensitive securities used more than 10,000 paths and monthly periods. Gradually, the standard went to 1,024 paths, and some analysts even dropped to 512 paths. Increased precision could be obtained by using more simulation paths, and it was found that fewer than 512 paths resulted in unstable estimated values, destroying confidence in those values.

However, using a great number of paths slows down a simulation analysis, requires more powerful computers, and makes valuation an exercise in patience. In the future, developments in computer technology undoubtedly will alleviate this concern, but today, it poses a problem. Therefore, a number of vendor firms have employed "variance reduction techniques" of various sorts in an attempt to reduce the number of paths necessary to obtain stable estimated values. One such method, developed by BARRA, is called "modified principal component" analysis and is able to obtain stable pricing that approaches the accuracy obtained from 10,000 paths with 64 or fewer paths.[10] Unless some such variance reduction technique is employed, it is safer to proceed with 1,000 or more paths for most applications. Otherwise, the analyst tends to get pricing that is sample-specific, and unreliable.

6.2 How Many Periods? How Long?

Most simulations today involve monthly time intervals, although for some shorter-term securities (e.g., five or fewer years to maturity), a finer time grid is employed. One reason for choosing the monthly time periods is convenience, because many financial securities, such as mortgage-backed securities, feature monthly cash flows. Another reason for the choice of monthly periods is that it has been shown to produce adequate pricing. Finer time divisions could be used, but at a cost of speed.

For 30-year instruments, the standard analysis involves monthly time intervals, or 360 periods. Few securities extend beyond 30 years, but many insurance policies do. In such cases, it is unnecessary to employ month-long time intervals in Monte Carlo simulations. Quarterly time intervals are more than sufficient to get adequate pricing. Keep in mind,

too, that the precision demanded by Wall Street is usually higher than that required by insurers. This is because Wall Street uses simulation pricing to identify and direct arbitrage transactions, where margins are often razor thin and high leverage is undertaken to enhance profits. An insurer performing simulation analysis for the purpose of asset/liability management or insurance policy pricing would not need such precision.

One variation on the theme is to generate time periods of differing lengths, with fine sampling in the early periods and less fine sampling in later periods. This is particularly helpful when using lattice valuation methods, where the number of computations quickly approaches millions for a long-term investment with many periods. For example, weekly or monthly periods may be used for the first years, and then quarterly periods thereafter until maturity. One leading valuation expert has obtained satisfactory results using 60 time periods, regardless of the maturity of the security. The time intervals are adjusted according to the time to maturity, with finer time sampling in the early years. Experimentation with the particular instrument to be valued should be done against a fine time grid benchmark in order to assess the loss in stability by making any of these compromises.

6.3 Number of Factors and Parameter Estimation Errors

As more factors are added, it is possible to obtain closer model fits to the prices of reference securities. However, with an increase in the number of factors often comes an increase in the number of parameters that need to be estimated. This can subject the parameter estimates to multicollinearity.

What tends to happen in such cases is that we can get very precise "in-sample" fits to our model prices, but "out-of-sample" fits are often abysmal due to the instability of the system of equations. For this reason, analysts often stop with only two, or perhaps a handful of factors in these simulations. For instance, some analysts use credit risk, foreign exchange risk, or liquidity risk as a third factor. One practice that can reduce the instability of parameter estimates is to use factors that are orthogonal to each other. If the factors chosen are not naturally orthogonal to each other, they can be transformed to be orthogonal.[11] In this way, the modeling process can produce better out-of-sample prices.

6.4 Credit, Liquidity and Prepayment Risk

In this monograph, we stated at the outset that our task was to describe valuation approaches to accommodate interest-sensitive cash flows, but that credit and liquidity risks would not be treated. Nonetheless, the same models that we have described in this monograph are often used to value corporate securities with both credit and liquidity risk. Moreover, they are used to model mortgage-backed securities, which often have minimal credit and liquidity risk, but exhibit substantial prepayment uncertainty.

Analysts make two types of adjustments for these situations. Let us consider first the case of mortgage-backed securities (MBS). These securities reflect the behavior of borrowers, many of whom do not optimally exercise their privilege to refinance their loans. In place of some refinancing rule based on optimal, arbitrage-free behavior, analysts insert a formula that describes observed prepayment behavior as a function of interest rate levels and their evolution. Arc tangent functions are commonly used for this purpose. Clearly there is uncertainty surrounding the actual state-contingent prepayment behavior of the mortgagees, but as long as their interest-sensitive behavior is captured by the formula, the uncertainty surrounding it is usually not modeled. No bias is injected into the valuation by this simplification; however, the uncertainty means that we no longer can rely upon the principles of arbitrage to ensure that our valuation will be correct. Nonetheless, analysts continue to use the arbitrage-free frameworks of lattices and simulation to estimate fair market values. Typically, a "fudge factor" known as an "option-adjusted spread" (OAS) is added to the short rates at each node in order to arrive at market prices. When the OAS is positive, it is often said that it is compensation for absorbing the uncertainty of prepayments. When it is negative, well... In the early and mid-1980s, OAS was almost always positive for MBS, but as familiarity with the instruments grew over time, much of this spread was eliminated. Today the OAS is often quite low, and sometimes even negative for some MBS. Sales people quip that negative OAS is a problem with the valuation model and not an indication of an overpriced security!

In the case of illiquidity, it is also common to add an OAS to reflect the fact that the owner of the security will not be able to capture easily certain trading profits that may arise. This is probably appropriate. However, in the case of credit risk, analysts often adjust (sometimes downward!) the assumed volatility in the simulation or lattice when computing an OAS. This practice is dubious at best. By adjusting the volatility, the OAS is no longer meaningful, because it is no longer a "spread to Treasuries." This is because the new simulation or lattice no longer correctly prices Treasuries.[12]

What they could do instead is adjust the promised cash flows to reflect their default risk. The promised cash flows should not be reduced to reflect only their expected losses, but should be reduced further to reflect their certainty-equivalent values.[13] Then these certainty-equivalent values can be input into a simulation or lattice and the valuation can proceed. Any resulting OAS would then have a meaningful interpretation.

6.5 Initializing the Parameters

In order to ensure that the simulation is consistent with arbitrage-free valuation principles, it is important to select carefully the parameters for the assumed processes. The general approach is to produce a simulation or lattice that correctly prices a set of Treasury securities, options on Treasury futures, and perhaps a set of interest rate caps. Treasury securities are chosen based on their liquidity and nearly default-free status. They are selected to cover a full range of maturities so that the interest rate process can be adequately modeled. In addition, options and caps are used to initialize the parameters of the valuation model. These securities are chosen because their values are extremely sensitive to the assumed interest rate volatility over time periods of varying lengths. If the model is correctly pricing them, the analyst has confidence that the assumed volatility is set at an appropriate level. Because options on Treasury futures are more liquid than interest rate caps, they are relied on more heavily to estimate the short-term volatility parameters.

7. Alternative Valuation Techniques on the Horizon

In this and in previous chapters, we have presented the techniques in common use for valuing interest-sensitive cash flows. There are,

however, alternatives appearing on the valuation horizon. While these techniques are in their infancy, they may, someday, become accepted valuation methods and eventually even supplant the approaches discussed in this monograph. Therefore, we will briefly introduce these two approaches before closing with some concluding remarks.

The first of these approaches, known as the low-discrepancy method, is similar to Monte Carlo simulation in some ways, and carries the same natural advantage of taking into account path dependencies in the cash flows.[14] As Paskov and Traub[15] correctly state, Monte Carlo simulation is little more than a technique to replace the integral of $f(x)$, which is a continuous average, by a discrete average over randomly chosen points. (Recall how the entire thrust of the Monte Carlo method was to obtain an average value over various interest rate scenarios.) But while Monte Carlo methods attempt to generate random paths of interest rates, and perhaps of other factors, we typically observe in practice regions where there are no points, even when a moderate number of simulation runs have been performed. A related computational disadvantage of Monte Carlo simulation is that its rate of convergence to a stable estimate is slow.

On the other hand, the low-discrepancy method chooses points as uniformly distributed as possible, and then attempts to approximate the integral by a discrete average. However, this average is computed based on low-discrepancy points. In many situations, this technique produces estimates of value that converge much more rapidly to a stable and accurate value than Monte Carlo simulation.[16] Thus, faster pricing is achieved and less computer power is required. More of such approaches based on number theory are expected to emerge over time.

The other alternative that is being suggested relies on multivariate density estimation (MDE) procedures to investigate the relation between security prices, the interest rate level, slope of the term structure and interest rates.[17] While traditional approaches to valuation depend crucially on the correct parameterization of interest-sensitivity of the cash flows, and on the correct model for interest rates, this alternative approach is a nonparametric, model-free approach, and that it is computationally much less onerous to apply. The method has been shown to produce reasonable security pricing without relying on the cash flow and interest rate models requisite for the other approaches. However, it does require substantial data on security market prices in order to develop viable multivariate density estimates for the prices of other securities. Therefore, the method can be used only for those classes of financial instruments for which liquid markets already exist.

8. Thoughts on the Valuation of Interest-Sensitive Financial Institution Liabilities

In this monograph we have shown how valuation models can capture the interest rate sensitivity of cash flows. Our focus has been mostly on traded financial assets. However, these methods are also used to estimate the fair values of liabilities, including financial institution liabilities that are nontraded or illiquid. Most bank, pension and insurance liabilities are not traded instruments, and therefore possess limited liquidity. Moreover, the lack of trading in these instruments inhibits arbitrage principles from ensuring convergent pricing.

These products are sold in markets characterized by imperfect information and consumers seldom exercise all of their options optimally.

These latter two features—imperfect information and suboptimal exercise of policy options—suggest that some financial institution liabilities are analogous to mortgage-backed securities in their valuation. Therefore, the expected future cash flows should be modeled to reflect their anticipated interest sensitivity. But the illiquidity of such liabilities relative to mortgage-backed securities suggests that a small OAS be included in the simulations or lattices used to value them. There is some theoretical support for including this illiquidity OAS. Because many financial institution liabilities are illiquid, and their customers do not "turn on a dime" in a rush to exercise their embedded options, it is cheaper to offer and fund such liabilities than those which must accommodate such exercise of options. Hence, it is proper to value them with a set of interest rates that are higher than those used for valuing liquid Treasury securities.

Financial institution liabilities are also subject to default. In our opinion, this should not be factored into the valuation of liabilities that are guaranteed by Federal and state insolvency programs. Rather, this default "put option" should be valued on the other side of the balance sheet as an asset.[18] For example, the valuation of insurance policies should reflect only what it would cost to fully fund them, on an expected present value basis. Indeed, this measure of value (which is, in essence, the present value of the exercise price) is a necessary input for determining the value of the default put option. (It is a separate matter to implement an asset-liability management investment program to ensure the payment of the liabilities.)

Surplus would be used to handle uncertainty in the mortality and morbidity rates, and in surrender, lapse, and policy loan utilization.[19]

We believe that two well-chosen factors should be sufficient to value most financial institution liabilities. More than this would be superfluous at this juncture, given the absence of more complete data regarding the liability cash flow interest rate sensitivities. While either lattice or simulation methods could be used, in our judgment the simulation method is the most natural choice. The chief advantage of the lattice approach is for exact pricing of American options. (Recall from end note 6 that this advantage is eroding, as innovations in simulation procedures are able to accommodate American options.) Because most financial institution liabilities are nontraded and illiquid, the need for lattices is not great; moreover, few instruments on the asset side of a financial institution's balance sheet require such modeling. In most cases, the financial institution is short an option (e.g., the corporation issuing a bond retains the option to call it), and the issuer, while long the option, typically does not exercise its options in exact accordance with the model assumptions regarding optimal timing. Moreover, the path dependencies of cash flows are more prevalent and important for the typical financial institution than the possibility of someone exercising their options optimally. Therefore, a simulation is probably adequate.

9. Concluding Remarks

Whether lattice, simulation or some combination of these methods is used in valuing assets and liabilities, the basic principles are similar. First, the behavior over time of interest rates and other economic factors is modeled. Adjustments may be made for the market price of various risks. Second, cash flows associated with assets or liabilities are mapped over time and across economic states and paths. Adjustments may be made to reflect their illiquidity and their default status. Third, the (default-adjusted or unadjusted) projected cash flows are discounted back to the current time by the sequence of short rates that could give rise to them, and these discounted values are averaged to get an estimate of market value (in the case of assets) or present value (in the case of liabilities).

Over time new and improved techniques will undoubtedly be developed that will aid us in valuing financial instruments with interest-sensitive cash flows. Also, advances in computer technology will remove some of the current obstacles stemming from the computational intensity that these methods require. Pushing the valuation science ever forward is the ongoing proliferation of financial instruments and insurance products. The next monograph on the valuation of interest-sensitive cash flows may have little resemblance to what we have discussed here. Undoubtedly, valuation technology will continue to improve. We look forward to what the future will bring.

End Notes

1. If this is not the case, the transformation is straightforward. For example, if the market price of interest rate risk is a constant, λ_r, it is merely subtracted from μ in the first term. If it is a function of the level of r, $\lambda_r(r)$, then κ is altered to reflect this functional relationship. See Jonathan E. Ingersoll, Jr., *Theory of Financial Decision Making* (Totowa, NJ: Rowman and Littlefield, 1987) for a discussion of the market price of interest rate risk. (Note, by the way, that if the market price of interest rate risk is a constant in this model, it will not preclude arbitrage; to avoid arbitrage, it would need to be a function of the level of r.) An analogous transformation would be applied to the equation denoting the random volatility process, and the market price of volatility risk, λ_v, or $\lambda_v(v)$.

2. Note that if the discrete steps between $t-1$ and t are too long, you no longer converge to the desired distribution, but you have created your own new process. Moreover, the longer the step, the more likely it is that negative interest rates and volatility will be generated over some time periods. There are alternate schemes that are more efficient, such as a stochastic Runge-Kutta scheme and others described in Peter E. Kloeden and Eckhard Platen, *Numerical Solution of Stochastic Differential Equations,* New York: Springer-Verlag, 1992. The more efficient the scheme, the longer the time interval can be used and still get the desired distribution.

3. A generalized procedure for multi-factor models with more than two factors is given in John C. Hull, *Options, Futures, and Other Derivative Securities,* 2nd ed., Englewood Cliffs, NJ: Prentice Hall, 1993, pp. 332-333.

4. The interested reader is referred to Richard Stanton, "Rational Prepayment and the Valuation of Mortgage-Backed Securities," *Review of Financial Studies* (Fall 1995), pp. 677-708; Scott F. Richard and Richard Roll, "Prepayments on Fixed Rate Mortgage-Backed Securities," *Journal of Portfolio Management* (1989), pp. 73-82; and Frank J. Fabozzi, editor, *CMO Portfolio Management* Summit, NJ: Frank J. Fabozzi Associates (1994).

5. See Peter E. Kloeden and Eckhard Platen, *Numerical Solution of Stochastic Differential Equations.*

6. In Panels A and B of Table 8.2, rows 14, natural e is raised to an exponent containing an integral. As we are using discrete-time simulation, it is necessary to approximate the integral. We use Rhomboid integration to make this approximation. This is accomplished by averaging the short rates at the beginning and end of each time interval and employing those averages in the exponent. For example, the Time 1 value of 0.93594370 shown in row 14 of Panel A equals $\exp[-(0.07+0.06239991)\div2]$. Similarly, the Time 2 value of 0.87842123 equals: $\exp\{-\{[(0.07+0.06239991)\div2]+[(0.06239991+0.06445826)\div2]\}\}$.

7. We should note here an exception. James A. Tilley, "Valuing American Options in a Path Simulation Model," *Transactions of the Society of Actuaries,* XLV (1993), pp. 499-520, has shown an innovative simulation approach that allows one to value American-style options with a path simulation model.

8. Path dependence of cash flows may be manifest in a variety of modes. Cash flows may depend not only on the level of short rates, but how they evolve over time. They may also depend on how long rates, average rates, or another reference rate (or combination of reference rates) of interest develop over time. In the case of adjustable-rate mortgage-backed securities, not only their prepayment behavior, but also the periodic coupon rate depend on how some reference rates of interest evolve over time. This is more pronounced if there are periodic and/or lifetime caps or floors on the coupon rates. Another kind of path dependence is exhibited in the cash flows received by holders of CMOs (Collateralized Mortgage Obligations). In creating CMOs, pools of passthrough mortgage-backed securities are used as collateral. The cash flow to be received by a particular CMO tranche in a given month depends on the outstanding balances of the other tranches in the deal. A history of prepayments is needed in order to calculate these balances, and the prepayments are themselves affected by interest rate levels and histories.

9. Examples of how these issues are treated in practice are given in Frank J. Fabozzi, *Valuation of Fixed Income Securities,* Summit, NJ: Frank J. Fabozzi Associates (1994), and Frank J. Fabozzi, Chuck Ramsey, Frank R. Ramirez, *Collateralized Mortgage Obligations: Structures and Analysis,* 2nd ed., Summit, NJ: Frank J. Fabozzi Associates, (1994).

10. The number of paths needed to obtain price convergence depends on the complexity of the cash flow stream being analyzed. See Deepak Gulrajani, Michael Roginsky, Ronald Kahn, "Advanced Techniques for the Valuation of CMOs," Chapter 7 of Frank J. Fabozzi, editor, *CMO Portfolio Management* Summit, N.J.: Frank J. Fabozzi Associates (1994). See also Phelim P. Boyle, "Options: A Monte Carlo Approach," *Journal of Financial Economics* (1977), pp. 323-338; and J. Hull and A. White, "The Pricing of Options on Assets with Stochastic Volatilities," *Journal of Finance* (1987), pp. 281-300.

11. For example, in the two-factor Brennan and Schwartz model discussed earlier, the two factors—

the short and the long rates—are correlated. Sometimes in implementing this model, the long rate factor is replaced by the spread between the long and short rates. This spread shows almost no correlation to the short rate.

12. See David F. Babbel and Stavros Zenios, "Pitfalls in the Analysis of Option-Adjusted Spreads," *Financial Analysts Journal* (July/August 1992), pp. 65-69.

13. Certainty-equivalent values are usually obtained by applying some utility function to the distribution of cash flow outcomes, transforming the uncertain cash flows into a single value which, if received with certainty, would leave the investor just as satisfied as if he were to receive instead the uncertain cash flows. The process is described in any theory of finance text, such as Jonathan Ingersoll, *Theory of Financial Decision Making.*

14. An excellent discussion of the theory of low-discrepancy points, with references to the literature, is contained in H. Niederreiter, "Random Number Generation and Quasi-Monte Carlo Methods," *CBMS-NFS*, 63, (1992). Applications of low-discrepancy points to the valuation of interest-sensitive cash flows, and comparisons of the approach to Monte Carlo simulation, are provided in Spassimir H. Paskov and Joseph F. Traub, "Faster Valuation of Financial Derivatives: A Promising Alternative to Monte Carlo," *Journal of Portfolio Management* (Fall 1995), pp. 113-120.

15. Paskov and Traub, "Faster Valuation of Financial Derivatives: A Promising Alternative to Monte Carlo."

16. Two such sets of low-discrepancy points that have been used in valuation experiments are Sobol points and Halton points. In some cases, use of these sets can generate accurate pricing with sample points reduced by a factor of approximately 10. More recently, application of generalized Faure sequences has been said to provide accurate pricing with sample points reduced by a factor of 1,000! This technique is said to match not only first, but higher moments of the distribution.

17. A full description of this procedure, and its application to the pricing of interest-sensitive mortgage-backed

securities, is given in Jacob Boudoukh, Matthew Richardson, Richard Stanton, and Robert F. Whitelaw, "Pricing Mortgage-Backed Securities in a Multifactor Interest Rate Environment: A Multivariate Density Estimation Approach," Stern School of Business, Working Paper (March 1995) and "A New Strategy for Dynamically Hedging Mortgage-Backed Securities," Stern School of Business, Working Paper (March 1995).

18. Recognizing that some insolvency programs are not perfect, and sometime indemnify the customers only after a considerable delay and with below-market returns, it is tempting to incorporate this into the valuation of liabilities. However, we believe that this complication can instead be reflected on the asset side of the balance sheet in terms of a reduced default put option value.

19. This viewpoint is more fully elucidated in David F. Babbel, "Thoughts on the Fair Valuation of Life Insurance Company Liabilities," *Fair Value of Insurance Liabilities,* Irwin T. Vanderhoof, editor, Burr Ridge, IL: Irwin Press (1996).

Practice Exercises

1. What are the advantages of the simulation approach to valuation of interest-sensitive financial instruments?

2. What are the disadvantages of the simulation approach to valuation of interest-sensitive financial instruments?

3. Why is it sometimes desirable to conduct a simulation through lattices?

Bibliography

Amin, Kaushik I. (1991), "On the Computation of Continuous Time Option Prices Using Discrete Approximations," *Journal of Financial and Quantitative Analysis* 26(4), pp. 477-495.

Amin, Kaushik I. and Robert A. Jarrow (1991), "Pricing Foreign Currency Options Under Stochastic Interest Rates," *Journal of International Money and Finance* 10(3), pp. 310-329.

Artzner, Philippe and Freddy Delbaen (1989), "Term Structure of Interest Rates: The Martingale Approach," *Advances in Applied Mathematics* 10, pp. 95-129.

Babbel, David F. (1988), "Interest Rate Dynamics and the Term Structure," *Journal of Banking and Finance* 12, pp. 401-417.

Babbel, David F. (1996), "Thoughts on the Fair Valuation of Life Insurance Liabilities," *Fair Valuation of Insurance Liabilities*, Irwin T. Vanderhoof, editor, Irwin Press, in press.

Babbel, David F. and Anthony M. Santomero (1996), *Financial Markets, Instruments, and Institutions*, Burr Ridge, IL, Irwin Press, 1996.

Babbel, David F. and Stavros Zenios (1992), "Pitfalls in the Analysis of Option-Adjusted Spreads," *Financial Analysts Journal* (July/August), pp. 65-69.

Bansal, Ravi and S. Viswanathan (1991), "No Arbitrage and Arbitrage Pricing: A New Approach," Working paper, Duke University.

Barnett, Arnold, "Optimal Control of the B/B/C Queue," Interfaces (August 1978), pp. 49-52.

Beckers, Stan (1980), "The Constant Elasticity of Variance Model and Its Implications for Option Pricing," *Journal of Finance* 35, pp. 661-673.

Bensaid, Bernard, Jean-Phillipe Lesne, Henri Pagés, and José Scheinkman (1992), "Derivative Asset Pricing with Transaction Costs," *Mathematical Finance* 2(2), pp. 63-86.

Bick, Avi and Walter Willinger (1988), "Dynamic Spanning Without Probabilities," Working paper, University of British Columbia.

Black, Fischer (1975), "Fact and Fantasy in the Use of Options," *Financial Analysts Journal* 31, pp. 36-41 and 61-72.

Black, Fischer, Emanuel Derman and William Toy (1990), "A One-Factor Model of Interest Rates and its Application to Treasury Bond Options," *Financial Analysts Journal* 46 (January-February), pp. 33-39.

Black, Fischer and P. Karasinski (1992), "Bonds and Option Pricing when Short Rates are Log-normal," *Financial Analysts Journal* (May/June), pp. 52-59.

Black, Fischer and Myron Scholes (1972), "The Valuation of Option Contracts and a Test of Market Efficiency," *Journal of Finance* 27, pp. 399-418.

Black, Fischer and Myron Scholes (1973), "Pricing of Options and Corporate Liabilities," *Journal of Political Economy* 81, pp. 637-659.

Bodie, Zvi, Alex Kane, and Alan J. Marcus (1996), *Investments*, 3rd Edition, Burr Ridge, IL, Irwin Press.

Boudoukh, Jacob, Matthew Richardson, Richard Stanton and Robert F. Whitelaw (1995), "Pricing Mortgage-Backed Securities in a Multifactor Interest Rate Environment: A Multivariate Density Estimation Approach," Stern School of Business Working Paper, New York University.

Boudoukh, Jacob, Matthew Richardson, Richard Stanton and Robert F. Whitelaw (1995), "A New Strategy for Dynamically Hedging Mortgage-Backed Securities," Stern School of Business Working Paper, New York University.

Boyle, Phelim P. (1977), "Options: A Monte Carlo Approach," *Journal of Financial Economics* pp. 323-338.

Boyle, Phelim P. and Stuart M. Turnbull (1989), "Pricing and Hedging Capped Options," *The Journal of Futures Markets* 9 (1), pp. 41-54.

Boyle, Phelim P. and Ton Vorst (1992), "Option Replication in Discrete Time with Transaction Costs," *Journal of Finance* 47(1), pp. 271-293.

Breeden, Douglas T. and Robert H. Litzenberger (1978), "Prices of State-Contingent Claims Implicit in Option Prices," *Journal of Business* 54, pp. 621-651.

Brennan, Michael J., and Eduardo S. Schwartz (1977) "Savings Bonds, Retractable Bonds and Callable Bonds," *Journal of Financial Economics* 5, pp. 67-88.

Brennan, Michael J., and Eduardo S. Schwartz (1979), "A Continuous Time Approach to the Pricing of Bonds," *Journal of Banking and Finance* 3, pp. 133-155.

Campbell, John Y. (1986), "A Defense of Traditional Hypotheses About the Term Structure of Interest Rates," *Journal of Finance* 41, pp. 183-193.

Constantinides, George M. (1992), "A Theory of the Nominal Term Structure of Interest Rates," *Review of Financial Studies* 5, pp. 531-552.

Conze, Antoine and Viswanathan (1991), "Path Dependent Options: The Case of Lookback Options," *Journal of Finance* 46, pp. 1893-1907.

Courtadon, Georges (1982), "A More Accurate Finite Difference Approximation for the Valuation of Options," *Journal of Financial and Quantitative Analysis* 17 (December), pp. 697-703.

Cox, John C. (1977), "Notes on Option Pricing I: Constant Elasticity of Variance Diffusions," Working paper, Stanford University.

Cox, John C. and Chi-Fu Huang (1989), "Option Pricing Theory and its Applications," in *Theory of Valuation: Frontiers of Modern Financial Theory*, volume 1, (Sudipto Bhattacharya and George Constantinides ed.), Totowa, Rowman & Littlefield.

Cox, John C. and Chi-Fu Huang (1989), "Optimal Consumption and Portfolio Policies when Asset Prices Follow a Diffusion Process," *Journal of Economic Theory* 49, pp. 33-83.

Cox, John C., Jonathan E. Ingersoll, Jr., and Stephen A. Ross (1981), "A Re-examination of Traditional Hypotheses about the Term Structure of Interest Rates," *Journal of Finance* 36, pp. 769-799.

Cox, John C., Jonathan E. Ingersoll, Jr., and Stephen A. Ross (1985), "An Intertemporal General Equilibrium Model of Asset Prices," *Econometrica* 53, 2, March, pp. 363-384.

Cox, John C. and Stephen A. Ross (1976), "The Valuation of Options for Alternative Stochastic Processes," *Journal of Financial Economics* 3(1), pp. 145-166.

Cox, John C. and Stephen A. Ross (1976), "A Survey of Some New Results in Financial Option Pricing Theory," *Journal of Finance* 31, pp. 383-402.

Cox, John C., Stephen A. Ross and Mark Rubinstein (1979), "Option Pricing: A Simplified Approach," *Journal of Financial Economics* 7, pp. 229-263.

Cox, John C. and Mark Rubinstein (1985), *Options Markets*, Englewood Cliffs, Prentice-Hall.

Cutland, Nigel, Ekkehard Kopp and Walter Willinger (1991), "A Non-Standard Approach to Option Pricing," *Mathematical Finance* 1(4), pp. 1-38.

Delbaen, Freddy (1992), "Representing Martingale Measures when Asset Prices are Continuous and Bounded," *Mathematical Finance* 2(2), pp. 107-130.

Dothan, M. (1978), "On the Term Structure of Interest Rates," *Journal of Financial Economics* 7, pp. 229-264.

Duffie, D., J. Ma and J. Yong (1995), "Black's Consol Rate Conjecture," Working paper, Graduate School of Business, Stanford University, forthcoming, *Annals of Applied Probability*.

Duffie, J. Darrell (1988), *Security Markets: Stochastic Models*, San Diego, Academic Press.

Duffie, J. Darrell and Philip Protter (1992), "From Discrete to Continuous Time Finance: Weak Convergence of the Financial Gain Process," *Mathematical Finance* 2(1), pp. 1-16.

Duffie, J. Darrell and Rui Kan (1995), "A Yield-Factor Model of Interest Rates," Working Paper, Graduate School of Business, Stanford University.

Dybvig, Philip and Chi-Fu Huang (1988), "Non-negative Wealth Constraints, Absence of Arbitrage, and Feasible Consumption Plans," *Review of Financial Studies* 1, pp. 377-402.

Eberlein, Ernst (1992), "On Modeling Questions in Security Valuation," *Mathematical Finance* 2(1), pp. 17-32.

Eisenberg, Lawrence K. and Robert A. Jarrow (1991), "Option Pricing with Random Volatility in Complete Markets: A Note," Working paper, Federal Reserve Bank of Atlanta.

Emanuel, David C. and J.D. MacBeth (1982), "Further Results on the Constant Elasticity of Variance Call Option Pricing Model," *Journal of Financial and Quantitative Analysis* 17(4), pp. 533-554.

Fabozzi, Frank J., editor (1994), *CMO Portfolio Management*, Summit, NJ, Frank J. Fabozzi Associates.

Fabozzi, Frank J. (1995), *Handbook of Fixed Income Securities*, Summit, NJ, Frank J. Fabozzi Associates.

Fabozzi, Frank J. (1994), *Valuation of Fixed Income Securities*, Summit, NJ, Frank J. Fabozzi Associates.

Fabozzi, Frank J., Chuck Rmsey, and Frank R. Ramirez (1994), *Collateralized Mortgage Obligations: Structures and Analysis*, 2nd ed., Summit, NJ, Frank J. Fabozzi Associates.

Föllmer, Hans (1981), "Calcul d'Itû sans Probabilitès," *Sèminaire de Probabilitès* XV, Lecture Notes in Mathematics 850, pp. 143-150.

Fong, H. Gifford and Oldrich A. Vasicek, (1991), "Fixed-Income Volatility Management: A New Approach to Return and Risk Analyses in Fixed-Income Management," *Journal of Portfolio Management* (Summer), pp. 41-46.

Galai, Dan (1978), "Empirical Tests of Boundary Conditions for CBOE Options," *Journal of Financial Economics* 6, pp. 187-211.

Gale, David (1980), *The Theory of Economic Models*, University of Chicago Press.

Garman, Mark B. (1976), "An Algebra for Evaluating Hedge Portfolios," *Journal of Financial Economics* 3, pp. 403-427.

Garman, Mark B. (1977), "A General Theory of Asset Valuation Under Diffusion Processes," Working paper, University of California, Berkeley.

Geske, Robert (1979), "The Valuation of Compound Options," *Journal of Financial Economics* 7, pp. 63-81.

Giddy, Ian (1983), "Foreign Exchange Options," *Journal of Futures Markets*, pp. 143-166.

Green, Richard C., (1986), "Positively Weighted Portfolios on the Minimum-Variance Frontier," *Journal of Finance* 51, pp. 1051-1068.

Harrison, J. Michael and David M. Kreps (1979), "Martingales and Multiperiod Securities Markets," *Journal of Economic Theory* 20, pp. 381-408.

Harrison, J. Michael, Richard Pitbladdo and Stephen M. Schaefer (1984), "Continuous Price Processes in Frictionless Markets Have Infinite Variation," *Journal of Business* 57(3), pp. 353-365.

Harrison, J. Michael and Stanley R. Pliska (1981), "Martingales and Stochastic Integrals in the Theory of Continuous Trading," *Stochastic Processes and Applications* 11, pp. 215-260.

He, Hua (1990), "Convergence from Discrete- to Continuous-Time Contingent Claims Prices," *Review of Financial Studies* 3(4), pp. 523-546.

He, Hua (1991), "Optimal Consumption-Portfolio Policies: A Convergence from Discrete to Continuous-Time Models," *Journal of Economic Theory* 55, pp. 340-363.

Heath, David, Robert A. Jarrow and Andrew J. Morton (1990), "Bond Pricing and the Term Structure of Interest Rates: A Discrete Time Approximation," *Journal of Financial and Quantitative Analysis*, Vol. 25, pp. 419-440.

Heath, David, Robert A. Jarrow and Andrew J. Morton (1992), "Bond Pricing and the Term Structure of Interest Rates: A New Methodology for Contingent Claim Valuation," *Econometrica* 60(1), pp. 77-105.

Ho, Thomas, S. Lee (1986), "Term Structure Movements and Pricing Interest Rate Contingent Claims," *Journal of Finance* 41(5), pp. 1011-1029.

Hull, John C. (1993), *Options, Futures, and other Derivative Securities*, 2nd ed., Prentice Hall, Englewood Cliffs, NJ.

Hull, John C. (1995), *Introduction to Futures and Options Markets*, 2nd ed., Prentice Hall, Englewood Cliffs, NJ.

Hull, John C., and Alan White (1987), "The Pricing of Options on Assets with Stochastic Volatilities," *Journal of Finance*, pp. 281-300.

Hull, John C., and Alan White (1990a), "Valuing Derivative Securities Using the Explicit finite Difference Method," *Journal of Financial and Quantitative Analysis* 25 (March), pp. 87-100.

Hull, John C., and Alan White (1990b), "Pricing Interest Rate Derivative Securities," *Review of Financial Studies* 3(4), pp. 573-592.

Hull, John C., and Alan White (1993), "One-Factor Interest Rate Models and the Valuation of Interest Rate Derivative Securities," *Journal of Financial and Quantitative Analysis* 28(2), pp. 235-254.

Hull, John C., and Alan White (1994), "Numerical Procedures for Implementing Term Structure Models I & II," *Journal of Derivatives* 1 (3), pp. 64-76.

Ingersoll, Jonathan E., Jr. (1987), *Theory of Financial Decision Making*, Totowa, Rowman and Littlefield.

Jacod, Jean and Albert N. Shiryaev (1987), *Limit Theorems for Stochastic Processes*, New York, Springer-Verlag.

Jarrow, Robert A. and Dilip B. Madan (1991), "A Characterization of Complete Security Markets on a Brownian Filtration," *Mathematical Finance* 1(3), pp. 31-43.

Jarrow, Robert A. and Dilip B. Madan (1992), "Valuing and Hedging Contingent Claims on Semimartingales," Working paper, Cornell University.

Jarrow, Robert A. and Andrew Rudd (1983), *Option Pricing*, Homewood, Il, Richard D. Irwin.

Karatzas, Ioannis and Steven E. Shreve (1988), *Brownian Motion and Stochastic Calculus*, New York, Springer-Verlag.

Karlin, Samuel and Howard M. Taylor (1975), *A First Course in Stochastic Processes*, Second Edition, San Diego, Academic Press.

Kim, I.J., K. Ramaswamy and S. Sundaresan (1992), "Does Default Risk in Coupons Affect the Valuation of Corporate Bonds? A Contingent Claims Model," *Financial Management* 22 (3), pp. 117-131.

Klemkosky, Robert C. and Bruce G. Resnick (1979), "Put-Call Parity and Market Efficiency," *Journal of Finance* 34, pp. 1141-1155.

Klemkosky, Robert C. and Bruce G. Resnick (1980), "An Ex Ante Analysis of Put-Call

Parity," *Journal of Financial Economics* 8, pp. 363-378.

Kloeden, Peter E. and Eckhard Platen, (1992) "Numerical Solution of Stochastic Differential Equations," New York, Springer-Verlag.

Kreps, David M. (1981), "Arbitrage and Equilibrium in Economies with Infinitely Many Commodities," *Journal of Mathematical Economics* 8, pp. 15-35.

Kreps, David M. (1982), "Multiperiod Securities and the Efficient Allocation of Risk: A Comment on the Black-Scholes Option Pricing Model," *The Economics of Information and Uncertainty*, (J. McCall, ed.), University of Chicago Press.

Kruizenga, Richard J. (1956), "Put and Call Options: As Theoretical Market Analysis," Unpublished doctoral dissertation, MIT.

Leland, Hayne E. (1985), "Option Pricing and Replication with Transaction Costs," *Journal of Finance* 11, pp. 1283-1301.

Longstaff, Francis (1990), "Pricing Options with Extendable Maturities: Analysis and Applications," *Journal of Finance* 45, pp. pp. 935-957.

McConnell, John J. and Eduardo S. Schwartz (1986), "LYON Taming," *Journal of Finance* 41, pp. 561-576.

Merton, Robert C. (1973), "The Relationship Between Put and Call Prices: A Comment," *Journal of Finance* 28, pp. 181-184.

Merton, Robert C. (1973), "Theory Of Rational Option Pricing," *Bell Journal of Economics and Management Science* 4, pp. 141-183.

Merton, Robert C. (1987), "Continuous Time Stochastic Models," in *The New Palgrave: A Dictionary of Economics*, (John Eatwell, Murray Milgate and Peter Newman, ed.) London, Norton.

Nelson, Daniel B. and Krishna Ramaswamy (1990), "Simple Binomial Processes as Diffusion Approximations in Financial Models," *Review of Financial Studies* 3(3), pp. 393-430.

Niederreiter, H. (1992), "Random Number Generation and Quasi-Monte Carlo Methods," *CBMS-NFS* 63, Philadelphia: SIAM.

Paskov, Spassimir H., and Joseph F. Traub (1995), "Faster Valuation of Financial Derivatives: A Promising Alternative to Monte Carlo," *Journal of Portfolio Management* (Fall), pp. 113-120.

Protter, Philip (1990), *Stochastic Integration and Differential Equations*, New York, Springer-Verlag.

Qi Shen (1990), "Bid-Ask Prices for Call Options with Transaction Costs," Working paper, The Wharton School.

Ramaswamy, Krishna and Suresh Sundaresan (1985), "The Valuation of Options on Futures Contracts," *Journal of Finance* 40, pp. 1319-1340.

Ramaswamy, Krishna and Suresh Sundaresan (1986), "The Valuation of Floating Rate Instruments: Theory and Evidence," *Journal of Financial Economics* (June), pp. 175-219.

Reisman, Haim, "Intertemporal Arbitrage Pricing Theory," *Review of Financial Studies* 5 (1992), pp. 105-122.

Rendleman, Richard J., Jr. and Brit J. Bartter (1979), "Two-State Option Pricing," *Journal of Finance* 34, pp. 519-525.

Richard, Scott F., and Richard Roll (1989), "Prepayments on Fixed Rate Mortgage-Backed Securities," *Journal of Portfolio Management*, pp. 73-82.

Ritchken, Peter H. (1985), "On Option Pricing Bounds," *Journal of Finance* 40, pp. 1219-1233.

Roll, Richard and Stephen A. Ross (1977), "Comments on Qualitative Results for Investment Proportions," *Journal of Financial Economics* 5, pp. 265-268.

Ronn, Aimee R. and Ehud I. Ronn (1989), "The Box Spread Arbitrage Conditions: Theory, Tests, and Investment Strategies," *Review of Financial Studies* 2, pp. 91-108.

Ross, Stephen A. (1978), "A Simple Approach to the Valuation of Risky Streams," *Journal of Business* 51, pp. 453-475.

Ross, Stephen A. (1987), "Finance," in *The New Palgrave: A Dictionary of Economics*, (John Eatwell, Murray Milgate, and Peter Newman, ed.), New York, Norton.

Rudd, Andrew and Mark Schroeder (1982), "The Calculation of Minimum Margin," *Management Science* 28, pp. 1368-1379.

Samuelson, Paul A. and Robert C. Merton (1969), "A Complete Model of Warrant Pricing that Maximizes Utility," *Industrial Management Review* 10, pp. 17-46.

Schroder, Mark (1989), "Computing the Constant Elasticity of Variance Option Pricing Formula," *Journal of Finance* 44(1), pp. 211-219.

Stanton, Richard (1995), "Rational Prepayment and the Valuation of Mortgage-Backed Securities," *Review of Financial Studies*, pp. 677-708.

Stein, Jeremy C. (1989), "Overreaction in the Options Market," *Journal of Finance* 44, pp. 1011-1023.

Stein, Elias M. and Jeremy C. Stein (1991), "Stock Price Distributions with Stochastic Volatility: An Analytic Approach," *Review of Financial Studies* 4(4), pp. 727-752.

Stoll, Hans (1969), "The Relationship Between Put and Call Option Prices," *Journal of Finance* 24, pp. 802-824.

Stoll, Hans (1973), "The Relationship Between Put and Call Option Prices: A Reply," *Journal of Finance* 28, pp. 185-187.

Stricker, Christophe (1990), "Arbitrage et Lois Martingale," *Annales de l'Institut Henri Poincaré æProbabilités et Statistiques* 26(3), pp. 451-460.

Stroock, Daniel W. and S.R.S. Varadhan (1979), *Multidimensional Diffusion Processes*, New York, Springer-Verlag.

Taqqu, Murad and Walter Willinger (1991), "Toward a Convergence Theory for Continuous Stochastic Securities Market Models," *Mathematical Finance* 1(1), 55-99.

Tian, Yisong (1992), "A Simplified Binomial Approach to the Pricing of Interest Rate Contingent Claims," *Journal of Financial Engineering* 1(1), pp. 14-37.

Tian, Yisong (1994), "A Rexamination of Lattice Procedures for Interest Rate-Contingent Claims," *Advances in Futures and Options Research* 7, pp. 87-111.

Tilley, James A. (1993), "Valuing American Options in a Path Simulation Model," *Transactions of the Society of Actuaries* XLV, pp. 499-520.

Turnbull, Stuart M. and Frank Milne (1991), "A Simple Approach to Interest-Rate Option Pricing," The Review of Financial Studies 4 (1), pp. 87-120.

Vasicek, Oldrich (1977), "An Equilibrium Characterization of the Term Structure," *Journal of Financial Economics* 5, pp. 177-188.

Whaley, Robert E. (1982), "Valuation of American Call Options on Dividend Paying Stocks: Empirical Tests," *Journal of Financial Economics* 10, pp. 29-58.

Williams, David (1991), *Probability with Martingales*, Cambridge University Press.

Solutions to Exercises

Chapter 1 Solutions

1. The implicit single-year forward rates of interest are:

$$f_1 = (1.07) - 1 \qquad\qquad = 7.0000\%$$
$$f_2 = (1.078^2 \div 1.070^1) - 1 = 8.6060\%$$
$$f_3 = (1.084^3 \div 1.078^2) - 1 = 9.6100\%$$
$$f_4 = (1.088^4 \div 1.084^3) - 1 = 10.0089\%$$
$$f_5 = (1.090^5 \div 1.088^4) - 1 = 9.8037\%$$

2. The cumulative value of a $1,000 4-year certificate of deposit would be:

$$\$1,000 \times 1.088^4 = \$1,401.25$$

3. The cumulative value of a $1,000 3-year certificate of deposit would be:

$$\$1,000 \times 1.084^3 = \$1,273.76$$

4. The implicit forward rate of interest extending from Time 3 to Time 4 would be:

$$(\$1,401.25 \div \$1,273.76) - 1 = 10.0089\%$$

5. The spot rates associated with the single-year forward rates given in this question are:

$$s_1 = (1.08) - 1 = 8.00\%$$

$$s_2 = (1.08 \times 1.089)^{1/2} - 1 = 8.4491\%$$

$$s_3 = (1.08 \times 1.089 \times 1.096)^{1/3} - 1 = 8.8314\%$$

$$s_4 = (1.08 \times 1.089 \times 1.096 \times 1.098)^{1/4} - 1$$
$$= 9.0727\%$$

$$s_5 = (1.08 \times 1.089 \times 1.096$$
$$\times 1.098 \times 1.099)^{1/5} - 1$$
$$= 9.2377\%$$

6. The implicit 3-year forward rate of interest, extending from Time 2 to Time 5, is:

$$f_{2\,\text{to}\,5} = (1.096 \times 1.098 \times 1.099)^{1/3} - 1$$
$$= 9.766596\%$$

7. "Short rates" are single-period rates of interest that may or may not arise in the future; "forward rates" are (typically) single-period rates of interest applicable to future time periods that are able to be "locked in" today by taking short and long positions.

8. The answer to this question depends on whether we are attempting to "lock in" a savings rate or a borrowing rate for the time period desired. To lock in today a future savings rate applicable to the time period extending from Time 3 to Time 4, we could purchase a 4-year instrument yielding the 4-year spot rate, while funding our purchase by simultaneously selling short a 3-year instrument yielding the 3-year spot rate. If we wished to lock in a borrowing rate for the same time period, we would purchase a 3-year instrument while short-selling a 4-year instrument with the applicable spot rates of interest.

9. There is little difference between internal rate of return and YTM. YTM is an internal rate of return, applied to a fixed income instrument

of some sort. Reported YTMs are sometimes different from IRRs due to Wall Street conventions, wherein YTMs are computed assuming semi-annual compounding, and then doubled to produce a "bond-equivalent yield." → annualized

10. Occasionally we *do* see term structures of interest plotted using YTM rather than spot rates or forward rates of interest. For example, the U.S. Treasury plots YTMs. However, when they do so, they typically adjust their data to reflect what they estimate YTMs would be if bonds were all selling at par value. In other words, they attempt to divine what the market YTMs would be if there existed bonds whose coupons were exactly equal to their YTMs. Of course, this kind of plot is based on a lot of guessing. When actual YTMs are plotted, they get a scatter plot with yields all over the map.

i.e. bond yield = market yield

(The uniqueness of YTM)

In general, YTMs cannot be used to value anything except the particular instrument with which they are associated. There is one exception. If bonds of all maturities were selling at par value, we could use their YTMs to derive spot and forward rates of interest, and then go about valuing other instruments with these derived rates of interest. This explanation will become clearer in Appendix 2.2, where we learn that YTM is based on a weighting scheme for spot rates of interest that depends on the size and timing of each cash flow. Since financial instruments usually spin off cash flows of different size and timing, the YTM of one instrument cannot be used to value another instrument with any high degree of accuracy, even if the two instruments have the same maturity and par value.

$$YTM \approx \frac{\sum DD\ of\ Bond\ i}{\sum DD\ of\ whole\ Port.} \times spot\ rate_i$$

Chapter 2 Solutions

1. The instrument's $1,500 cash flow that is received in two years would be worth $(1.5 \times \$890) = \$1,335$; its $2,000 cash flow that is received in five years would be worth $(2.0 \times \$720) = \$1,440$. Therefore, the instrument's value would be $\$1,335 + \$1,440 = \$2,775$.

$\frac{CF_t}{(1+\frac{y(0)}{2})^{2t}}$

2. The spot rates of interest are:

$$s_1 = (1,000 \div 950)^{1/1} - 1 = 5.2632\%$$
$$s_2 = (1,000 \div 890)^{1/2} - 1 = 5.9998\%$$
$$s_3 = (1,000 \div 830)^{1/3} - 1 = 6.4079\%$$
$$s_4 = (1,000 \div 770)^{1/4} - 1 = 6.7523\%$$
$$s_5 = (1,000 \div 720)^{1/5} - 1 = 6.7907\%$$

3. The implicit single-year forward rates of interest are:

$$f_0 = (1,000 \div 950) - 1 = 5.2632\%$$
$$f_1 = (950 \div 890) - 1 = 6.7416\%$$
$$f_2 = (890 \div 830) - 1 = 7.2289\%$$
$$f_3 = (830 \div 770) - 1 = 7.7922\%$$
$$f_4 = (770 \div 720) - 1 = 6.9444\%$$

4. The value of a bond paying a $100 annual coupon with a face value of $1,000, maturing in five years, would be:

$$\$100 \div (1 + 0.052632)^1 = \$95$$
$$\$100 \div (1 + 0.059998)^2 = \$89$$
$$\$100 \div (1 + 0.064079)^3 = \$83$$
$$\$100 \div (1 + 0.067523)^4 = \$77$$
$$\$1,100 \div (1 + 0.067907)^5 = \$792$$

The price of the bond is equal to their sum, $1,136.

5. The value of a $10,000 4-year zero would be:

$$\$10,000 \div [(1.052632)(1.067416)(1.072289)(1.077922)] = \$7,700$$

6. The value of a zero-coupon bond that pays $10,000 at the end of five years, whether short rates follow the first or second path, would be:

First path:
$10,000 ÷ [(1.08)(1.05)(1.04)(1.03)(1.06)]
$$= \$7,766.2348$$

Second path:
$10,000 ÷ [(1.08)(1.10)(1.14)(1.15)(1.11)]
$$= \$5,784.3943$$

Because the two paths are equally likely, the value would be:

$$(\$7,766.2348 \times 0.5) + (\$5,784.3943 \times 0.5)$$
$$= \$6,775.3146$$

Its YTM would be

$$(10,000 \div 6,775.3146)^{1/5} - 1 = 8.0971\%$$

(Note: This calculation does not take into account an adjustment for the "market price of risk," which will be discussed later in Chapter 3.)

7. The value of a zero-coupon bond paying contingent cash flows at the end of five years would be:

First path:
$15,000 ÷ [(1.08)(1.05)(1.04)(1.03)(1.06)]
$$= \$11,649.3522$$

Second path:
$5,000 ÷ [(1.08)(1.10)(1.14)(1.15)(1.11)]
$$= \$2,892.1971$$

Because the two paths are equally likely, the value would be:

$$(\$11,649.3522 \times 0.5) + (\$2,892.1971 \times 0.5)$$
$$= \$7,270.7747$$

To compute YTM in this case, we need to use the expected value of the final cash flow of $10,000 in place of the face value; thus,

$$\text{YTM} = (10,000 \div 7,270.7747)^{1/5} - 1$$
$$= 6.5820\%$$

(Note: This calculation does not take into account an adjustment for the "market price of risk," which will be discussed later in Chapter 3.)

8. The value of a zero-coupon bond paying contingent cash flows at the end of five years would be:

First path:
$5,000 ÷ [(1.08)(1.05)(1.04)(1.03)(1.06)]
$$= \$3,883.1174$$

Second path:
$15,000 ÷ [(1.08)(1.10)(1.14)(1.15)(1.11)]
$$= \$8,676.5914$$

Because the two paths are equally likely, the value would be:

$$(\$3,883.1174 \times 0.5) + (\$8,676.5914 \times 0.5)$$
$$= \$6,279.8544$$

To compute YTM in this case, we need to use the expected value of the final cash flow of $10,000 in place of the face value; thus,

$$\text{YTM} = (10,000 \div 6,279.8544)^{1/5} - 1$$
$$= 9.7514\%$$

(Note: This calculation does not take into account an adjustment for the "market price of risk," which will be discussed later in Chapter 3.)

9. The difference in values and yields arises from the fact that the end-of-Year-5 cash flows are different. The first path of short rates has lower average rates, and therefore values the cash flow more highly, while the second path of short rates exhibits higher average rates, and therefore values the cash flow lower. Depending on the pattern of cash flows across these two states, different prices and yields are generated. For instance, the highest yield among these three instruments is 9.7514%, which is generated because the high cash payment of $15,000 is received in the state where cash flows are valued less, while the low cash payment of $5,000 is received in the state where it is highly valued. The instrument with the lowest yield generates higher cash payments when they are more highly valued.

10. The first zero-coupon bond is worth $857,338.82, and the second zero-coupon bond is worth $385,543.29. The portfolio of these two bonds is worth $1,242,882.21. The exact YTM is 9.397564%. The dollar durations are −1,527,590.84 for the first zero-coupon bond, −3,723,195.60 for the second zero-coupon bond, and −5,250,786.45 for the portfolio of both zero-coupon bonds. The dollar-duration weighted estimate of YTM is therefore 9.418148%, or roughly 2 basis points too high.

If the 10-year spot rate is changed to 12%, the value of the first zero-coupon bond remains unchanged, but the value of the second zero-coupon bond is reduced to $321,973.24. The portfolio is now worth $1,179,312.06. The exact YTM is now 10.669704%. The dollar durations are −1,475,515.41 for the first zero-coupon bond, −3,278,564.73 for the second zero-coupon bond, and −4,754,080.14 for the portfolio of both zero-coupon bonds. (Note that the dollar duration changed for the first zero-coupon bond. Had we calculated it based on its own yield, rather than the yield of the portfolio, the dollar duration would not have changed, because its yield remained the same.) The dollar-duration weighted estimate of YTM is therefore 10.758527%, or roughly 9 basis points too high. The lower precision of this estimate of YTM, relative to the 2 basis points error on the first, is due to the larger spread between YTM and the spot rates that bracket it. Because the estimate relies on a linear approximation to a nonlinear function, the larger the spread in spot rates, the lower the precision of the YTM estimate.

Chapter 3 Solutions

1. The six possible values of the short rate at Time $t+5$ are 0.15259, 0.09766, 0.06250, 0.04000, 0.02560, and 0.01638.

2. The spot rates and implied forward rates are:

$s_1 = 0.05$	$f_0 = 0.05$
$s_2 = 0.050565$	$f_1 = 0.05113$
$s_3 = 0.051093$	$f_2 = 0.052151$
$s_4 = 0.051582$	$f_3 = 0.053049$
$s_5 = 0.052026$	$f_4 = 0.053806$

3. The price of the cap is $23,284.08.

4. When the current short rate is changed to 3%, the six possible values of the short rate at Time $t+5$ are 0.09155, 0.05859, 0.03750, 0.02400, 0.01536, and 0.00983.

The spot rates and implied forward rates are:

$s_1 = 0.03$	$f_0 = 0.03$
$s_2 = 0.030353$	$f_1 = 0.030706$
$s_3 = 0.030695$	$f_2 = 0.031379$
$s_4 = 0.031024$	$f_3 = 0.032012$
$s_5 = 0.031339$	$f_4 = 0.03260$

The price of the cap is $1,474.64. Notice that the term structure is still upward sloping but is shifted down. The price of the cap has dropped significantly because it is farther "out of the money" than it was when the short rate was 5%.

When the current short rate is changed to 7%, the five possible values of the short rate at Time $t+5$ are 0.21362, 0.13672, 0.08750, 0.05600, 0.03584, and 0.02294.

The spot rates and implied forward rates are:

$s_1 = 0.07$	$f_0 = 0.07$
$s_2 = 0.070759$	$f_1 = 0.071519$
$s_3 = 0.071444$	$f_2 = 0.072815$
$s_4 = 0.072048$	$f_3 = 0.073862$
$s_5 = 0.072565$	$f_4 = 0.074635$

The price of the cap is $86,357,14. Notice that the term structure is still upward sloping but is shifted up. The price of the cap has increased significantly because it is now "in the money" rather than "out of the money" as it was when the short rate was 5%.

5. When the volatility parameter is changed to 0.05, the six possible values of the short rate at Time $t+5$ are 0.06381, 0.05788, 0.05250, 0.04762, 0.04319, and 0.03918.

The spot rates and implied forward rates are:

$s_1 = 0.05$	$f_0 = 0.05$
$s_2 = 0.050027$	$f_1 = 0.050054$
$s_3 = 0.050052$	$f_2 = 0.050102$
$s_4 = 0.050075$	$f_3 = 0.050145$
$s_5 = 0.050096$	$f_4 = 0.050181$

The price of the cap is $130.37. Notice that the term structure is still upward sloping but is not as steep as when the volatility parameter was 0.25. The price of the cap has

dropped significantly. Because of the decreased volatility, it is far less likely that values of the short rate that lead to cash flows will arise.

When the volatility parameter is changed to 0.45, the five possible values of the short rate at Time $t+5$ are 0.32049, 0.15243, 0.07250, 0.03448, 0.01640, and 0.00780.

The spot rates and implied forward rates are:

$s_1 = 0.05$	$f_0 = 0.05$
$s_2 = 0.051573$	$f_1 = 0.053148$
$s_3 = 0.053063$	$f_2 = 0.056048$
$s_4 = 0.054433$	$f_3 = 0.058554$
$s_5 = 0.055650$	$f_4 = 0.060530$

The price of the cap is $62,001.45. Notice that the term structure is still upward sloping but is steeper than when the volatility parameter was 0.25. The price of the cap has increased significantly. Because of the increased volatility, it is far more likely that values of the short rate that lead to cash flows will arise.

6. When the probability of an up movement is changed to 0.46, the six possible values of the short rate at Time $t+5$ are 0.15259, 0.09766, 0.06250, 0.04000, 0.02560, and 0.01638.

The spot rates and implied forward rates are:

$s_1 = 0.05$	$f_0 = 0.05$
$s_2 = 0.050115$	$f_1 = 0.05023$
$s_3 = 0.050189$	$f_2 = 0.050336$
$s_4 = 0.050220$	$f_3 = 0.050312$
$s_5 = 0.050207$	$f_4 = 0.050155$

The price of the cap is $18,545.12. Notice that the term structure now has a single hump. The price of the cap has decreased from the base case. Because of the decreased probability of an upward movement in the short rate, it is less likely that values of the short rate that lead to cash flows will arise.

When the probability of an up movement is changed to 0.4, the five possible values of the short rate at Time $t + 5$ are 0.15259, 0.09766, 0.06250, 0.04000, 0.02560, and 0.01638.

The spot rates and implied forward rates are:

$$s_1 = 0.05 \qquad f_0 = 0.05$$
$$s_2 = 0.049442 \qquad f_1 = 0.048885$$
$$s_3 = 0.048855 \qquad f_2 = 0.047682$$
$$s_4 = 0.048241 \qquad f_3 = 0.046402$$
$$s_5 = 0.047603 \qquad f_4 = 0.045055$$

The price of the cap is $12,742.05. Notice that the term structure is now downward sloping. The price of the cap has decreased even further from the base case. Because of the decreased probability of an upward movement in the short rate, it is even less likely that values of the short rate that lead to cash flows will arise.

7. The values of the short rate and $Q(i,j)$ for the nodes of the lattice are as follows:

Node	Rate (%)	$Q(i,j)$
A	10.00	1.000
B	6.54	0.315
C	10.00	0.531
D	13.46	0.059
E	6.54	0.0904
F	10.00	0.411
G	13.46	0.314
H	16.93	0.0106
I	N/A	N/A
J	6.54	0.085
K	10.00	0.373
L	13.46	0.261
M	16.93	0.022
N	N/A	N/A

Notice that nodes I and N are not reached in this lattice due to the increase in the mean reversion parameter, a, to 0.4. The price of the interest rate cap is $1,971.09. This is much lower than the price of $4115.42 that was obtained using the parameter values from Figure 3.16 and Figure 3.17.

Chapter 4 Solutions

1. $\frac{1}{2}\sigma^2 P_{rr} + [\kappa(\mu - r) - \lambda(r, t)\sigma]P_r$
$$+ P_t - rP = 0$$

2.–5. The baseline case is given by Figure 4.2. The effect of parameter changes is discussed in the body of the chapter immediately following equation (4.26).

6. The valuation equation for an interest rate floor is

$$\frac{1}{2}a^2(r, t)P_{rr} + b(r, t)P_r + P_t - rP = 0$$

The boundary condition for $t = 0$ is

$$P(r,0) = \text{Max}(x - r, 0)$$

The boundary for r as it goes to infinity is

$$\lim_{r \to \infty} P(r, \tau) = 0, \tau > 0$$

The boundary at $r = 0$ is

$$b(r, t)P_r - P_\tau = 0$$

Notice that the only difference between the cap and the floor is the maturity condition. This simple difference is sufficient to uniquely identify the security being valued.

Chapter 5 Solutions

1. $4.54 Notice that $\alpha = r$ and that $\gamma = \sigma B(t,T)$.

2. $3.50.

3. Try changing each of the parameters of the model and observe the impact on the differential in prices. Notice that for some parameter values the Black-Scholes price is greater than the Vasicek price and for some parameter values the relationship is reversed. Why?

4. The coefficient matrix, analogous to the matrix in equation (5.41) is:

$$\begin{bmatrix} 1.0125 & -0.0125 & & & & \\ -0.00512 & 1.00068 & 0.02944 & & & \\ & -0.00432 & 1.016927 & 0.05406 & & \\ & & -0.00192 & 1.09392 & 0.058 & \\ & & & -0.00032 & 1.3605 \end{bmatrix}$$

The values analogous to the last column of Table 5.1 based on the parameters given in this question are 0.997348, 0.915793, 0.797912, 0.615142, 0.292325, and 0.

Chapter 6 Solutions

1. When inflation rates are relatively stable, the exclusion of the evolution of the inflation rate from a model of interest rates will not lead to serious errors. Alternatively, if the model of interest rates is sufficiently flexible, then the exclusion of an inflation rate factor will still not be a serious problem. An example is the Brennan and Schwartz two-factor model. In that model, the consol rate is highly correlated with the inflation rate. Therefore, the consol rate captures the influence of changing inflation.

2. The answer to this question is given in Duffie and Kan (1993). Assume that there are two underlying sources of uncertainty (factors) in the economy, v_1 and v_2. Choose two spot rates, r and l, that are uniquely determined as functions of the two factors so that

$$r = f(v_1, v_2)$$
$$l = g(v_1, v_2)$$

If these equations can be inverted so that

$$v_1 = a(r, l)$$
$$v_2 = b(r, l)$$

then r and l can be treated as if they were the underlying factors of the model. Essentially, inverting the functions f and g is solving for v_1 and v_2 as functions of r and l. The basic idea is that knowing the value and stochastic evolution of r and l is equivalent to knowing the value and stochastic evolution of v_1 and v_2. Therefore, it does not matter which pair is treated as the underlying factors in the model.

3. While a three-factor model would be more flexible and would fit a wider variety of term structures and volatility structures, it would be very difficult to implement. Increasing the number of factors increases the number of computations required to approximate solutions for security prices exponentially. So, in practice two factors are often used because the models are easier to implement and posses adequate flexibility.

Chapter 7 Solutions

1. In the case of the CIR two-factor model the level of the short real rate is independent of the level of the inflation rate. With the Fong and Vasicek model the level of the short rate depends on the level of the volatility parameter. Independence of the two factors can lead to a recombining lattice.

2. Because the rate of reversion for the single-factor models is higher than for the two-factor BrS model, the BrS model is likely to

generate a wider distribution of possible future short rates. This is true for two reasons. First, the lower rate of reversion will allow the short rate to wander more in the BrS model. Second, the short rate is reverting to a stochastic long-term rate in the BrS model while the short rate is reverting to a constant level in the single-factor models. The randomness of the level the rates revert to can pull the short rate over a larger range than if the short rate were reverting to a constant level.

Chapter 8 Solutions

1. The main advantages of the simulation approach to valuation of interest-sensitive financial instruments are discussed in Section 4 of Chapter 8.

2. The main disadvantages of the simulation approach to valuation of interest-sensitive financial instruments are discussed in Section 4 of Chapter 8.

3. The rationale for simulation through lattices is to model path-dependence of cash flows within a framework capable of valuing American-style options.

Index

fundamental issue in valuing, 26, 121
market price of risk, 42
with multiple cash flows, 49
reward to risk ratio, 66
types, 25
valuation using risk-free interest rate, 43
Interest rate paths simulation, 16-17
Interest rate risk
exposure measures, 96
market price, 121
Interest rates. *See also* Term structure of interest rates
continuously compounded, 58-59
hedging, 33
influence of inflation, 93
relationship to prices, 13
Interest-sensitive cash flow valuation
future trends, 121
principles, 18-20, 121

J

Jarrow, Robert A., 45, 53, 67, 89, 90, 106, 109

K

Kahn, Ronald, 122
Kan, Rui, 98
Kane, Alex, 9
Karasinski, P., 45, 53
Kim, I. J., 64, 67
Kloeden, Peter E., 122

L

Lattice methods
binomial, 31, 105-106
continuous-time, 87
discrete-time, 87
multi-factor, 101-107
recombining, 26, 102
simulations, 115-116
three dimensional, 101-102
trinomial, 45-51, 86-88
Lee, S., 44, 45, 53
Life insurance policies, 115, 116, 117, 120
Liquidity preference theory, 57-58
Liquidity risk, 118
Local expectations hypothesis, 57, 58-59, 61, 63
Low-discrepancy method, 119-120
Low-discrepancy points, 123

M

Ma, J., 98
Marcus, Alan J., 9
Market imperfections, 1
Market price of interest rate risk, 121
Market price of risk, 20, 61, 97
for all interest rate contingent securities, 42
and martingale probability, 44
Market value weighting *versus* dollar duration weighting, 23
Markovian process defined, 26
Martingale probability
adjustment from subjective probability, 44
defined, 43
market price of risk and, 44
Mean reversion, 105
Mean reversion model, 62
Merton, Robert C., 74, 89
Mesh points, 81
Milne, Frank, 51
Modified principal component analysis, 117
Monte Carlo simulations
advantages, 107, 108, 115
certainty-equivalent values, 119, 122-123
disadvantages, 115, 119
implementation issues, 116-119
in-sample *versus* out-of-sample fits, 118
through lattices, 115-116
model structures, 111-114
modified principal component analysis, 117
parameter selection, 119
time grids, 117
variance reduction techniques, 117
Mortgage-backed securities, 112, 115, 118
adjustable-rate, 122
Morton, Andrew J., 45, 53, 59, 67, 89, 90, 106, 109
Multi-factor lattices, 101-107
Multi-factor models
advantages and disadvantages, 91
characteristics, 51
continuous-time, 91-98
discrete-time, 101-109
stochastic factors, 91, 103, 106-107
Multiplicative binomial model, 26-30
with complex scenarios, 35-40
Multivariate density estimation procedures, 120

N

Niederreiter, H., 123
No arbitrage principle, 17

Nominal interest rate model, 104
Notational conventions, 3, 5, 55, 60
Notional amount, 32
Numerical solutions
    for multi-factor discrete-time models, 108
    for single-factor models, 79-87

O

Objective probabilities, relationship to risk-neutral proba-
    bilities, 90
Option-adjusted spread, 118-119, 120
Options. *See also* Call options
    American style, 115, 116
    equity, 72, 74-77
Ornstein-Uhlenbeck mean reverting process, 61
Orthogonalization process, 103

P

Parameter defined, 92
Partial equilibrium valuation model, 68, 69, 70-71
Paskov, Spassimir H., 119, 123
Path dependence of cash flows, 122
Path dependent models, 106-107
Path independent models, 101-106
Pension liabilities, 120-121
Platen, Eckhard, 122
Preference-free valuation methodology, 73
Preferred habitat theory, 57-58
Prepayment risk, 118, 122
Price of any default-free bond, notational convention, 60
Prices, relationship to interest rates, 13
Pure discount bonds, notational conventions, 55

R

Ramaswamy, K., 64, 67
Ramirez, Frank R., 122
Ramsey, Chuck, 122
Recombining lattice, 26, 102
Redundant securities, 71-72
Reward to risk ratio, 66
Richard, Scott F., 122
Richardson, Matthew, 123
Risk-free interest rate, 43
Risk-neutralized processes, 111
Risk-neutral probabilities
    defined, 43
    measures, 76
    relationship to objective probabilities, 90

Risk-neutral valuation methodology, 73
Roginsky, Michael, 122
Roll, Richard, 122
Ross, Stephen A., 44, 53, 55, 59, 64, 66, 67, 72, 90
Rounding errors, 52

S

Santomero, Anthony M., 9, 10, 109
Scholes, Myron, 73, 89
Schwartz, Eduardo S., 59, 67, 69, 72, 90, 98
Scientific yield method, 10
Short rates of interest
    characteristics, 94, 95
    defined, 5
    importance, 1
    movement over time, 1
    notational convention, 5
    probabilities of occurring, 5
    relationship to forward interest rates, 1, 5, 6, 20
    relationship to spot interest rates, 1, 6
    valuation using, 16-17, 18
Single-factor binomial branching model, 26-27
    short rates in, 26
Single-factor models
    continuous-time, 26, 51, 58-65
    discrete-time, 25-51
    limitations, 91
    simulation, 115
    solution approaches, 73-89
Sobol points, 123
Spot rate of interest
    difference from forward rates of interest, 2-3
    notational conventions, 3, 55
    relationship to short rates, 1, 6
    relationship to yield-to-maturity, 5, 22-24
    two-year, 30
    used as basis for forward rates, 4, 5
    valuation using, 14-15, 18
    yield curves, 7-8
Stanton, Richard, 122, 123
State-contingent claim, 68
Stochastic factors, 91, 103, 106-107
Stochastic Runge-Kutta scheme, 122
Strike level, 32
Strike price, 51
STRIPS
    for valuation comparison, 14
    valuation method, 28-30
Subjective probability, adjustment to martingale probabil-
    ity, 44
Sundaresan, S., 64, 67

T

Taxes, 1
Term structure of interest rates
    arbitrage-free models, 44-51
    in a certain economy, 55-57
    in continuous time, 58-59
    defined, 7
    importance of, 8
    model fitting compared, 87-89
    relationship to Treasury bond value, 25
    in an uncertain economy, 57-58
Thirty-year instruments, 117
Three dimensional lattices, 101-102
Tilley, James A., 122
Time period defined, 1-2
Time points
    defined, 1
    importance, 2
Toy, William, 44, 45, 53
T-period spot rate of interest, 2
Transaction costs, 1
Traub, Joseph F., 119, 123
Treasury bills
    call options, 77-79
    price volatility, 77-78
Treasury bonds
    call options on, 25
    characteristics, 25
Trinomial lattice method, 86-87
Turnbull, Stuart M., 51, 52
Two-factor lattices, 105-106

U

Underlying asset defined, 34
Underpriced securities, arbitrage opportunities, 35
U.S. government-issued securities, 7, 25, 77-79

V

Value additivity principle, 14, 18
Vanderhoof, Irwin T., 123
Variables, building correlation between, 105-106
Variance reduction techniques, 117
Vasicek, Oldrich, 44, 53, 55, 59, 64, 66, 67, 98
Vasicek one-factor model, 45-51, 78-79, 88, 93, 96
Volatility parameter as stochastic factor, 103, 106-107
Volatility risk exposure measures, 96
Von Neumann-Morgenstern expected utility, 69

W

White, Alan, 45, 51, 53, 55, 67, 87, 90, 98, 105, 109
Whitelaw, Robert F., 123
Wiener process, 59-60

Y

Yield curves defined, 7
Yield-to-maturity
    approximation, 10
    for bond price quotes, 22
    difference from bond equivalent yield, 10
    relationship to spot rates, 5, 22-24
    valuation using, 17-18
    zero-coupon bonds, 6, 10, 18
Young, J., 98

Z

Zenios, Stavros, 122
Zero-coupon bonds, 14
    notational conventions, 55
    pricing model, 70, 84-85
    tax treatment, 10
    yield-to-maturity, 6, 10, 18